Clash of Cultures

Warhafftige Contrafey einer wilden Frawen/mit jrē Töchterlein/gefunden in der Landtschafft/Noua terra genaṅt/vnd gehn Antorff gebracht/vnd von menigklich alda offendtlich gesehen worden/vnd noch zusehen ist.

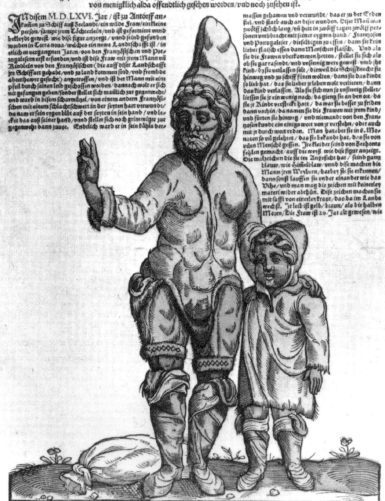

In disem M. D. LXVI. Jar / ist zu Antorff angeloffen zu Schiff auß Zeelandt/ein wilde Fraw/ein kleins persōn/sampt jrem Töchterlein/vnd ist geformiert vnd bekleydt gewest/ wie dise figur anzeyge/ vnnd seind gefunden worden in Terra noua/welches ein newe Landtschafft ist / in etlich en vergangnen Jaren/von den Franzöischen vnd Portugalesern erst erfunden/vnd ist dise Fraw mit jrem Mann vñ Kindlein von den Franzöischen (die auff diser Landtschafft jre Schiffart gehabe/vnd zu land kommen sind/vnd frembde abentheuer gesucht) angetroffen/vnd ist der Mann mit ein pfeil durch seinen leib geschossen worden/dannoch wolt er sich nit gefangen geben/sonder stellet sich mäülisch zur gegenwehr/vnd ward in disem scharmützel/von einem andern Franzöischen mit einem Schlachtschwert in der seyten hart verwundt/da nam er sein eygen blůt auß der seyten in sein hand/vnd bleßet das auß seiner hand/vnd stellet sich noch grimmiger zur gegenwehr dann zuuor. Endtlich ward er in sein kühle dermassen zehawen vnd verwundt/ das er zu der Erden fiel/vnd starb auch an diser wunden. Diser Mann war zwölff schůch lang/vñ hett in zwölff tagen zwölff personen vmbbracht mit seiner eygnen hand / Franzosen vnd Portugaleser / diselbigen zu essen / dann sie trincken lieber blůt vnd essen lieber flaisch dann Menschenflaisch. Vnd als sie die Frawen vberkommen hetten / stellet sie sich also ob sie gar rasendt vnd vnsinnig were gewest/ vmb jr Kind/ daß sie verlassen solt/ dieweil die Schiffknecht sie hinweg vnd zu Schiff füren wolten / dann sie das Kinde so lieb hat/ das sie lieber jr leben wolt verlieren/ dann das kind verlassen. Als sie sich nun so vnsinnig stellet/ ließen sie jr ein wenig nach/ da gieng sie an den ort/ da sie jr Kindt verstecket hart/ vnd war sie besser zu friden dann vorhin/ da nam sie die Frawen mit jrem Kind/ vnd füren sie hinweg/ vnd niemandt von den Franzosen kunde ein einigs wort von jr verstehen/ oder auch mit jr durch wort reden. Man hat aber sie in 8. Monaten so vil gelebt/ das sie bekandt hat/ das sie vnd vilen Menschen gessen. Jre Kleider seind von Zechonta feeln gemacht/ auff die weiß/ wie dise figur anzeige. Die malzeichen die sie im Angesicht hat/ seind gantz blaw/ wie Himelblaw/ vnnd dise machen die Mann jren Weybern/ darbey sie sie erkennen/ dann sonst lauffen sie vnder einander wie das Vihe/vnd man mag die zeichen mit keinerley materi wider abthůn. Dise zeichen machen sie mit safft von einerley kraut/das da im Lande wechst. Jr leib ist gelb/ braun/ als die halben Moren. Die Fraw ist 20. Jar alt gewesen/ wie sie gefangen ist worden/im 66. Jar/im Augusto/ dz Kind 7. Jar. Laß vns Gott dē Allmächtigen danck en für seine wolthat/ d er vns in seinem Wort erleüchtet hat/ das wir nicht so gar wilde Leüt vnd Menschen fresser seind/ wie in diser Landtschafft sein/ da diß Weib gefangen/ vnd heraußgebracht worden/ dann sie gar nichts von dem rechten Gott wissen/ sondern schier ärger dann das Vihe leben/ Gott wölle sie auch zu sein/ erkendtnuß bekeren/ Amen.

Getruckt zu Jngstpurg/durch Manheum Francken.

Clash of Cultures

Second Edition

Brian M. Fagan

AltaMira
PRESS

A Division of
ROWMAN & LITTLEFIELD PUBLISHERS, INC.
Walnut Creek • *Lanham* • *New York* • *Oxford*

ALTAMIRA PRESS
A Division of Rowman & Littlefield Publishers, Inc.
1630 North Main Street, Suite 367
Walnut Creek, CA 94596
www.altamirapress.com

Rowman & Littlefield Publishers, Inc.
4720 Boston Way
Lanham, MD 20706

12 Hid's Copse Road
Cumnor Hill, Oxford OX2 9JJ, England

Frontispiece: The first illustration of an Inuit woman and her child from Labrador, 1567. "In this year 1566 there arrived at Antwerp, by ship from Zealand, a savage woman (small person), together with her little daughter, and she is shaped and clothed as this picture shows, and was found near Terra Nova . . . They took the woman with her child and brought her away; and none of the Frenchmen could understand a single word of hers or speak with her at all. But she was taught enough in 8 months that it was known that she had eaten men. Her clothing is made of seal skins . . . the paint she has on her face is entirely blue, like sky blue . . . she knows nothing of the true God but lives almost more wickedly than the beast . . . "

Handbill printed in Augsburg, Germany. Translated by W. C. Sturtevant, *Inuit Studies* 4 (1–2): 48–49 (1980). Courtesy of the Department of Prints and Drawings of the Zentralbibliothek, Zürich.

British Library Cataloguing in Publication Information Available

Library of Congress Cataloging-in-Publication Data

Fagan, Brian M.
  Clash of cultures / Brian M. Fagan.—2nd ed.
    p. cm.
  Includes bibliographical references and index.
  ISBN 0-7619-9145-X (cloth)—ISBN 0-7619-9146-8 (pbk.: alk. paper)
    1. Europe—History—1492–. 2. Europe—Territorial expansion.
3. Culture conflict. 4. Discoveries in geography. I. Title.

D210.F25 1998
940.2—dc2   197-33837
                                                             CIP

Printed in the United States of America

♾™ The paper used in this publication meets the minimum requirements of American National Standard for Information Sciences—Permanence of Paper for Printed Library Materials, ANSI/NISO Z39.48–1992.

Again, there comes an experiment with the human work, the human design, by the Maker, Modeler, Bearer, Begetter:

…The time for the planting and dawning is nearing. For this we must make a provider and nurturer…So let us try to make a giver of peace, giver of respect, provider nurturer.

Dennis Tedlock (ed.), *Popol Vuh* (1995)

Contents

Preface and Acknowledgments

THIS BOOK IS AN ATTEMPT TO DESCRIBE some of the changing viewpoints about non-Western societies that colored Europeans' dealings with them between the fifteenth and late nineteenth centuries. This is a book about myth and reality, about often well-meaning people separated by vast gulfs of incomprehension and misunderstanding, a chronicle of noble deeds, scurrilous dealings, and bizarre thinking. Above all, it is a story of ordinary people pursuing their daily goals, making decisions in good faith that were to have tragic and unimaginable consequences for later generations. *Clash of Cultures* makes no attempt to be comprehensive. Readers seeking a global view of the momentous events that shaped the Age of Discovery and the Industrial Revolution should consult the references at the back of this book.

The research for this volume has involved selective reading in dozens of academic disciplines, in sources as varied as archaeological monographs, early Dutch colonists' diaries, even nineteenth-century New Zealand novels. I have traveled the world with Captain Cook, tried to master the intricacies of missionary literature, and admired the meticulous research of generations of historians and anthropologists. The result is a complicated but often grossly simplified narrative. To charges of naivete and simplistic analysis, I can only plead demands of multiple sources and space restrictions. I am satisfied, however, that *Clash of Cultures* covers the main points of a compelling and little-known chapter of world history; it also shows the importance of thinking of anthropology as a historical discipline, something that many theoreticians have tended to forget.

A morass of complicated theoretical viewpoints and complicated academic arguments surrounds the topic of this book. Eric Wolf has discussed the theoretical background to the subject in his magisterial survey of world history since 1400, *Europe and the People Without History* (Berkeley: University of California Press, 1982). Interested readers and scholars should consult this work for theoretical perspective. Much of the discussion is overwhelming even to the specialist, let alone the general reader. Anthropologists disagree violently with historians, archaeologists quarrel with them both, and ethnohistorians offer yet another perspective. It is for this reason that I have decided not to encapsulate this book within the framework of any particular theoretical perspective. Nor, indeed, am I intellectually qualified to do so. This book is designed to make one point, and I think it has succeeded in doing so—that many of our problems interacting with non-Western societies today have strong roots in historical processes that began over four centuries ago.

The second edition of this book comes at a time of increasing interest in this chapter of history. I have rewritten Chapter 1 to cover some of the recent thinking on the subject and to highlight central issues in later chapters. Chapter 5 adds a brief account of the changes in Japanese culture that resulted from European contact, filling a gap in the first edition. Chapter 6, "The Great Dying," discusses an emerging field of research that chronicles the devastating consequences of epidemic disease, specifically on native American populations. The book has also been updated and corrections made throughout. These changes are relatively minor, as the text has stood up well since the first edition in 1984.

So many people have helped with this project that I am at a loss to thank them all. I am especially grateful to James Belson and Bill Jersey, who struggled valiantly with a possible script treatment for a TV series that was never funded to production stage. I learned more from their ideas and companionship than I have from most other research experiences in my life. The photographs in this book owe a great deal to Jane Williams of Santa Fe, New Mexico, who traveled to many of the areas and took numerous shots of the landscape and people that supplemented my own extensive travels. I have gained not only a friend, but also profound insights into the difficulties of being a good photographer. Professor Elvin Hatch read through various drafts and freely shared his vast knowledge of the history of anthropological thought with me; I learned a great deal from his wisdom. Numerous scholars assisted with specific chapters, especially Professors Robin Fisher and Knud Fladmark of Simon Fraser University and Richard Elphick of Wesleyan University. I am grateful to Professors Robert McGhee, Douglas Oliver, and Leonard Thompson for reviewing the manuscript in its first draft. Mitch Allen of AltaMira Press commissioned the second edition, waving aside my objections with infectious enthusiasm. I am grateful for his support and tolerance of constantly postponed delivery dates. Jack Scott drew the maps with his customary skill.

The idea for this book came from the participants in an advanced undergraduate course at the University of California, Santa Barbara, in 1977. They became so enthusiastic about this then obscure topic that they cajoled me into writing this book. Since then, I have taught the course twenty times to an entire generation of undergraduates, who have embraced the subject eagerly, and taught me a great deal about societies I had never heard of. They have made teaching a joy, and the least I can do is dedicate this revised edition to them. Many of the ideas in *Clash of Cultures* were also honed in an advanced seminar at the University of Cape Town in July-August, 1982. Professors John Parkington, Andrew Smith, and others gave me valuable advice, and the University provided generous financial support for my visit to the campus.

Brian M. Fagan
Santa Barbara, California, June 1997

Author's Note

ANTHROPOLOGISTS TEND TO AVOID USING TERMS such as "native," "primitive," and "savage" on the grounds that they are pejorative expressions. I occasionally use them in the pages that follow, not in a negative sense, but simply because they were the words used at the time. Obviously, their presence here is a phenomenon of history, not of contemporary usage. Inevitably, too, there will be those who will cry "foul," "ethnocentrism," and "value judgement" at intervals during these pages. I have learned from hard experience that the topics covered in this book are inflammatory to many people, especially, oddly enough, anthropologists. Like everyone else, I have opinions and biases of my own. However, I have done everything I can to temper them. Where critical comments are quoted, they are (as is obvious to most thinking people) those of the people who wrote or said them at the time, not this writer's.

The descriptions of traditional cultures in this book are of necessity highly generalized. The reader should be aware that there are, or were, numerous local variations within each culture area and that human societies were never frozen in time. Thus, our portraits of, say, Tahitian society in 1769 are but fleeting impressions. They do not imply that island society was static. Far from it, for dynamic change has always been a characteristic of human culture everywhere.

Clash of Cultures concentrates on the first period of European exploration and settlement between A.D. 1488 and 1900. Normally, our story ends around 1900, by which time all of the societies described here had made major adjustments to Western civilization. This arbitrary date has been chosen simply because the primary focus of this book is historical. The same catastrophic processes of cultural change are still affecting non-Western societies today, compounded by the social, political, and environmental stresses of the late twentieth century.

PART I

The Age of Discovery

Whereas the making Discoverys of Countries hitherto unknown, and the Attaining a Knowledge of distant Parts which though formerly discover'd have yet been but imperfectly explored, will rebound greatly to the Honour of this Nation as a Maritime Power, as well as to the Dignity of the Crown of Great Britain, and may tend greatly to the advancement of the Trade and Navigation thereof...

British Admiralty Instructions to Captain James Cook (1768)

CHAPTER 1

Prologue

Land has grown, the sky has grown, and the ocean has grown; all these are filled with living creatures. The room for gods is filled with gods, and now what shall be done for the room for people?

Tahitian origin legend recorded in 1822,
quoted in Douglas Oliver, *Ancient Tahitian Society* (1974)

IN THE YEAR 1772, A SMALL BAND OF French seamen led by an explorer named Marion du Fresne landed on a sandy beach in southern Tasmania. As du Fresne's boat grounded, a band of about thirty aborigines carrying pointed sticks and sharp stones emerged from the trees to greet the strangers, exotic-looking people "in color black, the hair woolly and all were naked." It was perhaps surprising that the Tasmanians recognized their visitors as fellow humans. Marion du Fresne was the first outsider to greet them in at least 8,000 years.

The Tasmanians had been isolated on their remote island home by the rising waters of the Bass Strait at the end of the Ice Age. At the time of du Fresne's visit some 3,000 to 5,000 aborigines occupied Tasmania, divided into at least eighty different bands of thirty to fifty people (see Chapter 8). Their descendants survived less than a century of Western civilization. Branded as the most primitive people on earth, savages who were "the connecting link between man and the monkey tribes," the aborigines were decimated by exotic European diseases and literally hunted into extinction by land-hungry colonists. From the very beginning a vast chasm of incomprehension had separated the Tasmanians from their unwelcome visitors.

Du Fresne and his men advanced cautiously up the beach, while the locals piled up a heap of driftwood. The aborigines greeted the white men in a language that seemed to draw words "from the bottom of the throat." An officer offered them beads and other trinkets of the type carried by every expedition to the South Seas at the time. The Tasmanians rejected the gifts with scorn. When the French proffered live chickens, the aborigines flung them away in disgust and ran into the woods. Eventually du Fresne himself managed to prevail on them to return. The bandleaders again gestured at the woodpile. Confused, the captain set fire to the dry branches. The Tasmanians fled precipitately to the top of a nearby hillock and bombarded the astonished seamen with volleys of accurately flung stones. The French fled for their boats. Once safely out of range, they rowed along the shore looking for another place to land. The Tasmanians pursued them with showers of rocks. Du Fresne lost his temper when they hit two of his officers, and ordered a volley of musket fire. The Tasmanians scurried for cover, leaving one of their band sprawled on the beach. The expedition lingered in the cove for another six days in the hope that the aborigines would return. In the meantime, the officers laid out the abandoned corpse and measured it in the cause of science, noting that its owner was five feet, three inches tall, with "reddish brown hair." Then they sailed away to New Zealand, where Marion du Fresne was "devoured by natives."

Du Fresne's experiences with the Tasmanians were by no means unusual in the adventurous centuries of the Age of Discovery when Western explorers were penetrating every corner of the globe. In most cases, the first encounter with a hitherto unknown society was but a fleeting kaleidoscope of curiosity, sometimes horrified fascination, and often romantic excitement. The "natives" could be respectful and hospitable, even amorous. However, all too often they could act in seemingly unpredictable ways. Even navigators with a vast experience of exotic peoples like the celebrated Captain James Cook had difficulty understanding people like the Tasmanians and Australians. "They wander about in small parties from place to place in search of food," Cook wrote (Figure 1.1). "They are all together an ignorant, wretched race of mortals, though at the same time the natives of a country capable of producing every necessity of life, with a climate the finest in the world" (Reed 1969, 163). What bothered Cook and other observers most of all was that such people had no interest in improving their individual lot and were absolutely content with just "being." Such values were completely alien to goal-oriented, individualistic Westerners exploring the world with specific objectives in mind, whether a search for China, pure exploration, missionary activity, trade, or colonization.

We live in such a well-explored, familiar world that it is difficult to imagine what it is like to encounter a society that has never had contact with Western

*1.1   Australian aborigine with his lightweight hunting kit, from a drawing by
François Peron (1802)*

civilization before. The famed BBC traveler David Attenborough is one of
the few people who have had this experience in recent times. During the late
1960s he accompanied a party of government officials to the headwaters of
the Sepik River in New Guinea, where a bush pilot had reported mountain
dwellings where none were suspected to exist. After two weeks of marching
through unknown country, Attenborough's small party came across two sets
of footprints.

The group followed the footprints and laid out gifts in the forest. The
strangers left telltale spoors that showed they were watching constantly.
The Europeans cried out greetings in a known river dialect, but to no avail.
Eventually they lost the trail and almost gave up hope. Then suddenly one

1.2   Encounter with the Binai of New Guinea (courtesy of David Attenborough)

morning seven small, almost naked men appeared in the bush near their
camp. As the travelers tumbled out of their tents, the strangers stood their
ground. Attenborough recounts how he and his companions made hasty gestures of friendship, for the tribesmen did not understand any known river
dialect (Figure 1.2). Fortunately both sides had many gestures in common:
smiles, and eyebrows that could frown, signify wonder, disapproval, or ask a
question. The gestures were the only way to understand one another, to barter iron knives for fruit, to deepen the relationship between two absolutely
incompatible societies. Such gestures are one of the few common communication inheritances of humanity; the early explorers used them to the full.

The traveler of two centuries ago was much better versed in the procedures for landing on unknown shores and apparently deserted beaches. Indeed, the British Admiralty had standard instructions for its captains to
follow. A small party would land with the utmost caution, firearms within
easy reach, the ship's cannons and an armed pinnace at their back. If anyone
approached, an officer would offer gifts—perhaps iron tools, clothing, or glass
trinkets—and make appropriate gestures of friendship. Everyone held his
breath and waited for the local people to react. Sometimes they would accept the gifts or hang back until one bolder individual came forward to take

the offering. Sometimes violence would erupt or the group would take to their heels. Captain Cook and his contemporaries learned the value of expressive sign language, the irresistible lure of iron tools, the power of their own firearms. "Some of the men Grunted and Cryd lyke a Hogg then pointed to the others—others crowed Lyke cocks to make them understand that we wanted fowls," wrote one of Francis Drake's officers in the early years of the Age of Discovery (Shipton 1973, 14). After centuries of experience, and despite the overwhelming advantages of gunpowder and large ships, Europeans always feared the unpredictable and the unexpected, the fatal miscalculations that could bring sudden danger and terrible slaughter.

Historical Background

THE DISCOVERY OF THE EXTRAORDINARY BIOLOGICAL and cultural diversity of humankind between the so-called Age of Discovery between the late fifteenth and nineteenth centuries was one of the great intellectual watersheds of Western civilization. Long-term forces of history led to this discovery. After A.D. 1000, the rulers of western European states allowed merchants greater freedom and enhanced privileges, in marked contrast to those of the more centralized, tributary polities of the Near East and Asia. Western Europe was impoverished, on the periphery of a wealthy Asian and Mediterranean world. Merchants and their widespread networks were vital to ambitious European lords, for they provided the capital for warfare, conquest, and peaceful expansion. The same merchants had access to well-established river and sea routes, which provided cheaper, reliable transportation without all the tolls and other hazards of overland caravan travel. As the western Europeans expanded their sphere of mercantile operations, money turned over more rapidly and profits increased in the hands of people whom many historians regard as the ultimate founders of capitalism.

However, tributary surpluses continued to be the mainstay of rulers and their courts, of entire states. In New Spain (Spanish colonial Mexico), the conquistadors paid a fifth of their profits to the King. During the early centuries of the Age of Discovery, these tribute networks expanded dramatically, as producers in every part of the world—fur traders in northeastern North America, silver miners in Mexico and Peru, sugar plantations in the Caribbean—were drawn into vast webs of economic interdependency. In many areas, the merchants and visitors offered exotic commodities of little value such as glass beads, cotton cloth, or iron axes for raw materials. As the producers of these materials acquired a taste for exotic baubles, they became ever more dependent on those who bought their furs, slaves, or copper ingots. In many cases, merchants eventually supplied tools, even raw materials, receiving reimbursement in finished products in a system of unequal exchange that was a form of peonage. The African slave trade provided the labor to grow sugar, mine precious ores, and cultivate cotton.

From the fifteenth to eighteenth centuries, European voyagers traversed the sea-lanes of the world (Figure 1.3). They found sources of gold, silver, and precious stones. They found places where fur-bearing animals abounded and tropical savannas where large tusked elephants flourished. Wherever they sailed, they tapped into existing trading networks, linked them together, and manipulated them for maximum profit. Back in Europe, artisans working in villages and in sizable manufactories produced goods and commodities for overseas colonies and suppliers. Thus was born a global commercial network, a "World System," as many scholars call it, with roots in much earlier trading alliances in many areas of the world. Over many generations, societies large and small, Western and non-Western became linked in a vast web of interdependency and interconnectedness. With the notable exception of the Atlantic slave trade, these connections were mostly confined to merchants and missionaries, with a few settlers far from home, laboring in coastal communities close to well-established sea routes.

For four centuries, European commerce operated under the protection of its government sponsors, hedged around by a morass of constraints and monopolies. International trade flowed along predictable routes, most of the profits lying in commodities such as human beings, sugar, or elephant ivory rather than in manufactured goods. Throughout these centuries, the state was still a tribute-collecting organization, dominated by rulers who sought to enhance their wealth at the expense of their rivals. Then, in the late eighteenth century, the British textile industry turned mercantile wealth into capital with the dawn of the Industrial Revolution.

England had become a major wool producer in the fifteenth century, exporting its manufactures throughout Europe and further afield. As a result, landowners turned increasingly to sheep herding and more intensive agriculture. Communities of merchants and their financial backers dwelt in towns large and small, acting as middlemen in an increasingly more complex trade. By the eighteenth century, landowners and merchants were intermarrying, with major landlords and nobility controlling between 80 and 85 percent of the land. Increasingly, those who had once been medieval serfs, then tenants, were forced off the land. By the late seventeenth century, as much as 40 percent of the population had left the land, many of them going into manufacturing as salaried workers. The new, more commercial agriculture was capital-intensive, while at the same time merchants acquired more political power and held increasing control over rural craftspeople, who manufactured the goods they distributed elsewhere.

English society was changing rapidly, but the country's manufacturers faced stiff competition from the Dutch, who were expert wool finishers, and

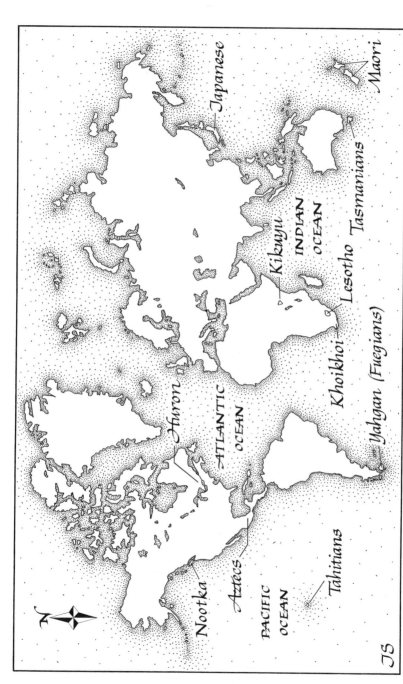

1.3   This map shows the major non-Western societies described in Clash of Cultures.

from Indian cottons and calicos, woven to suit European tastes. The English manufacturers responded to the Dutch by producing wool mixed with silk, linen, or cotton, and worsteds made with combed wool. They reduced their labor costs, first by moving their cloth production to the country, and then by increasing the mechanization of the production process. Indian competition was met politically by banning imports of calicos. At the same time, English manufacturers developed linen and cotton fabrics that were virtually identical to Indian cloth, using mechanization to undercut Asian labor costs with machine-made fabric. Provincial merchants and manufacturers began to exercise ever closer control over production techniques, using their wealth from other sources such as brewing and real estate to acquire the simple machines that were speeding up both weaving and finishing by 1750. Then, in 1779, Samuel Crompton developed the "mule," a machine that not only allowed a spinner to spin several threads of yarn simultaneously, but also wound the twisted fibers and drew them out. Eleven years later, this revolutionary device was powered by steam engines, resulting in a staggering increase in productivity. An Indian hand spinner would take about 50,000 hours to spin 100 pounds of cotton. Crompton's mule cut the time to 2,000 hours, while steam-powered machines reduced the time to 300 hours and could be operated by unskilled labor, mainly low-paid women and children. The figure fell even lower in the nineteenth century (Wolf 1982).

Inevitably, greater efficiency in the manufacturing process led to the abandonment of cottage industries and small workshops, which were replaced by well-organized factories. Factories gave the manufacturer much greater control over the entire process, as well as over the formerly kin-based, now wage-earning labor force. At the same time, pilfering could be controlled, transportation costs reduced, and delivery times shortened, while expensive machinery paid for with valuable capital was kept operating as intensively as possible. The changeover did not come easily. Many cottage workers strongly resisted the discipline and unrelenting labor of the new factories, many of which resembled prisons. Prolonged social unrest, indeed near-civil war, permeated English society after 1815, until the mid-nineteenth century saw the factory system develop its own institutions and factory labor forces stabilized.

The appearance of factories coincided with the growth of enormous textile-manufacturing cities, among them Manchester, which rose from a mere 24,000 inhabitants in 1773 to more than 250,000 in 1851. The new cities became magnets for immigration from the surrounding countryside, as well as from countries like Ireland. Displaced from the land and unable to find employment in the country, thousands of families moved to the new cities, where they worked for wages. Cotton textiles were the catalyst that produced the Industrial Revolution and the capitalism that went along with it. The ripples of the Industrial Revolution were felt throughout the world after the

Napoleonic Wars. By that time, half the total value of all British exports was cotton, and up to 20 percent of Britain's imports were raw cotton. By 1807, more than 60 percent of all this cotton came from the United States. The rise in production was staggering. In 1790, 3,000 American cotton bales reached England. By 1850, the figure had reached 4,500,000.

The Industrial Revolution, fueled by English textiles, brought a new social order based not on tribute, but on the deployment of capital, mechanized manufacturing, and the employment of laborers for hire. The reorganization of English agriculture created a huge reservoir of unemployed, free laborers, providing a unique work force, and a society not based on tribute or slavery, but on wages paid by deploying capital. The same capital financed railroads and steamships, improving communications, permitting the movements of raw materials, and of migrants, on an unprecedented scale. This same revolution created an insatiable demand for raw materials in many corners of the world, placing demands on native populations far from the factories of Lancashire and Yorkshire. At the same time, thousands of artisans and land-hungry farmers left their homeland and migrated to distant lands in search of wealth and new opportunity, and acreage of their own, "purchased" or seized from its long-term indigenous owners.

Non-Western societies in many parts of the world withered in the face of a flood of immigrant farmers, who believed they had the right to carve out a new life in an alien land without any reference to the indigenous population whatsoever.

The Age of Discovery connected all parts of the populated world to one another in lasting ways that still impact on our lives. These centuries of intermittent, then continual contact between Westerners and an enormous range of human societies dramatically changed European attitudes to the unusual and the exotic.

The Clash of Cultures

THE CHANGING ATTITUDES OF WESTERNERS to non-Western societies form a fascinating backdrop to what we may loosely term the *clash of cultures*. The clash was a progressive confrontation between an expanding, sophisticated civilization with radically alien beliefs and dozens of societies that lived in careful balance with the natural resources of their environments. The long centuries of Western discovery are a story of confrontation and non-comprehension, of cautious encounters between strangers, of searches for gold and brutal military campaigns, of profitable trading, land grabbing, and missionary endeavor. They are also a weary chronicle of pathos and tragedy, of bitter disillusionment between societies living in totally incompatible worlds. The intellectual, moral, and spiritual effects of the clash are with us to this day.

The clash of cultures played out against a backdrop of ever-changing attitudes towards, and expectations of, the non-Western world. By the same token, the perspectives of non-Westerners changed just as radically over the centuries.

At first, voyaging Europeans searched for paradise on earth, the last domain of a once universal Golden Age. At first, paradise was a remote and ancient dream, then it was located on earth, a mythical golden kingdom sometimes associated with Ethiopia, later with the Indies and the lands to the west. Ironically, the first Portuguese explorations brought Westerners in touch with the actual realities of some of the least complex of fifteenth-century human societies. Our story begins with the discovery at the southern tip of Africa of the Khoikhoi, simple herders whose way of life seemed so primitive that they soon became the epitome of savagery in European minds (see Chapter 2). The Khoikhoi seemed beyond Christian redemption.

Not so the American Indian, revealed to an astonished Europe by Christopher Columbus only a few years after the Portuguese reached the Cape of Good Hope. It was in the Indies and New Spain that images of the Noble Savage, of paradise and utopia, lingered to haunt peoples' minds for centuries. It was here also that the learned and greedy fought out their arguments over the morality of bringing Indians to the True Faith and to forced labor. Mexico was the land where the confrontation between Western civilization and the non-Western world was played out (see Chapter 3).

The Europeans who came to the New World, explored the Pacific, and coasted past Africa to India were members of a civilization that had only recently emerged from medieval feudalism. They were ruled by monarchs who governed rigidly stratified states. In this sense, the Spaniards or English were no different from the rulers of the Aztecs or Incas, who ran their empires on the premise that power and privilege were the right of only a few. Inequality and social stratification were for the common good, a tacit reality no one thought of questioning. But the Europeans were Christians, members of a faith that taught that individual freedoms and the equality of all people were fundamental doctrines for all humanity. To convert people to Christianity was to expose them to doctrines that in the long term undermined the established notion that inequality was a permanent condition. In due time these subversive teachings—for in a sense they were nothing less—were to overturn the colonial empires of every European nation.

Nearly five centuries have passed since the Conquest of Mexico, centuries during which the full diversity of humankind has been exposed to European eyes. While hundreds of societies underwent traumatic cultural change and the forces of reality played out on remote beaches and battlefields, philosophers and travelers developed a whole range of myths and stereotypes that plague our understanding of human diversity to this day. This strange dichotomy between myth and reality is ever present, ever-changing. Western perceptions of other societies have often fluctuated with the esteem in which Westerners held their own civilization. English and French philosophers sighed with nostalgia for a simple, uncomplicated life when Tahiti was discovered in 1769 (see Chapter 7). Noble Savages and people living with nature became fashionable in the eighteenth century, bursting on Western civilization with an intensity that is startling even today. By no means did everyone believe in nobility, however. It was but one strand in white perceptions of the non-Western world at the time. The Noble Savage gave way to disillusionment at the time of the Napoleonic Wars, when the Industrial Revolution and fervent nationalism changed global politics forever, bringing in their wake a new intellectual confidence about industrial civilization and its astonishing technological achievements (see Chapter 9).

Nineteenth-century Europeans believed, as had their predecessors, that Western civilization was the pinnacle of human achievement, a signpost of inevitable progress for the future. But their belief was now couched in far less tolerant terms. The non-Westerner became an even more inferior being in European eyes, often considered as having the intelligence of a ten-year-old child. From there it was a short step to the ardently racist doctrines of late nineteenth-century imperial Europe. Colonist and settler took refuge in doctrines of racial superiority to justify the annexation of tribal territories, or prime farming land, usually on specious arguments that the acreage was not used properly by its indigenous owners. The specious argument was simple and to the point: How could mere intellectual children learn the latest farming methods or govern themselves in a "civilized" manner? Leave such problems to a superior race, went the litany of imperial powers, with devastating consequences for the non-Western world. Hundreds of little-known societies, many hunter-gatherer cultures like the Tasmanians and Yahgan Indians (see Chapter 11), others elaborate societies like those of the Maori and Northwest Indians (see Chapter 14), were radically changed by contact with nineteenth-century missionaries, traders, and colonists. Some peoples, like the Khoikhoi of the Cape of Good Hope and the Tasmanians, vanished rapidly. Others, like the Aztecs and Maori, fell apart, the survivors becoming an impoverished and often oppressed minority on the fringes of the new society. Only a few non-Western societies managed to adapt with some success to a new world.

No one knows why some groups adapted better to European domination than others. A great deal depended on their political structure, for many non-Western societies, with their loosely structured, sometimes coercive, forms of government, were riven with factionalism, which made it hard for them to unite in the face of outside threat. Many of the societies that adapted with some success to the new order did so as a result of charismatic and shrewd leadership at the right moment.

1.4   An idealized portrait of King Moshoeshoe in 1833, from a drawing by a Parisian artist (1859)

King Moshoeshoe (1786–1870) of the BaSotho people of southern Africa was such a man (Figure 1.4). He was born into an isolated society of farming villages organized in small chiefdoms, a world that knew nothing of horses, firearms, or of white people. During his thirties, African refugees fleeing from the great Zulu ruler Shaka invaded his homeland and disrupted the centuries-old order. It was then that Moshoeshoe emerged as a leader. Through moral influence as much as military acumen, he rallied the survivors and built a small kingdom bounded by the massive Drakensberg Mountains of what is now Natal in South Africa. This kingdom he named Lesotho, the homeland of the Sotho people. Lesotho was still in its infancy when Western civilization expanded out of the Cape. For the rest of his life, Moshoeshoe grappled with the problems created by marauding plunderers, missionaries, British officials with treaties in hand, and Afrikaner farmers encroaching on his lands. He was a humane, self-disciplined man who ruled by popular consent and only resorted to warfare in self-defense or under extreme provocation. Above all, he was a realist who saw the selective advantages of such European innovations as guns, horses, European crops, and writing. This realism gave him a sophisticated understanding of changing power relationships in the Africa of his day. To survive, he navigated his people along a fine line, keeping one foot firmly in traditional society while embracing at least some evangelical Christian doctrine. The political and social reasons for his pursuit of such a course were so compelling that he was never baptized, despite frantic last-minute efforts by both Catholic and Protestant missionaries. He died as he had lived, in two worlds.

Moshoeshoe kept Lesotho together during a period of intense competition between Afrikaner and British interests for his lands. He fought bitterly with Afrikaner commandos, complaining to their leaders that he would not give his country away. "It belongs not to me, as you know yourself very well that every country in the world does belong to the people which dwells in it. If I remove the Basutos, I have nowhere else where I can establish them" (Thompson 1975, 294). His final diplomatic coup was to have his people annexed by the British, who had little interest in exploiting the BaSotho. Had the Afrikaners of the Orange Free State done so, they would have seized almost all their arable land. In the event, Lesotho was a British colony for nearly a century. The British forbade whites to own land and left the structure of society more or less intact. They did little to encourage economic development or higher education, or to prepare the country for independence. Moshoeshoe's family occupied most positions of power and prestige in the newly independent Lesotho on 4 October 1966. But the problems were and still are daunting: land shortages, an ever-rising population, and a single major export, mine labor for South Africa. A period of political instability followed, partly because Lesotho's new political institutions did not reflect the fine line that still bridged the new and traditional elements in BaSotho society.

But Moshoeshoe left a vital legacy behind him, for the BaSotho possess much more cultural integrity and social cohesion than their black neighbors who suffered for so long under the repressive rule of white South Africa. By shrewd political maneuvering, this great African king secured the best options for his people that he could, in a world where the options were at best unsatisfactory. Few other non-Western rulers achieved such a long-term legacy.

While many African and Asian societies were battered and profoundly changed by their encounters with European civilization, they managed to adapt and survive—as did the Japanese (see Chapter 5) or the Kikuyu of Kenya—emerging as the dominant society in a nation that has gained independence from colonial rule.

People Without History

CLASH OF CULTURES IS BASED ON ONE fundamental, and perhaps obvious, assumption: that world history during the past six centuries has not been merely the history of Western expansion, but of thousands of diverse human societies interacting with one another in an increasingly interdependent and interconnected world. This important point lies behind historians and social scientists' notion of a "world economic system" that was the consequence of the spreading tentacles of the Age of Discovery. The notion of a "world system" has some conceptual value, provided it is confined to the post-Medieval world, and not carried back into the remote world of the Late Bronze Age, as some archaeologists have suggested.

World systems theory argues that events in distant Europe could affect peoples thousands of miles away, who had never heard of London or even seen a white person. By the same token, a shortage of furs along North America's St. Lawrence River or reports of Maori cannibalism across the world in New Zealand could alter the course of European events in various ways (see Chapters 13 and 15). For instance, the international fur trade already had a long and highly profitable history that began when sixteenth-century European fishermen on the St. Lawrence River started trading for Canadian beaver pelts with the Indians along its banks. Beaver fur-wool was an immensely lucrative product, imported to Europe by the Dutch West Indies Company and later by the British and the French, and then redistributed throughout Europe. Canadian beavers revolutionized European fashion. The importers controlled redistribution so carefully that prices remained stable. Soon fur hats replaced the woolen headgear of earlier centuries. To own a beaver fur-wool hat was a sign of social status, even of political affiliation. Only in the early nineteenth century did the fur hat give way to silk and other materials.

From the very beginning, the North American fur trade involved not only competition between European powers, but between Indian groups as well. The frontiers of the trade moved rapidly, as one beaver population after another was hunted out, and the trappers had to move further into the interior. The new commerce had profound effects on both European and Indian society, as our essay on the Huron shows (see Chapter 13). At first the Huron profited from the trade. Their culture and ceremonial life were enriched. They and their confederacy partners controlled the fur trade over thousands of square miles, despite only minimal contacts with European colonists. However, as competition for furs intensified, both European powers and Indian groups competed for the rich harvest of pelts that flowed down the St. Lawrence. Eventually the Huron succumbed to the irresistible spiritual pressures of the Jesuits and fell prey to their fur-poor Iroquois neighbors, who took over their territory and the trade that went with it. Thus, men and women living hundreds, even thousands, of miles apart had their lives and their societies shaped by distant commercial and spiritual forces of which they were totally ignorant. It is both naive and simplistic to consider the history of either Western civilization or of the societies in these pages in isolation. Their destinies were shaped not only by their own actions, but by those of others as well.

World systems theory is conceptually useful for such broad issues, but does it have value on a smaller historical scale? It does, if it forces anthropologists, and archaeologists for that matter, to think in global and historical terms. As the distinguished anthropologist Eric Wolf pointed out in his magisterial study of capitalism and non-Western societies, *Europe and the People Without History* (1982), anthropologists have tended to ignore the forces of history in studying the non-Western world. He argues that events in Europe, as well as in remote lands, had a profound influence on the course of history, that the "people without history" were a major factor in global history. It is not enough, he argues, for anthropologists to study even the smallest of societies without considering their wider connections and their history, in whatever form it is recorded. In other words, anthropologists and historians should look at the world as a whole, not as a "sum of self-contained societies and cultures." Wolf speaks of unraveling "the chains of causes and effects at work in the lives of particular populations…[that] extend beyond any one population to embrace the trajectories of others—all others" (Wolf 1982, 385). Europe played an important role in this process, but what Wolf calls "chains of causation and consequence" within individual societies encompassed entire continents, and brought together the entire world.

Eric Wolf restored the "people without history" to the center stage of history at a general level, calling on a staggering array of scholarly sources to achieve his remarkable synthesis. The approach he calls for means researchers must venture far beyond documents and government archives into a realm of multidisciplinary scholarship unimaginable even a half century ago. Explorers' accounts, missionary journals, and Western sources tell but one side of a complex, multidimensional story. How can we correct this historical imbalance, examine the clash of cultures from both Western and non-Western perspectives, when many of the societies we study have completely different perceptions of history, and of the world around them? What weight can one place on oral histories, passed down from one generation to the text, on archaeological evidence, and on documents set down by native informants under the watchful eyes of Catholic friars? A new generation of multidisciplinary scholarship searches for fleeting clues. Australian historian Inga Clendinnen, herself the author of a memorable study of Aztec civilization, aptly calls us "Ahabs pursuing our great white whale." She adds: "We will never catch him...it is our limitations of thought, of understandings, of imagination we test as we quarter these strange waters. And then we think we see a darkening in the deeper water, a sudden surge, the roll of a fluke—and then the heart-lifting glimpse of the great white shape, its whiteness throwing back its own particular light, there on the glimmering horizon" (Clendinnen 1991, 275).

A Quartet of Sources

THE NEW SCHOLARSHIP RELIES ON UNSELFCONSCIOUS multidisciplinary thinking, which evaluates a patchwork of traditional and scientific sources to create a historical synthesis with many dimensions. Such approaches mean grappling with incomplete, often tantalizing, sources such as oral histories or material clues left in abandoned archaeological sites from contact times. As Clendinnen says, there are many things we will never know, such as the Tasmanians' reaction to Marion du Fresne. However, the sheer diversity of sources allows us to obtain at least glimpses of complex events and reactions. The detective work involves a quartet of major sources—historical sources, ethnohistory, anthropology, and archaeology—as well as insights from many other academic disciplines.

Historical sources are the conventional tools of the historian and come in many forms. Explorers' accounts of their voyages and travels, their journalism annotated and published by modern scholars, government archives, missionary accounts, early settler diaries, even the texts of treaties, all are the raw material of the events of the past five centuries. Almost invariably, they give the Western perspective and take on events, people, and societies.

Ethnohistory, traditional history derived from non-Western sources, is a burgeoning field of historical inquiry, involving not only analysis and collecting of hitherto unrecorded oral histories, but also the critical examination of native sources written down after European contact. The most important American ethnohistories come from Central America, where native accounts of Aztec and other societies were recorded by sixteenth-century friars, and sometimes by native speakers working under European supervision. Fray Bernardino de Sahagun used informants to set down a definitive account of Aztec civilization a generation after the Spanish Conquest. Sahagun's twelve-volume *General Things of the History of New Spain* covers the early history of Aztec civilization, its social, religious, and economic institutions, and ends with an account of the Conquest as seen through indigenous eyes. An entire academic specialty has developed around Sahagun's work alone, quite apart from other native documents such as the *Codex Mendoza*, an ethnographic account of Aztec society commissioned for the King of Spain in 1547.

Such sources bristle with scholarly challenges. Though Bernadino de Sahagun's *General Things* has an immediacy that comes from speaking to people who lived the traditional culture in their youth, he worked a full generation after the Conquest in a hostile political environment. While Sahagun considered his informants reliable, he edited their narratives for his book to meet his own Christian objectives. An intellectual chasm separated the informants and Sahagun's young Nahuatl interpreters, born since the Conquest into a quite different cultural environment. A similar gully divides modern scholars from the worthy friar. The modern Sahagun expert wrestles with the problems encountered by earlier scribes copying the prelate's original text and a hitherto unwritten language of highly inflected, compound words for the first time. Nahua discourse is full of allusions and unspoken implications, which escape us five centuries later. The Aztecs memorized their history through a combination of structured pictographs on codices and formal orations. This form of "alternative literacy" provided a reasonably standardized account of the Mexican past, which relied heavily on mnemonics and formal schooling, where pupils learned by rote, just as ancient Egyptian scribes did. The early friars wrestled with the complexities of a skeletal history transmitted by word of mouth. What follows is a summary of a once carefully managed past, for the Aztecs inherited a complex legacy of religious beliefs and philosophies from their predecessors, which their leaders refined for their own purposes.

Oral histories, whether recorded in textual form or captured by tape recorder, have serious limitations as historical documents. At their best, they echo with the resonance of confident memory, which lay easily in old mens' memories, and rolled easily from their tongues. The scientist has to reconstruct the context and content of their experiences from fragile oral clues and casual allusions. Most have an agenda—to legitimize a dynasty of chiefs, to make a political point, to lay claim to a piece of land. To dissect them requires extraordinary linguistic and critical skills, but a skilled expert can use oral traditions highly effectively to pinpoint memorable events such as solar eclipses or major population movements. Fortunately, the arrival of strangers from over the horizon in big ships was a major event by any standards, one quite out of the experience of human memory. The occasional oral traditions that have survived the centuries reflect a moment of shock, of gods perceived as arriving from outside the known world. A Maori chief in his old age remembered Captain Cook's men rowing backwards toward the shore like "goblins" with eyes in the back of their heads. Ethnohistories tell us that

European contact came as a rude shock, like a divine thunderbolt let loose in well-ordered, predictable worlds. How does one reconcile these accounts of visiting gods with the observations of hardened explorers? We can never be entirely sure. A long drawn-out controversy has surrounded Captain Cook's arrival and death in Hawaii. Did the Hawaiians actually greet him as their returning god Lono, or is this portrayal a figment of Europeans' imaginations or of anthropology itself? The debate surrounds both the reliability of contemporary European sources and scholars' preconceptions of other societies of which they are not members. On the whole, the veracity of the contemporary observers prevails in the debate.

Anthropology is the study of humanity in the broadest possible sense, ancient and modern. However, the societies first contacted by Westerners are long vanished, changed beyond recognition by exposure to industrial civilization. Our knowledge of pre-contact societies comes from contemporary sources such as Captain Cook's journals or pioneer missionary accounts, written long before prolonged interaction with Europeans. Such writings sometimes have an immediacy that reaches across the years, but their value varies infinitely from observer to observer, and inevitably reflect the biases of their authors. Cook was a sober chronicler of the Tahitians. His botanist colleague Joseph Banks was of romantic inclination, with a classical education and a penchant for the writings of the French philosopher Jean-Jacques Rousseau, who praised the natural state of humanity among savages.

Such accounts have value when combined with modern-day anthropological (ethnographic) studies undertaken by fieldworkers, who spent years living among their subjects. The scholar, however, must always remember there is no such thing as the "ethnographic present," a moment of first European contact when, say, Khoikhoi or Tahitian society was frozen in time in a "pristine" state. The so-called ethnographic present is a myth, for human cultures have changed constantly, ever since the first hominids fashioned stone choppers. European contact was simply another historical event that triggered cultural change, just as earlier innovations, such as, for instance, the Australian Aborigines' boomerang, sparked adjustments in hunting methods and society as a whole.

Ethnography provides a wealth of background information on the non-Western societies of the past five centuries, but we must never forget that each observation, each study, is but a snapshot of a brief moment in time. As Eric Wolf pointed out, relatively few anthropologists have a well-honed historical perspective, which contributed, and sometimes still contributes, to the impression that non-Western societies did not change dramatically over time.

Both ethnography and ethnohistory provide us with vital perspectives on the remarkably diverse worldviews of human societies. Many non-western societies share broadly similar cosmic views—a universe arranged in layers, a continuum between the living and spiritual worlds, and a central role for shamans and ancestors, intermediaries between the present generation and the intangible cosmos. These perspectives have deep roots in antiquity. Ancestor worship is well documented at early Jericho in western Asia at least 9,000 years ago. Bernardino de Sahagun's *General History* reveals an astounding complex Aztec pantheon and cosmos, many elements of which have survived the trauma of the Spanish Conquest to endure today in a subtle melding of Catholic and indigenous belief.

Westerners espouse a linear history, which unfolds over centuries and millennia, measured by major events, the reigns of kings and queens, the deeds of generals and statesmen. The relatively dispassionate historiography of modern Western scholarship that produces the recorded history learned by Westerners in school might serve political and ideological ends upon occasion, but is always a completely different conception of the past than that of the Tahitians, Huron, and other non-Western societies. The explorers of the Age of Discovery encountered cultures with a cyclical view of time and human existence, based on the eternal cycles of spring, summer, fall, and winter, of planting, germination, and harvest. This farming cycle replicates the verities of human life: procreation, birth, life, and death. Human existence unfolds in inexorable rhythm, through birth to death. One generation replaces another, in a world that the living inherit from the dead, and pass on to their successors, with the expectation that it will always remain the same. Everyone enjoys close material and spiritual ties to the land, which nurtures them and is the crux of cyclical human existence. Many non-Western societies have a linear sense of history, too, measured by glyphs or calendars as the Aztecs and Maya did, or remembered in oral tradition with reference to known ancestors, or major events such as solar eclipses or the arrival of outsiders. Such linear history serves to subdivide time, to justify imperial ambitions or the rule of lords, or is simply the stuff of generational memory, something quite different from the long time spans of Western history compiled from centuries of documents and millennia of archaeology. Reconciling the cyclical and linear views of history is a major challenge for a historian of the Age of Discovery.

Archaeology is unique among all academic disciplines in its ability to describe and explain cultural change over long periods of time. For example, excavations in southwestern Tasmania chronicle human occupation in the southern extremities of Australasia by at least 32,000 years ago, during the late Ice Age. Recent research by archaeologist Herbert Maschner in southeast Alaska has shown that coastal native American societies in that region varied dramatically in their cultural complexity and forms of settlement over time. His research suggests that the elaborate contact-period societies of the country's northwest coast may not have been long established in all areas.

Archaeology provides a long view, and is also a powerful ally when used in conjunction with historical documents to reconstruct life at early European settlements, like, for instance, the fifteenth-century Portuguese fort at Elmira on West Africa's Ghanian coast. Evidence for interaction with outsiders is harder to find in indigenous sites, except in the form of exotic artifacts of unquestioned foreign manufacture such as the imported glass beads, sea shells, and other baubles used in long-distance trade from Africa's coasts into the far interior. Historic period Huron and Iroquois archaeological sites in the St. Lawrence Valley also provide evidence of trade between Europeans and native American groups that predate, and are contemporary with, the expansion of the fur trade.

By its very nature, archaeology is an anonymous discipline, concerned with the generalities of human culture rather than the deeds of individuals, providing relatively little information on European contact. However, excavations, field surveys, and meticulous analyses of historic and prehistoric artifacts can provide extremely valuable information on the earlier origins of societies such as the Khoikhoi or the Aztecs.

This formidable quartet of historical sources provides the tapestry for our story. However, remarkable, and sometimes startling insights come from unexpected sources: the florid prose of Victorian adventure novels, children's books, the artistic styles used by explorers' artists such as the Scottish colors used by Cook's first artist to evoke Tahitian landscapes, even handbooks for explorers and official directions to government expeditions. Biological anthropologists provide forensic and medical data; linguistic researches give clues to ancient migrations; and fragments of animal bones and long discarded seeds reveal dietary stress or evidence for human diets modified when fisheries are exhausted or crops fail in the face of cycles of drought. The list of potential, and sometimes imaginatively developed sources is unending. Five centuries of sometimes dramatic and always complex culture contact provide a unique opportunity for creative and unconventional research. These inquiries are still in their infancy.

Even in today's global world, few people find it easy to accept those who are different from them, whether the difference be that of color, creed, or simply ways of thinking. This inability of humankind to comprehend others heightens the tensions in our industrial and nuclear world. *Clash of Cultures* uses contemporary scholarship and nine human societies to explore some of the ways our forebears reacted to human diversity. Our present attitudes to non-Western cultures are colored by powerful and little known forces of history that developed in medieval times and reached a crescendo in the imperial heyday of the late nineteenth century. We live with the legacy of racist doctrines and stereotypes that developed over a century ago, sharpened by the events of the twentieth century.

CHAPTER 2

The Khoikhoi of the Cape of Good Hope

They are very piggish in their eating...when the Dutch kill an ox they beg the guts, from which they do but draw the dung between the fingers and scrape it out, and so lay it on the fire; and when it is not yet half roasted they bite into it with such appetite that is a horror to see.

1653 account of the Khoikhoi,
quoted in R. Raven-Hart, *Cape Good Hope* (1971)

WESTERN EUROPE WAS BORN THREE THOUSAND years ago. For millennia it had been a geographical outpost of Asia, on the fringes of civilizations and empires based on the Near East and Mediterranean lands. Twenty-five centuries ago it became a western peninsula with a consciousness and identity all its own. This consciousness was born of Greek civilization, nurtured on the battlefields of Marathon and Salamis, and matured still further in later European victories against the Huns, Turks, and Moors. Europe faced eastward, its intellectual and political frontiers terminating at Alexandria and Constantinople (Byzantium). The philosophies and thoughts of the Greeks had spread from the Mediterranean deep into Western Europe, creating a European spirit that was opposed to Asia, but looked towards it. Part of this philosophy was Aristotle's famous notion that the world was divided into Greeks and barbarians, those people who were by nature free, and those who were destined to be slaves. The encounter between Westerners and the Khoikhoi herders of South Africa's Cape of Good Hope, described in this chapter, epitomizes early European views of other societies.

35

The World Without

THIS ATTITUDE TOWARDS OTHER SOCIETIES was one of the forces that gave Europeans a curious ambivalence about the outside world. One part of their psychology filled them with a sense of hostility and rejection towards foreigners, and a need to protect themselves against intruders. Yet at the same time, Judeo-Christian doctrines taught that one should love one's neighbor—even one's enemy—as oneself. In time, the same Christian teachings encouraged a deep sense that the individual was as important as the state, and fostered leanings towards justice and equality that were ultimately to revolutionize Europe's relationships to its non-Western neighbors. An increasing sense of individualism and adventure bred an intense curiosity about the outside world. What peoples lived south of the endless wastes of the Sahara Desert? Were there distant lands beyond the boundless horizons of the western ocean?

As late as the fourteenth century, the European world was a relatively small and familiar place, bounded by the shores of the Mediterranean, limited by the eastern steppes and the unknown Sahara, by the limitless wastes of the Atlantic to the west. True, the Norsemen had voyaged far westward beyond Greenland and Labrador in the eleventh century A.D. The thirteenth-century *History of Norway* spoke of "small people" living to the north of the west coast of Greenland who "possess no iron, but use walrus tusk for missiles and sharpened stones instead of knives" (McGhee 1983, 122). The Norse intention had been to sail west and settle the newly discovered lands. But the colonists met their match in the local people. The land was ideal for colonization, but "there would always be fear and strife dogging them on account of those who already inhabited it" (123). Fear of the fighting abilities of the eastern American Indians was to deter European expansion into North America for five centuries.

For most Europeans, the center of the medieval world was thought to be Jerusalem, the biblical city of the Holy Land set "in the midst of the nations and countries that are round about." The unknown lay without, a teeming wilderness of land and water peopled by giants, monstrous birds, and fierce sea serpents (Figure 2.1).

For centuries, long before classical times, people had looked back over the tumultuous millennia of history with nostalgia towards a Golden Age, to a mythical past when the earth gave of its plenty and everyone lived lives of ease and luxury. A deeply felt belief that all humanity had fallen from grace in the Garden of Eden permeated European consciousness. The angel with the flaming sword who guarded the gates of the garden shut the door of paradise to a civilization condemned to live with the knowledge of its fall from grace. This sense of degeneration was to dominate Western thinking until the sixteenth century and beyond. It also fuelled an intense curiosity about the world beyond. Had all humanity suffered in the Fall? Were there still

2.1 Medieval monsters by an anonymous artist

people living in a natural state, untrammeled by the burdens of civilization? Was paradise still to be found on earth?

At first the notion of paradise had no founding in contemporary reality, lying only in the teachings of Christianity and the past. But the Crusades and the travels of the Venetian Marco Polo and his ilk had drawn up the curtain on a dazzling and tantalizing world all around, a world of gold and jewels, of rich spices and dazzling fabrics. As Europe's horizons widened, a new myth was born—that of paradise on earth. One prime candidate was Ethiopia, the strange African land where the Nile had risen, the blessed kingdom of the elusive King Prester John, who ruled from East Africa to the Indus. Thus, paradise was thought to lie in the east, perhaps between the Nile and the Indus, the Tigris and the Euphrates (Genesis 2:11–15). One of the principal aims of Portuguese exploration of the West African coast was to open a channel of communication with Prester John. So pervasive was the belief in this paradisal kingdom that Vasco da Gama, who opened the route to India, actually carried letters from the king of Portugal to the fabled monarch.

The Age of Discovery dawned in the fifteenth century, when Prince Henry the Navigator of Portugal and other monarchs of his age were motivated to exploration. For the most part their motives were commercial and political— to find spices and new markets, to search for fresh allies against the forces of Islam. They had high-minded motives, too—to perform great deeds for the glory of God and a profound wish to propagate the Faith. But however practical their objectives, they were also moved by an irrational, psychological urge to make great discoveries, to find places known in myth and legend.

By the middle of the sixteenth century, European seamen had sailed most of the great oceans of the world in search of these golden lands. As the Portuguese voyaged southward around Africa and eastward towards Asia and the Spaniards explored the New World, they encountered a new and unsettling world, a world densely settled not with godlike, paradisal beings, but with a new and confusingly diverse heathen humanity engaged in "dayly tumultes, fears, doubts, suspitions, and barbarous cruelties." The ethnocentric teachings of Aristotle and others cast most of these peoples in bestial modes as people without civilization, social order, or religion. A few societies, like the West African kingdoms, were described as orderly; "Monarchical, living under Laws, Order, and Princes," wrote John Ogilby in his *Africa* (1670, 34). The remainder were "sway'd on all occasions like tumultuous Herds, and at other times like tame Cattel feeding, and following their idle pleasures" (34). These were far from paradisal images, but descriptions penned out of ignorance, superstition, and a widespread belief that most savages were little more than beasts. These were the "bad savages," the counterpoint to the magnificent human societies that still flourished beyond human ken. It was only in later centuries that the tendency to equate the primitive with the bestial gave way to more humanitarian viewpoints that saw non-Westerners as childlike human beings, but at least as human.

The diverse Western images of savages and barbarism were forged from these early discoveries. Eventually it became clear that Prester John was a fable, and that paradise did not exist on earth. So the quest for paradise became a search for a utopian kingdom where people were still high-minded and filled with brotherly love. Slowly, the Golden Age turned from a nebulous dream into a detailed, idealistic image of a society where primitive children of nature inhabited a heavenlike country beyond the seas. The explorer no longer searched for paradise, but for utopia, for a nostalgic place where the pressures of Western civilization could be forgotten.

The myths of paradise and utopia, of lands of gold, were to persist for centuries, part of the elaborate tapestry of fables and idealistic stereotypes that were to evolve into tales of the Indian braves and dusky maidens so beloved of nineteenth-century American novelists. Such myths were fabricated at home, far from the remote shores and islands where explorers confronted hostile tribes and ravaged local villages for gold and slaves. All that was needed was for a few romantic, imaginative travelers to return home, and rumors were born—of lands rich in gold, of great kings, cannibals, and vast, rich cities, of people living simple lives untrammeled by the degenerate cares of Western civilization. The myth of the noble savage was born; it was to color European thinking about the non-Western world right into this century.

For five centuries, Westerners have looked at non-Europeans with a curious ambivalence. Philosophers extolled the virtues of primitive children of nature living in a perfect state of happiness only twenty days' sailing from Europe. This was the world of myth and illusion, the realm of the conquistador, the sea captain, and the missionary; the harsh realities entailed massacres, land grabbing, forced conversion, and forced labor. There was always a duality about the non-Western world: on the one hand it was a physical world that could be of practical use, on the other an ideal, nostalgic world where Europeans could project their idealism, vent their dissatisfactions, and dream of unattainable paradise. This outside world was to remain infinitely variable, ever susceptible to different interpretation, the victim of our ever-changing, ever-convoluted thoughts about other societies.

"A People of Beastly Living"

THE REALITIES OF THE OUTSIDE WORLD struck home at the very beginning of the Age of Discovery, when Europeans first sailed around the west coast of Africa. During the 1420s and 1430s, Henry the Navigator, prince of Portugal, organized annual voyages southward from Europe deep into tropical latitudes. His captains claimed the Azores, Madeira, and the Canaries. They coasted down the west coast of Africa and rounded the great western bulge in 1433. Henry's objective was to outflank the Islamic merchants who controlled the Saharan caravan trade and the lucrative gold trade between West Africa and the Mediterranean world. By the 1450s, the Portuguese were in direct contact with tropical Africans, not only with the relatively sophisticated West African kingdoms of what are now Ghana and Nigeria, but also with other peoples who were "all Blacke, and are called Negroes, without any apparel saving before their privities" (Hakluyt 1903–05, 10:15). Soon African slaves were working on Portuguese farms in Europe, on the Canary Islands, and Madeira. The king's ships ventured ever southward until Bartolemeu Diaz rounded the Cape of Good Hope in 1488, and Vasco da Gama followed him and sailed across to India in 1497–8. Diaz and da Gama encountered the Khoikhoi, the notorious "Hottentots" of the Cape of Good Hope, who were aimlessly roaming cattle herders with few possessions and no apparent religious beliefs. Inevitably, the Khoikhoi became the very epitome of everything that was savage, evil, and primitive, with little in common with the rest of humankind (Figure 2.2).

The untutored seamen who frequented quayside taverns embellished the practical realities of Africa with tales of cannibalism and the fantastic, of mysterious apelike creatures, and of "libidinous" blacks. The Portuguese and Spanish had been in close contact with North Africa for centuries. The impact of the black people of the southern tropics was perhaps less powerful in their minds than in that of northerners and particularly Englishmen. Yet many chroniclers marveled at the astounding diversity of skin colors in Africa and the New World. "One of the marveylous thynges that god useth in the composition of man, is colour: whiche doubtlesse can not bee consydered withowte great admiration in beholding one to be white and an other blacke, being coloures utterly contrary," wrote one Spanish observer in 1555 (Arber 1885, 338). One thing was clear: the Africans were no paradisal "Ethiopians," but an alien people of a color that was repulsive to many Europeans' eyes.

To a sixteenth-century Englishman, no other color (except perhaps white) had such ingrained meaning as black. While white was the color of purity, virginity, and beauty, black was its polarity: filthiness, sin, and baseness. Blackness did not necessarily make the Africans repulsive savages, but it did make them the object of intense curiosity. How had they acquired their black color? Was it because of the torrid African climate or because God had cursed Ham for gazing on Noah's nakedness? The Africans' black skins started off as a scientific mystery. It was only later, in the days of the slave trade, that it became a social reality, an object of discrimination. But from the very beginning the Africans' black skins set them apart as people from a distant, pagan continent. And their apparent lack of religion isolated them from the mainstream of Christian civilization. Some English writers went as far as to link their

2.2 A wild man on the Cape de Bona Speranza, from a sixteenth-century Dutch engraving, whose description states that the Khoikhoi clucked like turkeys (anonymous)

paganism with savagery and blackness. They were, wrote one observer, "A people of beastly living, without a God, lawe, religion, or common wealth" (Hakluyt 1903–05, 6:167).

The Africans were set apart not only by their color, but by their entire way of life and morality, which differed dramatically from that of Europeans. They were discovered at a time when Europeans had an insatiable interest in the wonderful and the exotic, in the adventurous and often miraculous world that lay beyond the Mediterranean and the Western Ocean. African savagery was not so much an issue (as it was to become at the height of the slave trade) as an observed and accepted fact that set blacks apart as radically different kinds of people. They were frequently described as "brutish," "bestial," or "beastly." Pages and pages of early travelers' tales abound with stories of cannibalism, warfare, horrible diets, and dreadful tortures. Perhaps this is hardly surprising, for Africa was a continent of mystery, teeming with savage beasts and exotic monsters.

It was also the home of strange humanlike creatures, tailless apes that walked around like people. Europe was introduced to the chimpanzee and the Negro at the same time and in the same place. Hardly surprisingly, many scholars began to speculate about the relationship between two apparently related creatures that inhabited the medieval bestiaries, the ape and the Negro. No one was left in any doubt of the ape's character—it was libidinous and lustful, as were men "that have low and flat nostrils." They were "Libidinous as Apes that attempt women, and having thicke lippes the upper hanging over the neather, they are deemed fooles like the lips of asses and Apes" (Topsell 1607, 18). The comparison between Negroes and apes was irresistible and inevitable, given the long held assumption that Africans were more highly sexed and that there was sometimes a "beastly copulation or conjuncture" between apes and blacks. This, of course, was not to say that the Africans were beasts, for they clearly possessed speech and powers of reasoning that separated them from all other animals. The Great Chain of Being of the medieval philosophers that linked all living things to God in heaven provided a convenient framework for placing apes, Khoikhoi, and Africans in a close relationship, the last only a short distance above the chimpanzee and far below Europeans.

The virtual avalanche of geographical discoveries during the fifteenth and sixteenth centuries not only transformed the known world; it also led scholarship in new directions. Increasingly, scholars turned away from a preoccupation with their own salvation towards a curiosity about the outside world and about human diversity. As time went on, the physical differences between people assumed heightened significance. How was one to create order out of human diversity? How had humanity risen above bestiality? Were there lesser orders of humans below the Westerner? The question was to fascinate European thinkers for centuries.

Few people were in any doubt as to which savages lay at the bottom of the human ladder. If a vote had been taken, the Khoikhoi of the Cape of Good Hope at the southern tip of Africa would have won the prize by a wide margin.

They ranked far below the Negro in scientific esteem. "Of all People they are the most Bestial and Sordid," wrote sea captain John Ovington in 1689. "They are the very reverse of Human kind…so that if there's any medium between a Rational Animal and A Beast, the Hotantot lays the fairest Claim to that Species" (Ovington 1696, 284). The Khoikhoi were to become the epitome of savagery. They were firmly entrenched low on the Great Chain of Being that was to dominate European thinking about savagery in the seventeenth and eighteenth centuries. Just as the American Indian and later the South Sea islander were to be associated with the search for paradise and the nobility of the "natural" savage life, so the simple, and not even black-skinned, Khoikhoi, and later the Tasmanians and Fuegians, were to be cast as unredeemable primitives. The Khoikhoi did not long survive the onslaught of European settlement, but their undeserved reputation for near-bestiality lasted until this century.

The Discovery of the Khoikhoi

IN MARCH 1488, TWO BATTERED PORTUGUESE SHIPS under the command of Bartolemeu Dias came to anchor in a sheltered bay east of the Cape of Good Hope. Weary from a thirteen-day storm, the sailors gazed at a fertile landscape dotted with peacefully grazing cattle. The people tending the herds stared in astonishment at the strange ships. "Since they had no language which could be understood, we could have no speech with them; but rather they drove off their cattle inland, as if terrified at such a new matter, so that we could learn no more of them that they were blacks, with woolly hair like those of Guinea" (Raven-Hart 1967, 1). Dias named his peaceful anchorage Angra dos Vaqeiros (now Mossel Bay), raised anchor, and returned to Portugal without any further contact with the cattle herders. His arduous voyage had opened the gateway to India.

In 1497, five years after Columbus's departure to the New World, four more Portuguese ships under Vasco da Gama anchored in the same bay. It was several days before the cattle herders appeared. Da Gama had come to blows with a few of them in an anchorage north of the Cape of Good Hope. They were people who ate seal and whale meat and lived off wild vegetables. "They have many dogs like those of Portugal which bark as do those," one of the party wrote. Following long established practice with West Africans, da Gama and his well-armed sailors hovered just outside the breakers. They made gestures of friendship and threw small bells and other trinkets ashore. The herders made welcoming signs, so the Portuguese landed at a spot where a surprise attack was impossible. Gifts of ivory bracelets and red caps were exchanged without incident, but the locals shook their heads when shown gold and spices. Two days later the Khoikhoi serenaded the Portuguese with flutes and dancing, and the sailors played trumpets and danced their jigs in return. Da Gama watched every move and tried to avoid misunderstandings, for his position was precarious at best. When some of the herders objected to the use of their water, he fired his cannons. The people fled in a panic, only returning stealthily to collect their cloaks and cattle. A few days later Vasco da Gama sailed on to East Africa and India. He returned to Portugal in 1499 to place the eastern spice trade in his sovereign's hands.

Year after year, small fleets of Portuguese ships were dispatched to the Indian Ocean via the Cape, ordered to offer peace and friendship to anyone who would accept Christianity and trade, and war to those who did not. By the 1590s, Dutch and English ships had begun to follow in their footsteps. They would stop at the Cape, replenish their water casks, collect firewood, trade for beef and mutton, and rest their crews. Sometimes the crews would fight with the Khoikhoi, who acquired a reputation for ferocity and military prowess. In 1510, a Portuguese force that attacked a herding camp was repulsed with heavy losses. Fifty Europeans were killed in the foray by Khoikhoi who moved "so lightly they seemed like birds." The Portuguese now avoided the Cape, but the British and Dutch visited it regularly after 1590, for they had no secure bases in the Indian Ocean. They traded with the locals for cattle, but never trusted them. For their part the herders were suspicious of Europeans, afraid of their firearms, and especially anxious to prevent them from moving inland. On the whole, the Cape became a peaceful place, largely because no gold or silver were to be found, and the land was perceived as being of no particular value. Its inhabitants continued to live as they had done for centuries. An occasional visiting ship would barter trinkets for cattle or sheep. "We bought an ox for two knives, a calf for a knife, and a sheepe for a knife; and some we bought for lesse value than a knife," recalled a Lieutenant Edmund Barker, who stopped off in Mossel Bay in 1591 (Raven-Hart 1967, 15). The tribesmen acquired a reputation for thievery and stealth. "They passed by us as we returned, without our being ware of them, so cleverly can they pass through the bushes," wrote a Dutch visitor in 1595 (17). Not that trading was easy, for the Khoikhoi were reluctant to part with anything but surplus beasts, so beef prices rose sharply. The British attempted to control the trade by taking a local man named Coree to London in 1614. He was to learn English and then become a middleman in the trade. Coree hated England, but was shrewd enough to note the low value the English placed on the trade goods that were landed at the Cape. He promptly told the Khoikhoi they were being cheated. "Itt were better hee hadde been hangd in Englande or drowned homewarde," said one Englishman in disgust (84).

Above all, the inhabitants of the Cape acquired a reputation for extraordinary primitiveness (Figure 2.3). "The inhabitants of the country towards the point of the Cape are, I believe, the most miserable savages which have

2.3 A Man and Woman at the Cape of Good Hope. *This sixteenth-century drawing of two Khoikhoi bears no resemblance to reality. (Thomas Herbert, 1627)*

been discovered up to now," wrote Augustin de Beaulieu of the Strandloopers in 1620. "They eat certain roots, which are their chief food...Also they go along the seashore, wherever they find certain shellfish, or some dead fish, however putrified it may be, and this they put on the fire for a little and make a good meal of it" (Raven-Hart 1967, 100). The people lived in crude shelters of brush and sticks, and sometimes in caves. Visitor after visitor were horrified when they saw the herders pick up even decaying cattle or seal entrails and swallow them with apparent relish. Soon the herders acquired the name "Hottentot," a label derived from a persistent word in one of their dance chants. They called themselves Khoikhoi, the term used by scholars to describe them today. So degraded and irredeemably savage appeared the

Khoikhoi to visitors that the word "Hottentot" soon passed into Western vo-cabularies as a pejorative term. Even today the *Shorter Oxford Dictionary* de-fines a Hottentot figuratively as "a person of inferior intellect or culture." "Hottentot" was a common term of abuse in the eighteenth century: Lord Chesterfield once called the celebrated Samuel Johnson a "respectable Hottentot." The word persists even today. In a curious but self-consciously humorous bit of linguistic usage, *Hottentottentententoonstellingsterrein* ("an exhibition ground for Hottentot huts") is said to be the longest word in the Dutch language.

Most visitors to the Cape were repelled by the Khoikhoi. They were clothed in animal skins and coated with stinking grease. Many of them wore animal entrails around their necks. "They are very piggish in their eating" was a common reaction, a description applied to pagan peoples in many parts of the world. "They eat lice, which they neatly pull out of their hair and bite in their teeth...very large and fat" (Raven-Hart 1971, 1:130). They seemed to "eat everything that we find loathsome." The Khoikhoi habit of eating raw entrails gave them an immediate reputation as cannibals. One Dutch party that got into a fracas with some Khoikhoi and lost thirteen of their number, stood to arms all night in their camp "being belegred with Canibals and Cowes." The impression of savagery was heightened by their strange language, which few Europeans even began to master. "When they speak they fart with their tongues in their mouths," wrote a contemptuous visitor in 1660.

With their strange click language and seemingly primitive way of life, the Khoikhoi seemed to represent the nadir of humankind, the most barbarous of all humans. Some scholars wondered if the Khoikhoi were human beings at all. Their cardinal sin was their casual religious beliefs: "It is not known what their religion is, but early, when it is nearly day, they come together, and hold each other's hands, and dance, and shriek in their tongue towards heaven: from which it may be assumed that they must have had some knowledge of God," wrote Dutchman Johan Jacob Saar in 1659 (Raven-Hart 1971, 29). Fifteen years later another writer described them eloquently and contemptuously as more resembling "the unreasonable beasts than unreasonable man."

"The inhabitants of these lands are yellowish"

DESPITE MORE THAN A CENTURY OF sporadic research, the Khoikhoi are still a little known people. Most of what we know about them comes from early travelers' accounts and historical records, from pioneer anthropological re-searches and a few archaeological excavations. One reason we know so little about the herders is that they were constantly on the move. "They have no fixed dwellings at all, but wander around...taking wives and children with them, and all their gear," recorded Jan Nieuhof in 1654, two years after the

Dutch colonization of the Cape. Not only was their way of life apparently primitive and aimless, but the Khoikhoi were thought to be of uncouth appearance. "The inhabitants of these lands are yellowish, like the Javanese, smearing themselves with some grease which makes them very ugly, indeed horrible, with around their necks the guts of beasts plaited two or three times together, with the skin of a beast around their upper bodies but otherwise naked except for that their male organs are covered with a small scrap of skin about a hand wide and a span long," wrote one traveler in 1609 (Raven-Hart 1971, 6). Both men and women wore slain aprons, those of males little more than penis sheaths. Skin cloaks known as karosses kept the herders warm in cold weather. These versatile garments doubled as carrying bags to transport nuts, shellfish, and other foods. Everyone wore sturdy leather sandals to protect their feet on long marches. Copper and ivory ornaments, small leather bags, and other trinkets hung around the neck and adorned their hair.

The Khoikhoi were of moderate stature, with light, yellow brownish skins and sparse body hair. Their short, black hair was arranged in a spiral fashion on top of their heads, their bodies slender with long legs that enabled them to run fast, something vital when hunting small game. The women displayed two characteristics that fascinated Europeans. Their buttocks were covered with thick layers of fat, a condition known as steatopygia, thought to be an adaptation to the cycles of feast and famine that sometimes characterize the hunter-gatherer lifeway. Some women had elongated labia minora as well, a physiological feature that caused much curiosity among the early Dutch. Photographs of this condition were regularly suppressed from early twentieth-century textbooks on anthropology.

The impression of simplicity and primitiveness was reinforced not only by the people's appearance, but also by their simple artifacts and material culture. Like all herders constantly on the move, the Khoikhoi relied on the simplest of portable artifacts: pointed stone or wood spears, bows and arrows, and throwing sticks for hunting. They made leather bags and wooden milk bowls, and manufactured baglike clay pots incised with lines or dots. The herders obtained rare and highly prized supplies of copper and iron for spearpoints and ornaments from distant peoples in the far interior. They eagerly traded cattle for European metal once this became available from visiting ships. Not only their artifacts but their houses were portable as well. The Khoikhoi lived in light huts fashioned of a circular sapling framework bent together at the center to form a beehive shape (Figure 2.4). The framework was covered with withies and specially woven mats to form a serviceable and highly portable shelter that was sometimes lined with skins. The entire hut could be rolled up and carried to a new campsite on the back of an ox. The herders laid out their encampments in a circle, often enclosed with a thorn fence to protect people and their stock from animal predators and raiding parties.

2.4 A Khoikhoi encampment from W. J. Burchell, Travels in the Interior of Africa *(London: Longman, Hurst, Orme, and Brown, 1822). Burchell traveled in the interior long after the Cape Khoikhoi had vanished, but the inland encampments were much the same as those described for the coast.*

"A poor miserable folk, who went quite naked...They clucked like turkeys and smeared their bodies so that they stunk disgustingly..." (Raven-Hart 1967, 29). Traveler after traveler commented on the aimless and primitive life of a people who seemed to do little more than wander aimlessly near the shores of the Cape. But even a cursory examination of Khoikhoi society from the records available to us reveals that it was far more complex and subtle in its adaptation to the complex Cape environment than Europeans ever realized. The herders' ostensibly random wanderings were far from random to the Khoikhoi themselves, for they knew from long experience when grazing grass was at its best and when vegetable foods were in season. The Khoikhoi understood the minute seasonal changes in their homeland. They scheduled their annual round very carefully to make the most effective use of the resources in their territory and to avoid overgrazing valuable pasture. This implicit strategy was based on generations of cultural and ecological precedent of living within the natural limits of the environment. These precedents were to be drastically disrupted by European settlers.

Cattle and sheep were the staples of Khoikhoi existence, the main reason why the herders were constantly on the move, driving their herds to fresh pastures and near reliable water supplies. Their apparently aimless migrations defied all Dutch attempts to understand them. At times the Khoikhoi were widely dispersed over the countryside; at times they lived at close quarters. Judging from the accounts of eighteenth-century observers, the Khoikhoi used all manner of subtle signs in their annual round, signs like the flowering of common plants, the breeding seasons of rock rabbits, and the rainfall patterns that nourished grazing grass. To add to the apparent confusion, Khoikhoi settlement patterns were determined not only by environmental factors, but by subtle and inconspicuous ritual observances and social considerations, as well as deaths in the family that forced people to abandon their camp sites in short order.

Recently, archaeologist Andrew Smith has tried to reconstruct seasonal movements using early travelers' diaries. He argues that the Khoikhoi lived in the coastal areas near Saldanha and Table Bay during the winter months. During the summer they would move inland to the valley pastures west of the Cape mountains where water was abundant and good grazing grass available (Figure 2.5). This traditional pattern was eventually disrupted by the regular visits of European ships to Table Bay, for the herders would travel to the coast to trade their stock for metals. This pattern of transhumance played a vital role in conserving pasture and using the land to carry the highest density of cattle possible. "The grass is nowhere eaten off too close," wrote Andrew Sparrman in the eighteenth century (Sparrman 1787, 2:54). Khoikhoi herding practices contrasted dramatically with those of European ranchers, who concentrated their herds within much smaller areas and systematically overgrazed vulnerable pastureland. In contrast, the Khoikhoi would disperse widely over the drier areas of the inland Karroo Desert during the winter rainy season and early dry months. They would feed on game and vegetable foods, while their cattle grazed on the growing vegetational cover. Then, as the surface waters evaporated, they would concentrate in areas where permanent water was available and pasture plentiful during the lean months. This was a climate of seasonal extremes, in which the Khoikhoi were obliged to make their activities and settlement distribution coincide with the fluctuations of rainfall and vegetational cover. It never occurred to Europeans that Khoikhoi life was finely tuned to the climatic vagaries and carrying capacity of Cape land.

Although game, vegetables, and shellfish were vital to the Khoikhoi diet, cattle and sheep were dominant forces in all aspects of Cape life. Cattle were powerful social instruments, too. Few Dutch settlers ever realized that the Khoikhoi herds served as wealth on the hoof and as such were rarely slaughtered or traded indiscriminately. Surplus beasts were killed on special occasions—at weddings, or to honor special visitors. Both cattle and sheep were exchanged to fulfill social obligations, as dowry, and as gifts. Wealthy men used surplus milk to make butter that they smeared liberally all over their bodies. Cattle served as much more than food and symbols of wealth. They were used as pack animals, occasionally ridden, even trained as lowing phalanxes to charge and confuse the enemy in times of war.

Not surprisingly, Khoikhoi society was flexible, highly mobile, and in a constant state of flux. What Europeans thought was aimless wandering was in fact a constant adjustment to ever-changing environmental and social conditions. Society itself was held together by ever changing kinship ties and informal rankings that preoccupied every member of society. Most Khoikhoi families lived with others claiming common descent from similar ancestors. These "clans" were in turn organized into loose groupings that can be called

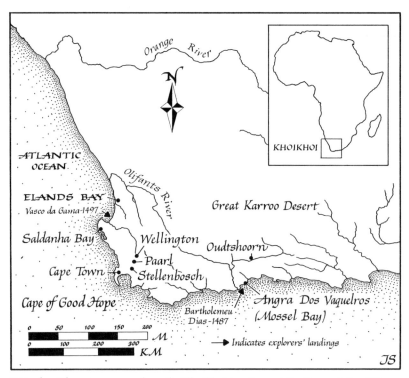

2.5a–b   These two maps show the Khoikhoi territory at the Cape of Good Hope.

"bands." The Dutch grouped the Khoikhoi into at least nine "nations," but had great difficulty in pinning down their identity, partly because Khoikhoi clans changed names, waxed rich and poor in cattle, split off from one another, or amalgamated. The herders themselves recognized their important hereditary leaders, wealthy men liberally smeared with fat and often polygamous. Otherwise, the Dutch were confused to find little that distinguished them in material terms from their subjects. The Khoikhoi appeared to be an aimless, leaderless people.

It was this very flexibility that made the Khoikhoi a viable society. Cattle and pasture rights were so important that the stronger and more successful clans were usually those who excelled at warfare and raiding. Cattle theft, quarrels over grazing land, and the abduction of women—all were cause for war. Khoikhoi wars rarely lasted more than a day. The warriors would join in pitched battle, hurling spears, stones, and sticks at one another with considerable precision. Sometimes the attackers would drive charging wedges of cattle into the fray, controlling the stampeding herds with their owners' calls. Sudden guerrilla raids were highly effective tactics, too, as the cumbersomely

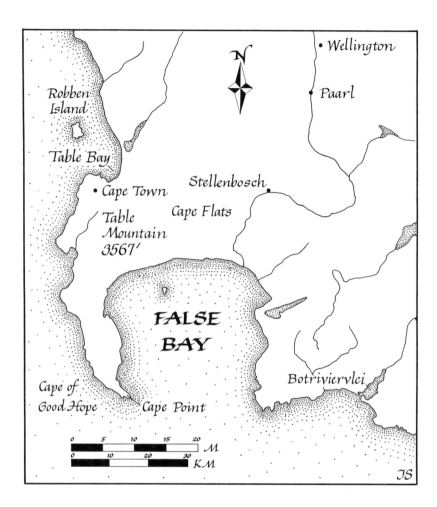

armed Dutch ranchers found to their dismay. The attackers would descend in fury, attack, and then rapidly melt away into the bush.

No one knows exactly where the Khoikhoi came from, nor how long they lived at the Cape. Recent archaeological researches have established that they have been living near the southern tip of Africa for at least eighteen hundred years. Their language and culture are very close to that of the San, hunter-gatherers who have lived in southern Africa for at least ten thousand years, and perhaps much longer. Some scholars have gone so far as to describe the Khoikhoi as San with cattle, a description that is not strictly accurate. However, Khoikhoi who were deprived of their cattle probably became hunter-gatherers again, so the distinction between the two was probably somewhat blurred on the frontiers between Khoikhoi and San territory to the north of the Cape. Considerable controversy surrounds the origins of cattle and sheep at the Cape. The Khoikhoi probably acquired them from pastoralists far to the north and west of the Cape, or, conceivably, from trading contacts with farming peoples in more fertile areas in the far interior. It is certain, however, that the Khoikhoi herded cattle for centuries before Europeans arrived, enjoying a culture that changed constantly over the generations.

The Europeans who settled at the Cape in 1652 were confronted with a far more complicated set of local cultures than they realized. Our description of Khoikhoi society is at best simplistic and generalized, for the herders were in a constant state of cultural flux. There were others who exploited the Cape's rich environment. The Strandloopers were people who lived off wild vegetables and shellfish, but not cattle. Then there were the San hunter-gatherers, who lived in the mountains and deserts surrounding the Cape and were in constant contact and competition with the Khoikhoi. While the dynamics of Cape life were complicated, there is no reason to believe that the apparently simple, but in fact highly sophisticated Khoikhoi society could not have continued to flourish indefinitely had not European settlers arrived. Unfortunately, neither Khoikhoi nor San society was compatible with that of the Dutch seamen, sedentary farmers, and traders, who believed in individual ownership of land. Once Europeans settled at the Cape, they competed directly for the same grazing grounds. Their plows, firearms, and superior technology gave them the upper hand. In time, the Dutch imported Malay slaves, and other Europeans settled at the Cape, adding still more cultural strands to an already highly complex situation. The Khoikhoi were faced with the almost impossible task of finding a place within the new and highly stratified social order.

"From us they have learned blasphemy"

FOR 164 YEARS, THE KHOIKHOI REMAINED in sporadic contact with passing European ships, a mild and primitive curiosity on the fringes of the known world. The herders were fearful of white settlement at first, then lulled into a sense of false security as a constant kaleidoscope of visitors passed by. Then, in 1652, Jan van Riebeeck erected a Dutch East India Company fort at the foot of Table Mountain. The Dutch were merely anxious to found a trading and refreshment station for their ships. They wanted nothing more than to trade quietly and live in peace with their new neighbors. But direct competition for land, grazing grass, and even cattle was inevitable. Inevitably, too, the weaker society lost. The trouble was that the Khoikhoi possessed fresh meat on the hoof, craved by sailors after months at sea. Their culture was soon impoverished by ever accelerating demands for cattle, by wholesale annexation of pastureland, and by the occasional cattle raids and local wars that pitted European against herder. Within a century, most of the Cape Khoikhoi had vanished. Many were wiped out by exotic European diseases such as smallpox. Some herders reacted to European settlement by moving ever further into the interior. Those who remained were either assimilated into the fringes of Dutch society as laborers, retainers, and domestic servants, or were killed in cattle raids or by European diseases.

Few colonists had any interest in the welfare of the Khoikhoi; indeed, many whites believed they would never absorb European culture. Van Riebeeck himself was determined to acculturate at least some Khoikhoi. He took a woman named Eva into his family as an interpreter. She was a great success as long as only a few of the local people spoke Dutch. Van Riebeeck left for Batavia in southeast Asia in 1662, and Eva was now on her own. By this time, dozens of Khoikhoi spoke Dutch, so her services were less valuable. Eva took to prostitution and bore two children of European fathers. Two years later she married a young surgeon named Pieter van Meerhoff, superintendent of the convicts on nearby Robben Island. She bore her husband three children, but found the island too confining and took to drink. Then her husband was killed on an expedition to Madagascar in 1668. Eva became a prostitute again, until the disgusted governor banished her to Robben Island, just off the coastline and notorious as a prison in recent times, where she lived until her death in 1674.

Before 1713, only a handful of Khoikhoi were fully exposed to European life. Many visitors and colonists were so repelled by their appearance that they would not consort with them. The few Khoikhoi who mingled with whites felt considerable stress. Several committed suicide, others took to drink and prostitution. One Khoikhoi man was converted to Christianity by a Dutch minister and taken to Holland, where he was baptized. He later returned to the Cape, where he behaved so badly that he was banished to Robben Island. The few ministers at the Cape were so busy working with the whites that they had little time for the Khoikhoi, whose language was exceedingly difficult for Europeans to master.

Many Khoikhoi lived in Cape Town under even more degraded conditions than slaves. They eked out a living as beggars, often boarding visiting ships, where they made a beeline for the galley to beg grease and animal entrails. The amused sailors would watch while they covered themselves with the cook's leftovers. Then, plied with alcohol and tobacco, they would dance to entertain the crew, hopping on each foot and chanting "Hotantot, Hotantot" again and again. Some would show their genitals to visitors, for rumor had it that Khoikhoi men had but one testicle. These activities added to the general disdain with which "Hottentots" were held throughout the world.

At first the 8,000 or so Khoikhoi living at the Cape prospered off the stock trade. They supplied hundreds of surplus beasts to the Dutch in exchange for copper or other commodities that they then traded further inland for additional cattle. The herders were shrewd traders who managed both to increase the size of their herds and to triple the price of cattle and sheep in the first few years. So adept at understanding Dutch did the Khoikhoi become that van Riebeeck warned his successors never to say anything of importance in their presence. The trouble began when the Company's insatiable demands for cattle began to exceed the supply of surplus animals. The unimaginative officials who administered the trade had no conception of Khoikhoi attitudes towards cattle, nor of the care with which they guarded their breeding stock. They simply thought in terms of more and more head. They began encouraging Europeans not only to enter the trade, but to start off as ranchers as well. Soon European herds under individual ownership were encroaching on communally owned Khoikhoi lands and disrupting age-old transhumance patterns. The company also outlawed cattle raiding, an edict that altered literally overnight the dynamics of Khoikhoi clan life and upset their flexible social order. The demands of the European cattle trade further disrupted Khoikhoi society by bringing white traders into contact with ambitious, but previously socially insignificant, herder middlemen who enriched themselves and now vied with the established chiefs for wealth and prestige.

The herders' first reaction was to declare war on the colonists. They harassed the Dutch in 1659 by stealing their plow oxen and carrying out raids on wet days when Dutch muskets would not fire. Even when peace was restored, the Khoikhoi complained constantly about the annexation of their pastures. As the white frontier expanded outward from the Cape in the late seventeenth century, the carefully regulated official cattle trade became a free-for-all. Large-scale meat contractors operated on the frontier and took up thousands of acres of Khoikhoi pasture that they promptly overgrazed. The Khoikhoi responded by raiding their neighbors. Bloody fighting and cattle raiding persisted until the late eighteenth century, when the settlers wore down the surviving bands by sheer force of bloodletting.

Archaeologist Carmel Schrire has excavated a remote provisioning outpost for passing ships founded by the Dutch East India Company on Saldanha Bay's Churchhaven Peninsula. The Oudepost site was occupied from 1669 to 1732, what Schrire calls a "rough frontier settlement occupied by lads working off their contract to the Dutch East India Company" (Schrire 1995, 99). But Schrire's main concern was with the interactions between colonists and local Khoikhoi at Oudepost, which she infers from associations of indigenous and colonial artifacts. She studied these interactions through animal bones, which give graphic proof of the devastating effect of firearms on game, birds, and other animals, a shift from the Khoikhoi's small, persistent culling to wholesale onslaught. But the remains found in the site itself were misleading, for the colonists dumped the butchered carcasses of larger animals, including large numbers of cattle, into the nearby ocean. The bones at water's edge document the deep inroads the colonists made into the Khoikhoi's indigenous stock base, which was one of the primary causes of the breakdown of their society. The beads found in the excavations encode the inequitable nature of a trade in baubles on one side and basic commodities in the other, a barter system that ensured the Khoikhoi could never compete as equals.

By 1700, white farmers occupied most of the herders' territory in the Cape Peninsula. Most Cape Khoikhoi had lost their cattle, either through the cumulative effects of trading, or through raiding and then selling their booty to Europeans. By now they were unable to recoup their losses. There were too few cattle in circulation within their own society. Many herders took jobs on white ranches in an attempt to regain some head of cattle. But they were removed from the mainstream of their own culture, which depended on a constant flow of cattle between different groups and a regular seasonal round of hunting, foraging, and herding. So pervasive were the pressures to become wage earners that most of the herders of the western Cape were totally dependent on the Dutch economic system by 1713.

In that year, smallpox epidemics swept over the Cape, killing off perhaps as much as 30 percent of the Khoikhoi population, which had no built-in immunity to the unfamiliar disease. The herders may have fared somewhat better than the Europeans, for they lived in dispersed settlements where the risk of infection was lower. But this epidemic and later ones left what remained of Khoikhoi society in even more disarray.

For all the raiding and armed resistance, most Cape Khoikhoi opted to attach themselves to white society. They became domestic servants and agricultural workers on European farms. The mainstay of Dutch military commandos were Khoikhoi levies, who served as soldiers, interpreters, trackers, and guides. The Khoikhoi were much less successful within European society itself, for they ranked among the lowest of the low. The colonists had found the herders unwilling to work for them, so they imported Malay slaves instead. While some Khoikhoi achieved a measure of prosperity within Cape society and adopted the language, religion, and many of the customs of their white neighbors, their culture, appearance, and religion set them apart from the settlers and their slaves. Deeply felt racial prejudice condemned them to the lowest paying menial jobs and to near-serfdom. There were few opportunities for upward mobility. Many Khoikhoi succumbed to alcoholism and psychological stress from political and social pressures placed on them by European government. Part of the present Cape colored population of the region resulted from interbreeding between locals and whites in the eighteenth century. Then, as until recently, they were a subordinate class in European society.

The rapid disappearance of the Khoikhoi excited little attention at the time. Only a few settlers, often people with a jaundiced view of their own society, rose to their defense. "From us they have learned blasphemy, perjury, strife, quarrelling, drunkenness, trickery, brigandage, theft, ingratitude, unbridled lust for what is not one's own, misdeeds unknown to them before, and among, other crimes of deepest die, the accursed lust of gold," wrote one Dutch pioneer (Elphick 1977, 198). Most people thought of them as miserable, primitive folk who were merely a convenient source of farm labor. The Khoikhoi hovered somewhere between animals and humans, people thought to have "no better predecessors than monkeys." The story of their struggle for survival held none of the drama and romance that has attracted historians or novelists to the Zulu warrior tribes of Natal or to other spectacular contacts between blacks and whites. Yet the processes of the Khoikhoi decline are important to understand. As historian Richard Elphick points out, European subjugation began "not because statesmen or merchants willed it, nor because abstract forces of history made it necessary; but because thousands of ordinary men, white and brown, quietly pursued their day-to-day goals, unaware of their fateful consequences" (239). The trouble was that the Khoikhoi possessed resources that were vital to European survival on the way to India. They were, quite simply, in the way.

The Khoikhoi came into Western consciousness just as an entire new world was opening up to the west. Not even the most romantic traveler could claim they were the glittering subjects of the great Prester John. They were not the kind of people who triggered the sort of intensive self-examination that the discovery of the American Indian engendered in Spanish circles only a few short years after Bartolemeu Dias anchored in Mossel Bay. Nor were they eradicated immediately by conquerors hungry for gold or land. Instead, they became an anthropological curiosity, a people thought to be so primitive that they were little better than animals, the epitome of the "bad" savage. Many European stereotypes of non-Western societies were honed on a diet of travelers' tales about the primitive inhabitants of the Cape of Good Hope. The Khoikhoi quietly faded away on the frontiers of the known world.

In contrast, the Aztec Indians of Mexico were to amaze Europe with the magnificence of their civilization, a civilization whose capital was compared, to the latter's disadvantage, to Seville or Salamanca. Yet this sophisticated society collapsed like a stack of cards when confronted with the same inexorable forces that destroyed the Khoikhoi. We must now look at the impact of Western exploration, not only on the Aztecs, but also on the great debates that raged about the morality of colonizing the New World.

CHAPTER 3

The Aztecs

It was all so wonderful that I do not know how to describe this first glimpse of things never heard of, seen, or dreamed of before...But today all that I then saw is overthrown and destroyed. Nothing is left standing.

Bernal Diaz, *The Conquest of New Spain* (1963)

ON 12 OCTOBER 1492, ONLY FIVE YEARS after Bartolemeu Dias sighted the Khoikhoi at the Cape of Good Hope, Christopher Columbus landed on San Salvador Island in the Bahamas. There he encountered "a people guileless and unwarlike," with speech that was "the sweetest and gentlest in the world." Within a generation, Europeans were gazing at a dazzling, new, and exotic world, a world of myriad islands and of a vast, unknown continent that stretched to the shores of the Pacific. This "New World," as Amerigo Vespucci called it, was a "continent more densely peopled and abounding in animals than Europe or Asia." The discovery of the American Indian and of the Americas has been described as the most significant event in European history, one that had a momentous intellectual impact on Western philosophy, science, and theology.

Columbus carried some American Indians back with him to Spain. They paraded through the streets of Seville in front of enormous crowds, and their very appearance triggered intense speculation. The learned and wise began to speculate about the strangely clad Indians. Where had these extraordinary people come from? Did God create them? Had they originated in the Garden of Eden, or "had the devil decoyed these miserable savages hither?" Should one consider them animals or humans? Above all, were they capable of receiving the Christian faith? The uncomfortable questions about savages posed by the Khoikhoi and other African peoples were magnified tenfold by the remarkable diversity of the American Indians. The discovery of the New World triggered a prolonged, agonizing, and little-known controversy about the treatment of non-Christian societies that was to rage for much of the sixteenth and seventeenth centuries. This controversy erupted in the quarter century after Columbus as the conquistadors explored the West Indies, settled Cuba, and voyaged westward across the unknown ocean to the Yucatán and the sophisticated Aztec civilization in highland Mexico. The repercussions of this debate were to be felt for generations after a handful of adventurers and friars overthrew the Aztec ruler Moctezuma and ravaged his capital in 1521.

The horde of Spanish soldiers of fortune, government officials, and clerics who descended on the Indies had characters that tended to great extremes. The Spaniards were devout people with a passion for legalism and an unshakable belief in the rightness of their divine mission to colonize "New Spain" for the glory of God and the crown as well as for personal gain. At one end of the spectrum were rapacious adventurers who came for the gold and a life of ease. "As if they were monkeys they seized on the gold," remembered an Aztec chronicler. "It was as if their hearts were satisfied, brightened, calmed. For in truth they thirsted mightily for gold; they stuffed themselves with it; they starved for it; they lusted for it like pigs" (Sahagun 1975, 19). Most of the adventurers were quite open about it. The conquistador Francisco Pizarro, who subjugated the Inkas of Peru, told an ecclesiastical critic that he came "to take away their gold." Bernal Diaz, who wrote an immortal chronicle of the conquest of Mexico, admitted, "we came here to serve God, and also to get rich." The vast majority of the Spaniards who descended on the Indies were not interested in the welfare of the Indians. Most believed they were little better than beasts whose chief desire was "to eat, drink, worship heathen idols, and commit bestial obscenities." Thus, the Spaniards argued, it was entirely in order for them to commandeer the Indians' possessions and to compel their services.

At the other extreme was a vociferous and powerful faction of Spaniards who believed that the crown's divine mission was to carry Christianity to all corners of the world. All other considerations were secondary to this God-given task. The Dominicans and Franciscans argued that the Spanish Crown's primary responsibility was the conversion and welfare of the Indians. "The aim," wrote Dominican Bartolomé de las Casas, "is that the natives of these regions shall hear the faith preached in order that they may be saved. And the means to effect this end are not to rob, to scandalize, to capture or destroy them, or lay waste their lands, for this would cause the infidels to abominate our faith" (Hanke 1949, 24). Both schools of thought realized that their views would only prevail if they could acquire political influence at court, so they lobbied constantly to keep the issue alive. No colonial power has ever engaged in such a prolonged debate about the legality and morality of its imperial policies. Unfortunately, the debate and the legislation that arose from it had relatively little effect on the direction of events thousands of miles across the Atlantic. The government lacked the local authority or the regular communications to enforce its laws designed to protect the Indians, who were the first non-Westerners to feel the full impact of European expansion and colonization.

The Spanish theorists were puzzled by societies that apparently lacked many ingredients of European culture, including Christianity, organized government, and legal codes. Nearly everyone who thought about the problem in coming centuries assumed that the Indians were inferior to Europeans. Where exactly did the Indians belong in the scheme of things? Were these "copper-colored people" rational human beings? Or, like the Khoikhoi, should they be regarded as barbarians intermediate between humans and animals? Theologians wondered whether the Indians were pagans or lapsed Christians, who had been missionized centuries earlier during a visit to New Spain by the apostle Saint Thomas. Then there was the complex question of slavery. Had God created the Indians as free people, or were they to be considered slaves under the principle long enumerated by Aristotle? He had argued that certain people were born "inferior by nature" and it was only just that they be governed by wiser leaders, who might use their services. If these issues were not enough, many prominent jurists with a concern for legal formality worried whether Spain had valid title to its new possessions and whether the conquistadors were legally justified in waging wars against the Indians. All of these issues smoldered as the Spaniards conquered and exploited their way to the Yucatán; they came to a head when the conquistadors found themselves confronted with the magnificent sophistication of the Aztec civilization

The Rise of the Aztecs

THE DRAMATIC RISE OF THE AZTECS FROM total obscurity to brilliant mastery of Mexico spanned a mere four centuries. Unfortunately, the Aztecs were brilliant propagandists, so it is often difficult to separate historical fact from fiction. Their recorded history began when the Moors still ruled much of Spain and the Toltecs were the masters of highland Mexico (Figure 3.1). In 1150, the Aztecs (often called the Mexica) were a minor nomadic group living on the fringes of the Toltec world. Three centuries later they were the masters of a vast empire (perhaps better described as a tribute-gathering organization) that extended from the Gulf to the Pacific and from the Basin of Mexico to fringes of Guatemala. Their dramatic rise to imperial splendor is one of the great epic stories of world history. Fortunately, a few Spanish friars collected some of the legends and oral histories that commemorated the Aztec past before they could vanish in the confusion and chaos that followed the Conquest. Their accounts provide an incomplete, and sometimes biased view of Aztec history and society, which is a blend of actual historical events and of legends, dreams, and aspirations.

An Indian chronicle written nearly a century after the Conquest describes how the Aztecs came forth from the womb of the earth, a rock named Chicomoztoc, "which has holes on seven sides; and there came forth the Mexicans, carrying their women." The seven caves were to be found near a mythical place called Aztlan, "the Place of Whiteness," an island on a lake to the northwest of the Basin of Mexico where the people had once fished and lived as hunters. The Aztecs' wanderings began in the early twelfth century, following the sacred medicine bundle of their god Huitzilopochtli, "humming bird of the south," borne by four priests. The wanderers were caught up in the confusion that followed the fall of the Toltec empire half a century later and lost themselves in "the mountains, the woods, and the place of crags." After 1168 they came into increasing contact with the Acolhuas and Tepanecs, the dominant peoples in the Basin of Mexico. Both shared a common culture deeply rooted in Toltec civilization, a sacred calendar of 260 days, and a theology that revered a complex divine pantheon and sanctified human sacrifice as a means of sustaining the gods and the world.

The landless Aztecs were unwelcome visitors among the competing kingdoms of the Valley, but finally settled on a hill named Chapultepec ("Hill of the Locust") by the end of the thirteenth century. There they enjoyed a magnificent view of Lake Texcoco, but an uneasy relationship with their neighbors. By now the Aztecs were an aggressive people who believed they were the chosen ones of the war god Huitzilopochtli. After repeated battles, they were forced to flee from Chapultepec in about 1319, and were allowed to settle on some desolate land near the town of Culhuacan, where their neighbors hoped they would starve to death. Far from dying of starvation, the Aztec leaders became successful traders and soon acquired the airs and polish of nobility from their Toltec lineage. Inevitably, they quarreled with their hosts. This time they were forced to retreat into the swamps of Lake Texcoco, taking the idols of Huitzilopochtli with them.

Now, legend tells us, the god appeared before one of the priests and ordered him to search for a cactus where a great eagle perched. This, said the god, was Tenochtitlán, "the Place of the Fruit of the Cactus" (Figure 3.2). The priests recognized the symbolism of the place, for the eagle was the symbol of the sun—Huitzilopochtli himself—while the red cactus fruit was in the

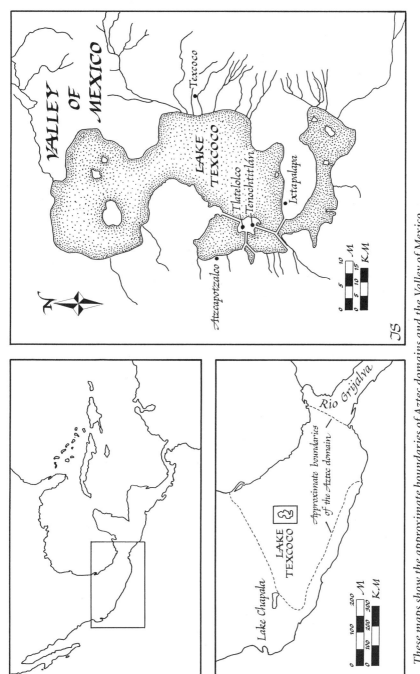

3.1   These maps show the approximate boundaries of Aztec domains and the Valley of Mexico.

3.2   The founding of Tenochtitlán, from the Codex Mendoza *(courtesy of the Bodleian Library, Oxford. MS. Arch. Selden A.1 folio 2)*

shape of the human hearts that the god devoured. Immediately they erected a reed temple to the god on a low sod platform. This temple was founded in the Aztec year Two House, probably around A.D. 1325, although some authorities place the date twenty years later. Tenochtitlán was an ideal choice for the capital, not only because of abundant food supplies and water, but because of its obvious strategic position. Less than two centuries later Tenochtitlán was the largest city in the Americas.

At first the Aztecs lived in the shadow of the Tepanecs, who dominated the Basin until about 1428. They fought on the Tepanec side, acquired some mainland territory, and developed vast networks of cultivated swamplands around their capital. By the mid-fifteenth century, Tenochtitlán and its neighbor Tlatelolco boasted of impressive ceremonial buildings and fine stone dwellings for the nobility. The year 1428 was a turning point, for the Aztec rulers adopted new, aggressive policies aimed at dominating their neighbors. After lengthy diplomatic exchanges, the Aztecs created a Triple Alliance with the cities of Texcoco and Tacuba, an alliance that was to last for generations. But the Aztecs were the masters. They used their new allies to crush the Tepanecs in 1531. Now the Mexican world lay at their feet, a world that was not theirs by sudden conquest or by dramatic feat of arms, but because they had spent generations consistently strengthening their position in an ever-shifting political landscape. A series of great, conquering rulers gazed beyond the confines of the Basin of Mexico and took their armies to the lowlands and to the Gulf Coast and the Pacific, and far southward towards Guatemala. Their generals would demand tribute from local leaders. When this was refused, the army would move in and the tribute was taken by force.

Perhaps the greatest architect of Aztec hegemony was Moctezuma Ilhuicamina I, "the angry one, the archer of the skies," who reigned from 1440–1468, and who gave the Aztecs control over thousands of acres of fertile lands and created an empire where control of the land was vested in the hands of the nobility. He and his successors used land to ensure the loyalty of local lords and to reward service to the state. Moctezuma proclaimed that war was to be considered the principal occupation of the Aztecs, a means of supplying prisoners to feed the insatiable gods. The immediate consequence was almost continual warfare. By this time the Aztec empire was big business, a complex organization that required the services of thousands of petty bureaucrats simply to keep track of the multitudinous tribute payments and commercial transactions that passed through Tenochtitlán and its satellite communities. Moctezuma himself created a complex government system that governed not only tribute, but also clothing, rank, and personal contact. He based his rules of society on two criteria: birth and bravery in battle. Everything consolidated the power of the king and his nobles. Moctezuma himself assumed all the remoteness and dignity of a mighty potentate, adorned in the finest jewels and raiment, with dazzlingly bright tropical feathers in his headdress. His administrative reforms extended to a harsh code that regulated everything from adultery to drunkenness as well as more serious offenses. The severity of Aztec law surprised the Spaniards. Even thieves could be executed or forced to serve as slaves to their victims.

Such ruthlessness is not surprising, for the Aztec empire was not a colonial entity but a loosely structured, superbly efficient tribute-gathering machine. The state allowed conquered local rulers considerable latitude and power, provided they paid their annual assessments. The hated Aztec tax collectors went almost unarmed. They went about their business secure in the knowledge that nonpayment of tribute would bring swift and savage reprisal. Between 1440 and 1519, Moctezuma I and his successors created a web of political and military alliances that was held together by the ruthless and cynical use of vassalage, heavy taxation, and a combination of military power and terror. The extravagant use of human sacrifice was but one instrument of conquest. Diaz and others leave us in no doubt that every subject city in the empire lived in fear of the Aztecs. Vassal leaders were invited regularly to Tenochtitlán to witness festivals involving human sacrifice. The fifteenth-century friar Diego Duran tells us that the ruler Ahuitzotl dedicated the expanded temple of the war god Huitzilopochtli in 1487 with human sacrifices that lasted from dawn to dusk through four long days (Figure 3.3). He distributed the equivalent of a year's tribute to his guests, including no less than 33,000 handfuls of exotic feathers. Every public display was designed to ensure that the Aztecs' enemies "should be conscious of the greatness of Mexico and should be terrorized and filled with fear."

By 1502, when thirty-four-year-old Moctezuma Xocoyotzin II was elected to the throne, Tenochtitlán was a vast city with an imposing ceremonial precinct surrounded by a fortified wall. This proud and haughty man had a reputation as a brave warrior and a wise counselor. He presided over an empire that fed on conquest, more conquest, and still more conquest. What had begun as a strictly commercial operation had now become an obsession with prestige, appeasement of the gods, and military prowess. The Aztecs were locked into a vicious circle that forced them to expand and conquer simply to obtain more sacrificial victims and to ensure a steady flow of tribute. Moctezuma was a deeply religious man who was convinced of his mission to feed the ever-hungry gods. He presided over a brilliant empire of uneasy vassals who were all too ready to rebel against established authority. The theological forces that were fueled by mass human sacrifice and further conquest were so powerful that no Aztec ruler, however prestigious, could hope to develop new, more centralized forms of government that would lead to long-term political stability and provide the insatiable Huitzilopochtli with a more temperate diet.

3.3   Human sacrifice, from the Codex Magliabechiano, *folio 70*

Moctezuma was obsessed with theological dogma, which made it impossible for him to deviate from the policies of his conquering predecessors. He had himself declared a god and tried to consolidate earlier territorial gains. He also engaged in obsessive wars with Tlaxcala, a city east of Tenochtitlán that was to become one of the Spaniards' staunchest allies. All of Moctezuma's efforts were devoted to securing all the reins of Mexican power in his hands, and in his hands alone. Soon the lonely and xenophobic ruler began having visions and seeing evil portents on every side. When coastal Indians sighted "mountains" moving on the sea in 1517, the omens, perhaps the figment of Moctezuma's terrified imagination, assumed new and sinister dimensions. Certain of his divine powers, the paranoid Moctezuma turned to the familiar truths of the symbolic world he lived in. These truths provided the only precedents for dealing with phenomena that lay right outside the Aztec's cultural experience.

The Fifth Sun

THE AZTECS LIVED IN A DEEPLY SYMBOLIC and mystical world where every act, however prosaic or trivial, had a ritual significance. Even the basic principles of Aztec metaphysics, philosophy, and religion defy our close understanding, separated as we are from their wise men by four-and-a-half centuries and the disruptions of the Conquest. They formulated their beliefs in the language of the ancient myths, through the metaphor of poetry and song. Their orators recited poems that told of five Mexican worlds, the fifth of which was the present cosmos. Each of the four previous worlds had been ruled over by one of the great gods of the Aztec pantheon. The deities had quarreled with each other constantly until the birth of the Fifth Sun at the abandoned city of Teotihuacán, centuries before. This time, the competing gods had reached some form of uneasy cooperation. But the Fifth Sun, like the earlier worlds, was destined for eventual destruction on a fateful day, *Nahui ollin* (the Aztec four-day movement):

> *The old people say*
> *That in this age earthquakes will appear*
> *And there will come starvation*
> *And we shall perish.*

(Leon-Portilla 1963, 64)

The Aztec priests used a complicated secular and religious calendar to measure the progress of the months and days along a series of fifty two-year cycles that ticked off the progress of the Fifth Sun towards nemesis. In the meantime, they fed the sun daily with *chalchihuatl,* the vital sacrificial fluid that came from the human heart, the very symbol of life. The Aztec world was based on the assumption that everything was ephemeral, transitory, and destined for oblivion. "Although it be jade, it is broken, although it be gold, it is crushed," the ancient myths insisted.

Convinced that the physical world was really a dream, the Aztec wise men took refuge in a metaphysical world, *topan,* "the world above and beyond us." The influence of *topan,* of the cosmic forces of good and evil, was felt not only by the Aztecs as a whole, but by every member of society. Everyone lived by the sequences of astronomical portents that succeeded each other in the days, months, and years of the sacred calendar. One might reasonably expect such a symbolic world to belong to a pessimistic people, obsessed with impending disaster and cruel fate. In fact they were a vigorous, enthusiastic society, driven by a powerful, mystic imperialism to war, conquest, and to their sacred mission of nourishing the sun. So ceremonial warfare and sacrifice became the very core of national life.

The Aztecs worshipped a complicated pantheon of deities, many of whom were ill-disposed towards humanity. They were invisible, but had at least partially human forms. Most of them had several dimensions of cardinal direction, color, and personal association. Huitzilopochtli, for example, was associated with warfare and Tlaloc with rainfall. Aztec religion had three major cult themes. The first held that the gods were supernatural magicians, responsible for creating the world and the dreaded forces of night and darkness. A second theme was associated with rainfall and the fertility of agricultural land. The rain god Tlaloc and many deities associated with him were worshipped throughout the empire. The Aztecs believed that the forces of nature acted for both good and evil, and they personalized these elements as gods and goddesses. They would make offerings to these deities and perform symbolic acts to incur their favorable disposition to the nation. The fertility of land and the occurrence of rainfall were closely bound up with the Aztec belief in cycles of life, from birth to maturity and then to death, and the endless cycles of the seasons. Thus, it fell to them to watch the cycles of nature very closely, so that the forces of the environment never caught them by surprise or overwhelmed them.

The third and most pervasive theme of Aztec religion was that of nourishment of the earth and the sun, the life-giving elements in the Mexican world. This theme was closely associated with human sacrifice, for the blood of human victims kept the sun fed and ensured that the world would not end. The sun god Tonatiuh was associated closely with human sacrifice. He was the patron deity of the warrior societies that provided the cream of the Aztec armies. Three other major divinities were widely venerated: Tezcatlipoca, sometimes called "Smoking Mirror;" Huitzilopochtli, the great war god of the people of Tenochtitlán; and Quetzalcóatl, "Feathered Serpent." Quetzalcóatl, the god of creation and civilization, and the ancient, revered "saint" of the Toltec, was to play a vital role in the drama of the Conquest.

The Aztecs as a society had developed a simple economy and material culture as well as a flexible social organization to enable everyone to live harmoniously together. Nobles, merchants, warriors, or commoners all maintained close ties to their own local kin group. Local identity was a major player in the effectiveness of Aztec society, linking the central government and authority to local residential wards within the city, and to communities large and small without. Individual liberty, personal wealth, and freedom of action were unknown, indeed alien, to Aztec thought. Everyone's position in society was defined by visible signs, by the cloaks they wore, permissible jewels and ornaments for certain ranks, and so on, giving everyone instant recognition of status, and a respect for authority.

Much of the extravagance and xenophobia of Aztec society can be explained by its preoccupation with maintaining the correct order of the universe and the world around it, by the balancing of the forces of light and darkness. Existence for both the nation and the individual was a matter of divine favor. When the Spaniards confronted the dazzling glitter of Aztec power, the people blindly followed their devout leaders to destruction. They were not conditioned to think for themselves; rather, they had a blind faith in the strength of their institutions. As anthropologist George Vaillant once wrote: "An Aztec would have been horrified at the naked isolation of an individual's life in our Western world." When confronted by strangers who espoused totally alien values and beliefs and conducted their business with steel and gunpowder, Moctezuma and his people fell back on the metaphysical values of their symbolic world. Once this familiar world was challenged and overthrown, the temples razed, codices burnt, and images of the gods thrown down, the people believed they themselves had perished as well.

Cortés and Moctezuma

IN THE YEAR 1517, A QUARTER CENTURY after Columbus landed on San Salvador, some Spanish ships under the command of Francisco Hernandes de Cordoba arrived off Mexican Yucatán. They coasted along the densely populated coast, landed several times, and took away some "idols of baked clay, some with demons' faces...and others equally ugly which seemed to represent Indians committing sodomy with one another" (Diaz 1963, 19). They also collected some gold ornaments, found evidence of human sacrifice, and fought with the local people before returning to Cuba with glowing reports of new, rich lands to the west.

Reports of the white, bearded foreigners soon reached Moctezuma in the distant highlands of the Basin of Mexico. When the strangers returned a year later, Moctezuma sent three important nobles to receive them. His ambassadors found four ships anchored offshore under the command of Juan de Grivalja. With admirable concern for correct protocol, the emissaries burned incense and presented him with the ceremonial capes accorded to a god. They were astonished when Grivalja waved them aside and refused food as well (by coincidence it was a fast day). Aztec gods never refused their regalia or nourishment. Instead, Grivalja offered glass beads and indicated with signs that the Indians should bring gold. They complied at once. "During the six days that we stayed there they brought more than sixteen thousand pesos' worth of low-grade gold worked into a variety of shapes" (Diaz 1963, 36). The gold ornaments merely excited Spanish avarice. Grivalja's men glimpsed great, snowclad mountains far to the west, behind which, it was said, the richest Indians lived, in a land named Mexico.

Moctezuma and his councilors were completely mystified by the strange behavior of the visitors. They appeared far from devout, totally uninterested in the regalia and gifts that every Mexican god hungered for. Unlike other enemies, the Spaniards could not be bought or seduced into the Aztec empire. Yet they had come from across the sea, from the eastern horizon where, centuries before, the divine Quetzalcóatl, the Feathered Serpent, vanished, in one of the great legends of Aztec history.

This legend went as follows: Quetzalcóatl was the deity of wind and the morning star, the very essence of Mexican piety. Centuries before, he had been one of the gods of Teotihuacán and had made the Toltec city of Tula his favored home. Its priest-rulers adopted his name and nourished the god with human sacrifice. The legend tells how a high priest named Topiltzin embarked on an austere reform of Toltec religion. Topiltzin was a fanatic, who believed in penitence rather than human sacrifice and bloodshed, in holiness rather than war. He and his reformers soon ran afoul of the powerful warrior class who espoused more militaristic policies. The alienated nobles turned away from Quetzalcóatl to the worship of his powerful, bloodthirsty rival, the war god Tezcatlipoca. After vicious internal strife, Tezcatlipoca prevailed. His sorcerers got Quetzalcóatl so drunk and befuddled that he slept with his own sister. Whatever happened, Quetzalcóatl in the person of Topiltzin and his followers fled from the Toltec capital, burning or burying all the wealth of the temples. The god went first to the nearby city of Cholula, then to the Gulf Coast, "thereupon he fashioned a raft of serpents. When he had arranged [the raft], there he placed himself, as if it were his own boat. Then he set off going across the sea" (Sahagun 1953, 3:12).

Sahagun's Aztec informants told him that Quetzalcóatl's conqueror Tezcatlipoca prophesied that Quetzalcóatl would return to claim his domains, in the Aztec year 1 Reed. In fact, no native histories refer to this prophecy, and many scholars are convinced it was created after the Spanish Conquest by Aztec historians who were trying to make sense of the arrival and victory of the newcomers. Anthropologist Susan Gillespie has argued convincingly that they rewrote the past out of their deep conviction that history ran in cycles, a central part of the Aztec worldview. So they rationalized the Conquest with a prophecy of a returning god.

We have no means of knowing what Moctezuma thought of the newcomers. Clearly, the strangers posed a threat to the kingdom. But there were cosmological and historical associations of potential importance. Exotic in appearance, with unfamiliar weapons, and a cavalier disregard for established protocol and rules of behavior, the newcomers arrived from the east, the direction of authority in Aztec belief. Furthermore, they arrived over the ocean, the primordial mother of waters. The year 1 Reed was important in the Aztec cosmos as it bore the cosmological sign of a plumed serpent. And the Aztec wise men remembered that they themselves had arrived as mysterious conquerors, and, in a cyclical world, history could well repeat itself. According to Sahagun's informants, Moctezuma pondered over the white visitors and became convinced that "this was Topiltzin Quetzalcóatl who had come to land. For it was in their hearts that he would come, that he would come to land, just to find his mat, his seat" (Sahagun 1975, 9). In fact, he probably considered them a potential threat and played it safe by greeting them with royal honors, just in case an ancestral ruler was returning to claim his kingdom.

A far larger party of strangers arrived off the Yucatán in the spring of 1519. This time eleven ships anchored, carrying five hundred and eight soldiers, a hundred seamen, sixteen horses, and some artillery under the leadership of a thirty-four-year-old adventurer named Hernán Cortés. Cortés has been depicted by some historians as a great, almost legendary general, by others as little more than a gold-hungry robber. A "somewhat bowlegged," grave man, Cortés was a born adventurer, "a good horseman and skillful with all weapons." By all accounts he was a popular, courageous, and charismatic commander. That he was a man of great cunning and shrewdness is unquestionable, for his dealings with the Aztecs show how well he understood the weaknesses of his adversaries. His official instructions were to explore the country, take possession of the land in the name of the crown, and to persuade the Indians to accept the Christian faith.

Moctezuma responded to news of the invasion by obeying religious protocol to the letter. He sent five princely emissaries with the ceremonial regalia of Quetzalcóatl and his rival Tezcatlipoca. They burned incense in front of Cortés, and "thereupon they arrayed the Captain. They put him into the turquoise serpent mask with which went the quetzal feather head fan... And they put him into the sleeveless jacket" (Sahagun 1979, 12:15) (Figure 3.4). Cortés responded in a friendly way, but made sure that the diplomats were treated to a demonstration of the firepower of Spanish cannons and shown the cavalry. A chanting friar celebrated Easter Mass in their presence. Then Cortés told the chiefs he wished to visit Moctezuma. They demurred, so the Spaniards presented the messengers with beads, agates, a carved wooden armchair, and a crimson hat with a medal of Saint George and the Dragon for Moctezuma.

The returning emissaries did little to dispel the confusion in Tenochtitlán. Moctezuma sacrificed two captives in their presence, in case the ambassadors had gazed on the faces of gods. He sampled sweet Spanish food and heard tales of cannons that thundered, of fierce hunting dogs, and of deer (horses) that "were as tall as roof terraces." So he ordered the people to shower the strangers with gifts of as much food as they could eat. A new party of ambassadors set out with munificent gifts, including "a disk in the shape of the sun, as big as a cartwheel and made of very fine gold." Moctezuma also sent "captives so they might be prepared: perchance [the Spaniards] would drink their blood" (Sahagun 1979, 21). The Indians were thunderstruck when Cortés and his men were nauseated by the victims and sacrificial food soaked in blood. Moctezuma intended these gifts as statements of dominance and liberality. The Spaniards thought they were bribes. The abundant food and

3.4 The Aztec emissaries make offerings to Cortés, from the Florentine Codex, *volume 12 (courtesy of University of Utah Press)*

gleaming gold now convinced Cortés that he must see Moctezuma as soon as possible, not only to find more gold, but to campaign against human sacrifice and idolatry.

Meanwhile, Cortés learned that the local people were far from favorably disposed towards the Aztecs, who oppressed them greatly. Shrewdly, he persuaded them that they would be better off under his protection. His position was greatly strengthened when he prevailed upon a local chief to imprison five of Moctezuma's tax collectors with apparent impunity. With these allies on his side, he now began to make active plans for a journey to the Aztec capital. But first Cortés founded the town of Veracruz in friendly territory, a small settlement of "a church, a marketplace, arsenals, and all the other features of a town," and built a fort. Then he boldly arranged for all his ships to be grounded and burned. With no escape route behind them, the Spaniards had only one way to go—into the interior. Helplessly outnumbered, with no accurate knowledge of the countryside before him, Cortés and his men set out on their epic journey to Mexico on 16 August 1519.

A generation later, a scholarly friar named Bernardino de Sahagun embarked on a lifelong study of Aztec society in the belief that such knowledge was essential to successful missionary work. He worked closely with aged informants, people who had witnessed the Conquest. Using questionnaires and interviews, Sahagun pieced together the story of the rise and fall of Aztec civilization in twelve volumes, his immortal *General History of the Things of New Spain*. The last volume is an Aztec account of the coming of the Spaniards and of the downfall of the empire, written in Nahuatl (the Aztec lingua franca) and paraphrased in Spanish. This strange and moving account of the Conquest through Indian eyes is a unique, thoroughly partisan document, but one that reveals a surprisingly tolerant attitude towards the victors. It enables us to look at the stirring events of 1519–21 from the incomplete perspectives of both sides.

Moctezuma watched quietly as the Spaniards moved towards the highlands. Rumors swept through Tenochtitlán. "There were terror, astonishment, expressions of distress, feelings of distress." Moctezuma himself was indecisive and at a loss as to what to do. Eventually he simply waited upon fate, for he simply could not make up his mind whether he was dealing with human or immortal enemies.

The Spaniards were unopposed until they reached Tlaxcala, over seven thousand feet (2,100 m) above sea level, a city that was a bitter enemy of the Aztecs. They were confronted by an enormous army of brightly dressed warriors. Sporadic fighting continued for nearly two weeks before the chiefs of Tlaxcala surrendered. By keeping their ranks closely knit and making effective use of their horses and ordinance, the Spaniards were able to weather mass attacks. The Indians were confused by the cavalry and snarling dogs, and unused to the smoke and noise of cannon and the terrible wounds it inflicted. Nevertheless, the Tlaxcalans might have worn down the Spaniards by sheer numbers had not internal dissension caused much of the Indian army to defect. Once peace was established, the Tlaxcalans became some of Cortés's most loyal allies. Emissaries from other unwilling Aztec vassal kingdoms hastened to visit his camp.

Tlaxcala lay but a short distance from Cholula, a large town loosely allied with the Aztecs, where Moctezuma tried to arrange a massacre of the Spaniards by bribing the local leaders. Cortés entered Cholula expecting treachery and was not disappointed. Forewarned of a plot to massacre his men, Cortés summoned the nobles to a conference in a walled compound. The Spaniards then slaughtered the assembled company. This act was a calculated strategy on Cortés's part. "They received a blow they will remember forever," wrote Bernal Diaz.

There was no doubt in Cortés's mind that Moctezuma was behind the plots against his small army, for his spies were everywhere. The reports they sent back recorded apparently bizarre behavior on the part of the conquerors. Moctezuma was astonished when Cortés instructed his Indian allies to release all their prisoners instead of sacrificing them, as was the normal Aztec practice. The Spaniards ordered the Cholulans to abandon their pagan idols, "to stop sacrificing and eating human flesh, to give up robbery and their customary bestialities." Cortés made a point of reminding the Indians how their gods had deceived them, how the sacrifices made before battle had been in vain. He ordered the destruction of "cages of stout wooden bars that we found in the city, full of men and boys who were being fattened for the sacrifice." Everything Cortés did seemed to attack the very core of Aztec religious beliefs (Figure 3.5).

So Moctezuma continued to vacillate. Playing for time, he sent more emissaries bearing rich gifts, in another display of wealth and power. The gold and fine jewelry merely made the Spaniards even more determined to visit Tenochtitlán. Eventually Moctezuma gave in and assured Cortés that he could visit his capital. But he still tried to stall his progress. In desperation, he sent soothsayers to the Spaniards. Sahagun's informants tell us the emissaries encountered a vision of the war god Tezcatlipoca disguised as a drunkard with a rope around his waist leading the invaders. Tezcatlipoca called out to them: "Why in vain have you come walking here? Nevermore will there be a Mexico; it is already [gone] for ever…" When they looked around it was as if "all the temples…all the houses in Mexico were burning; and it was as if already there was fighting." As for Moctezuma, "when he heard it, he only bowed his head; he only sat with bowed head…he only sat dejected for a long time, as if he had lost hope" (Sahagun 1975, 34)

The Spaniards advanced towards the Basin of Mexico along roads lined by hundreds of people who came from far and wide to look at the strangers. Eventually, they gazed over the fertile Basin. "And when we saw all those cities and villages built in the water, and other great towns on dry land, and that straight and level causeway leading to Mexico, we were astounded," wrote Bernal Diaz in one of the immortal passages of American literature. "These great towns…and buildings rising from the water, all made of stone, seemed like an enchanted vision… Indeed, some of our soldiers asked whether it was not all a dream… It was all so wonderful that I do not know how to describe this first glimpse of things never heard of, seen or dreamed of before… when we entered the city of Iztapalapa, the sight of the palaces in which they lodged us! They were very spacious and well built, of magnificent stone, cedar wood, and the wood of other sweet-smelling trees, with great rooms and courts,

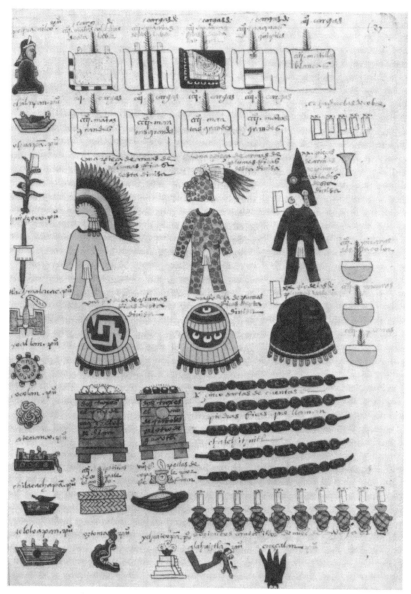

3.5 *Six grades of Aztec warriors and their prisoners, from the* Codex Mendoza *(courtesy of the Bodleian Library, Oxford. MS. Arch. Selden A.1, folio 65)*

which were a wonderful sight, and all covered with awnings of woven cloth...
I say again that I stood looking at it, and thought that no land like it would
ever be discovered in the whole world, because at that time Peru was neither
known nor thought of. But today all that I then saw is overthrown and destroyed. Nothing is left standing" (Diaz 1963, 214–15).

Tenochtitlán

MOCTEZUMA TOOK NO CHANCES WITH THE strangers in his midst. He admitted the strangers into the city so they could appreciate the extent of his greatness. Sahagun's informants tell us the ruler himself greeted Cortés as if he
were the returning Quetzalcóatl: "Thou hast come to arrive on earth. Thou
hast come to govern thy city of Mexico; thou hast come to descend on my
mat, upon my seat, which for a moment I have watched for thee, which I
have guarded for thee... And now it hath been fulfilled; thou hast come"
(Sahagun 1975, 12:44). The conquistadors were escorted to a palace in the
central plaza. They found themselves in a city that Cortés thought was "as
large as Seville or Cordoba." In fact, Tenochtitlán was the largest of nineteen
island communities on Lake Texcoco. It covered an area of about six square
miles (15.5 sq. km) and was connected to the mainland by three long causeways. Well over 600,000 people lived in or near the city with its enormous
markets and extensive agricultural systems. "At the time of Cortés's coming,
Mexico was a city of sixty thousand houses," his secretary tells us. "Those of
the king and lords and courtiers were large and fine; those of the others small
and miserable without doors, without windows, but however small they might
be, seldom containing fewer than two, three, or ten inhabitants, so that the
city had an infinitely large population" (Gomara 1964, 156). Moctezuma's
palace was close to the great ceremonial precincts that were the hub of
Tenochtitlán. "It had twenty doors opening on the square and public streets,
and three large courtyards, in one of which was a beautiful fountain" (164).
There were over a hundred rooms in the two-story building, as well as many
baths. The walls were painted, floors covered with mats. The ruler himself
lived in great state, attended by dozens of servants. Only a handful of key
officials were allowed to address him directly.

The capital was in fact two cities, Tenochtitlán itself and Tlatelolco, where
the conquistadors found an enormous market. "We were astounded at the
great number of people and the quantities of merchandise, and at the order-
liness and good arrangements that prevailed." There were dealers in gold and
silver, fabric merchants and chocolate sellers. Food stuffs, animal skins, pottery, timber, even canoe loads of human excrement used as fertilizer were for
sale. Specially appointed officials regulated the bartering and mediated disputes. Tenochtitlán and Tlatelolco lay at the hub of a sophisticated marketing

and tribute system that brought products from many different ecological zones into the great city markets. Maize came from the Veracruz lowlands, beans from Puebla, and tropical plants and cotton from the south. Cholula sent painted vessels and jewelry. Slaves, gourds, cloth capes, tropical feathers, obsidian knives, salt, and a host of other commodities and luxuries flowed across the causeways to Tenochtitlán.

The conquistadors found that Tenochtitlán was divided into four great quarters, corresponding with the cardinal directions of the Aztec world. Each was further divided into *barrios,* residential wards each *calpulli* lived in, each with its own temples, markets, and administrative buildings. Tenochtitlán was a highly organized city, with an army of officials who regulated everything from drinking water to tribute lists. "Everything was so well recorded that no detail was left out of the accounts," wrote Diego Duran. "There were even officials in charge of sweeping" (Duran 1964, 183). Nothing was left to organizational chance in a community where power depended on one's ability to control the minds and hands of one's subjects.

The entire state was based on Tenochtitlán and run for the benefit of the gods and a tiny elite of nobles, warriors, and priests. Only the nobility owned land, and then only by permission of the ruler. They maintained power by controlling individual ownership of land and by inculcating everyone with symbolic and theological beliefs that made the feeding of the gods the key to survival in a world that was one day destined to destruction. One of the most pervasive instruments of social control was human sacrifice.

"A Reminder of Death"

EVERYWHERE THEY LOOKED, THE CONQUISTADORS found themselves in an alien, highly organized world, where the individual and his ambitions counted for nothing. The great temple pyramids towered over the lake like artificial mountains (Figure 3.6). Moctezuma took Cortés on a tour of the temples the day after his arrival. Tenochtitlán's temple precinct "was a square, measuring a crossbow shot to the side." The causeways that gave access to the city ended at the great temple enclosure. The temple itself consisted of a stepped pyramid, "a structure of earth and heavy stones, square like the [temple] enclosure itself, measuring fifty fathoms to the side." The summit of the temple pyramid was a flat platform about 40 feet (12 m) square, reached by a great staircase on the western side which had 114 high steps. "To see the priests climbing and descending them during some ceremony, or carrying a man up to be sacrificed, was a spectacle to behold" (Diaz 1963, 240). Recent excavations near the Zocalo in Mexico City have revealed the ruined facade of the Templo Mayor, the latest in a series of shrines that go back to the very first humble temple erected when Tenochtitlán was little more than a tiny hamlet.

3.6   A reconstruction of the central plaza of Tenochtitlán by architect Ignacio Marquina (courtesy of the American Museum of Natural History, negative no. 326597)

Cortés and his friars were shocked by the bloodstained, stinking shrines on the summits of Tenochtitlán's pyramids. They learned that sacrifices to Huitzilopochtli were conducted on two large altars placed at the very edges of the temple platform. Each was associated with a "very pretty chapel painted of carved wood, and each had three lofts, one placed above the other, quite high, of carved panelling" (Diaz 1963, 236). The precincts below contained a number of smaller temples, and a skull rack where the grinning crania of human victims were displayed. The conquistadors counted the gruesome trophies. "Andres de Tapia, who described it to me, and Gonzalo de Umbria counted them one day and found them to number 136,000 skulls, including those on the poles and steps," reported Cortés's secretary (Gomara 1964, 167). Undoubtedly the number was much exaggerated.

Accustomed as they were to bloodshed and butchery, to say nothing of systematic torture, even the conquistadors were totally unprepared for the raging appetites of the Aztec gods for human flesh. The Aztecs have been labeled as bloodthirsty cannibals ever since the Conquest, partly because they slew their victims by ripping out their hearts on the summits of Tenochtitlán's pyramids. Then the priests would roll the corpses down the steps, where the bodies were dismembered and the parts "divided up in order to eat them." The famous historian William Prescott did not help the Aztec image when he described Sahagun's relatively sober accounts of human sacrifice and embellished them into "a banquet teeming with delicious beverages and delicate viands, prepared with art and attended by both sexes" (Prescott 1843, 421). We shall never know how important cannibalism was to the Aztecs, or exactly what role it played in their society. Unfortunately, the consumption of human flesh, like exotic sexual habits, polygamy, and other customs alien to Westerners, tends to raise violent and often distinctly unintellectual passions in the scholars who examine the custom. Some anthropologists, like William Arens, deny that the Aztecs were cannibals at all. Others, like Michael Harner of the New School for Social Research, believe that the Aztecs used human sacrifice and cannibalism as a means of providing vital meat protein for a population living in an environment where sources of animal food were scarce. There was, of course, no way that the Aztec leadership could supply all protein needs by human sacrifice, but Harner argues that they resorted to cannibalism in times of famine to keep the people quiet. The Harner hypothesis suffers from the objection that the Aztecs acquired more than adequate supplies of protein from beans and other sources, and that they did not need animal protein as much as Europeans did. Few scholars agree with either Arens or Harner. Most feel that the Aztecs may well have practiced some form of ritual cannibalism. The only conclusive evidence for the consumption of human flesh can come from archaeological excavations in residential areas that might yield human bones deliberately broken up for food. So far such excavations have not been carried out.

The Western word "sacrifice" covers a variety of Nahuatl word clusters, which denote different forms of human offerings, among them the ritual shedding of blood by individuals in the presence of sacred images, and dying for the gods, notably in the "Flowery Death," either in battle or as a sacrificed prisoner of war. Central to Aztec notions of sacrifice were ideas of repaying a debt to the gods, or of laying out and giving gifts at feasts and festivals. Ritual performances and feasts in which sacrificial victims dressed as gods were a central part of major Aztec festivals. Great public rituals and ceremonies were performance art, a vital work of the gods which bound together the diverse strands of Aztec society.

Human sacrifice profoundly affected the ways the Aztecs waged war. Moctezuma and his predecessors went to war for defense, to gain economic advantage, and to suppress rebellions. All their tactics had one overriding objective: to obtain prisoners of war for sacrifice to the gods. Most battles consisted of mob attacks in which untrained levies tried to overwhelm each other by sheer force of numbers and hand-to-hand combat. The Aztecs fought with wooden clubs edged with sharp obsidian blades, and with javelins. Their body armor of brine hardened, padded cotton was so effective against spears and arrows that the Spaniards soon adopted it instead of their hot and confining steel armor. The limited objectives and crude tactics of Indian warfare put their warriors, however brave, at an immediate disadvantage when confronted with Spanish soldiers who fought to kill, and with long-term tactical gain in mind. To the Aztecs, warfare was a ritual event, an earthly reenactment of the great struggle between the forces of darkness and light, a struggle in which the sun lived and died a sacrificial death each day to ensure the survival of humankind. People with this perspective on warfare were ill-equipped to resist the onslaught of Cortés's small band of brutal, campaign-scarred veterans.

The Fall of Tenochtitlán

MOCTEZUMA ACCORDED CORTÉS DIVINE honors, but soon discovered that his visitors were interested in gold to the exclusion of almost anything else. We are told the beleaguered ruler readily agreed to send regular tribute to Cortés's sovereign, but this seems unlikely, unless Moctezuma realized the account was only due when payment was enforced. Far worse were the theological demands made by the strangers, for they had the temerity to urge that the idols to Huitzilopochtli be thrown down and replaced with their own cross-like symbols. Moctezuma was shocked when Cortés said he would destroy the idols if the priests continued to sacrifice people to the gods. It seemed grotesque for anyone, even a returning god, to question the propriety of human sacrifice.

Moctezuma began to plot the Spaniards' destruction. Cortés realized that his position was a vulnerable one, housed as he was in a palace surrounded by pyramids and causeways that could easily be used to blockade and starve out his tiny force. Then he heard that Indians had killed a band of his men on their way to the coast. So he went to Moctezuma's palace with a small band of armed men and accused the ruler of plotting against him, offering him the choice of death or accompanying him to the Spaniards' quarters. Moctezuma reluctantly agreed to captivity, where Cortés ordered him bound in chains while the offending Indians were burned at the stake. Weeks before, the conquistadors had discovered the great treasure store that lay close to their quarters. Moctezuma magnanimously, and one must assume, in desperation, gave the contents to Cortés. Nearly all the treasure was melted down. Much of it, except the king of Spain's statutory one-fifth, ended up as gambling stakes. In 1520, the celebrated artist Albrecht Dürer saw a portion of the crown in Brussels: "a Sun all in gold, as much as six feet in diameter and a moon all in silver…there were two chambers full of armor used by these people, and all kinds of weapons…All these things were so costly that they are estimated at 100,000 florins in value" (Fagan 1977, 11).

The Aztecs now realized that Moctezuma was but a puppet in Cortés's hands. Their generals now attacked the conquistadors' lodgings in June, 1520. Moctezuma perished in the ensuing melee. The Spaniards were forced out of Tenochtitlán. Only a quarter of Cortés's soldiers reached the mainland safely. The conquistadors recuperated at Tlaxcala, while Cortés exploited the divided loyalties of surrounding cities and raised a large army of Indian allies. Then he advanced on Tenochtitlán, pulling down houses to fill in canals and allow his horses and artillery to advance against the defenders. The city fell after a brutal ninety-three-day siege, during which the conquistadors saw their comrades captured and sacrificed to the war god. "The Indian butchers...flayed their faces, which they afterwards prepared like glove leather, with their beards on," wrote Bernal Diaz in vivid memory (Diaz 1963, 387). The Aztecs sent their grisly trophies around the neighboring towns, but to no avail. Tenochtitlán was razed to the ground, its inhabitants reduced to complete starvation. "The city looked as if it had been ploughed up," wrote Diaz. Overwhelmed by a tiny force of ruthless soldiers with commanding technological advantage and by the treachery of their own allies, the Aztecs yielded to impossible odds and surrendered to Spanish rule. Aztec civilization collapsed like a pack of cards and Hernán Cortés found himself the master of a new, complex land. As for the Aztecs themselves, it was as if the Fifth Sun had come to an end, for, as one priest remarked to the Spaniards, "there is life because of the gods, they gave us life." Now the gods were destroyed and the people faced an uncertain fate in the hands of alien rulers.

The effects of European contact with the Aztecs were far more drastic and immediate than they were on the Khoikhoi. The Cape herders had little to offer their unwelcome visitors except cattle and sheep. The Dutch colonists soon bred their own herds, gradually taking over Khoikhoi grazing grounds and destroying the very fabric of herder life. It took nearly two centuries of sporadic contact and about fifty years for the Europeans to destroy their traditional lifeway on the Cape peninsula; the Aztecs, however, felt the immediate impact of Western civilization. The conquistadors were hungry for gold, land, and wealth. The Church was eager to convert the thousands of Indians who worshipped at great temples reeking of human sacrifice. Within a few generations, almost nothing remained of Aztec civilization, except the memories of those who had witnessed the events of the Conquest. Chapter 4, "The Consequences of the Spanish Conquest," examines the aftermath of the Conquest in more detail and shows how the Indians were affected by a drastic new social order.

The Consequences of the Spanish Conquest

As long as the world will endure, the fame and fortune of Mexico-Tenochtitlán will never perish.

Domingo Chimalpahín Cuauhtlehuanitzin, *Memorial breve de la fundacíon de la cuidad de Culhuacán* (1965)

THE SIEGE OF TENOCHTITLÁN ENDED in August 1521, with Cortés and about a thousand Spaniards the uneasy masters of the Aztec empire. A year later the Spanish Crown confirmed Hernán Cortés as captain general and governor of New Spain (Figure 4.1). By this time, he had already made himself lord of a huge estate, entitled to the services and tribute of 23,000 Indians. The new governor found himself in a difficult position, caught as he was between the official policies of the Crown that stressed justice and order, and his own loyal followers, who were out for quick profit at any cost. He also inherited the legacy of decades of debate about the Indians and the most appropriate way to handle them. A plethora of laws, decrees, and bureaucratic procedures dictated how he should deal with the Indians, all of them designed to grapple with the grave intellectual and moral problems that confronted the Spanish Crown in the New World. High-minded as many of these regulations were, few of them worked in practice.

4.1 Hernán Cortés, *drawn by medalmaker Christoph Weiditz in 1529 (courtesy of the Regents of the University of California)*

Encomiendas and the Laws of Burgos

ON 3 AND 4 MAY 1493, POPE ALEXANDER VI issued two famous papal bulls entitled *Inter Cetera*. These decrees gave Spain and Portugal the right to direct the secular and religious affairs of their newly discovered possessions in the Indies. Thus the Spanish Crown assumed the responsibility of saving millions of Indians from paganism, as well as governing them according to European principles of morality and justice. At first the Crown and its officers assumed that the decrees gave them the legal power to manipulate the Indians in any way they wished, provided they made at least nominal attempts to convert them. The king's Council of the Indies never thought of the Indians as noble savages. Council members argued that the proper relationship between Europeans and Indians was that of master to servant. So they took advantage of an existing legal institution known as the *encomienda* to accommodate the relationship.

The word *encomendar* means "to give in trust." The *encomienda* had been originally invented in Spain as a temporary grant of rights to gather tribute. It seemed logical to use it in the Indies as a convenient way of entrusting the Christian welfare of the local people to Spanish colonists. Under this system, the Crown granted a group of Indians to a settler, who had the right to extract tribute or forced labor from them in exchange for religious conversion and protection. Inevitably, the *encomienda* resulted in terrible abuses and cruelty, for the settlers could get away with just about anything in the privacy of their estates thousands of miles from Spain. The few officials responsible for enforcing government policy in the Indies were just as anxious to enrich themselves and did little to stop even the most flagrant abuses.

On the Sunday before Christmas, 1511, a Dominican friar, Fray Antonio de Montesinos, denounced the colonists' treatment of the Indians from the pulpit of his grass-roofed church on the island of Hispaniola. He took as his text the words "I am a voice crying in the wilderness," and denounced the settlers for mortal sin in their dealings with the Indians. "Tell me, by what right of justice do you keep these Indians in cruel and horrible servitude," he thundered. "On what authority have you waged a detestable war against these people, who dwelt quietly and peacefully on their own lands?...Are these not men? Have they not rational souls? Are you not bound to love them as you love yourselves?" (Hanke 1949, 17). His passionate sermon sparked off a storm of protest that resulted in a royal order forbidding further such preaching. But Antonio de Montesinos and his fellow Dominicans were far from cowed by royal displeasure. They fought back and argued the case of the Indians at court for generations (Figure 4.2).

The Dominicans' first success came a year after the Montesinos sermon. The Crown promulgated the famous Laws of Burgos on 27 December 1512, the first legal code ever formulated for dealing with indigenous peoples. The laws provided meticulous instructions on the running of *encomiendas*, the regulation of Indian diet, housing, and religious instruction. The colonists were forbidden to beat Indians with clubs or whips, or to call one "An Indian 'Dog'" or any other name unless it is his real name." Not that the

4.2   *An Indian at the Spanish court, drawn by medalmaker Christoph Weiditz in 1529 (courtesy of the Regents of the University of California)*

laws were easy on Indians: an amendment a year later compelled them to give nine months labor a year to the Spaniards "to prevent their living in idleness and to ensure their learning to live and govern themselves like Christians" (Hanke 1949, 25). No one in the Indies took much notice of the Laws of Burgos. They were honored more in the breach than in the observance.

At the time, the king was more concerned with the legality of Spain's right to fight and conquer the Indians. Teams of lawyers searched for precedents, arguing that the king "might very justly send men to require those idolatrous Indians to hand over their land to them, for it was given to him by the pope. If the Indians would not do this, he might justly wage war against them, kill them, and enslave those captured in war" (Hanke 1949, 32). In its passion for legalism, the Crown ordered all leaders of military expeditions in the Indies to read an official manifesto known as the *Requirement* to hostile Indians before attacking them. This curious document spelled out the legal right of the Crown to fight and convert the Indians. The *Requirement* gave the Indians two options. They could acknowledge the Church and the Crown and be allowed to leave in peaceful vassalage. Those that did not would be punished. "We shall take you and your wives and your children, and shall make slaves of them…and we shall take away your goods, and shall do all the harm and damage that we can…" (33).

The *Requirement* became an essential part of every conquistador's baggage, even though it was regarded as bureaucratic nonsense. If the *Requirement* was read, as it often was, to an empty village, a group of prisoners, or a hidden audience, an official notary witnessed the process. Few expeditions took the *Requirement* seriously, except when, like Cortés, they were looking for excuses to enslave large numbers of rebellious Indians. On the face of it, the *Requirement* seems a somewhat hypocritical document. Yet this is not entirely fair, for the officials who compiled it were genuinely concerned with the legality of Spain's actions on both legal and theological grounds. Unfortunately, they knew little of the realities of life in the Indies and New Spain.

The Laws of Burgos were the first stage of a long and unsuccessful campaign for Indian rights waged by the Dominicans and their supporters. The legal and theological debates focused on a single, basic question: were the Indians rational human beings? The Dominicans had lengthy experience of the Indians, through their untiring missionary efforts in the Indies, and impressive intellectual resources to draw on. Their scholars argued passionately that the "Indians exercise, in their own way the use of reason. This is manifested, because they have established their things according to a certain order. Besides they also have a kind of religion and do not fall in error about things evident to others, which indicates the use of reason" (Hanke 1949, 44). The great Dominican theologian Francisco de Vitoria (1492–1546) went on to argue, "…though they appear to us so stupid and dumb this is due in large part to their bad and barbarous education, because even among us, rustics not dissimilar from animals are not uncommon…" (63). Vitoria's arguments were not based on romantic or noble conceptions of the Indians, but on what was thought to be solid logic. The Dominican carried his powerful arguments about rationality to the Pope himself. After prolonged debate, the Holy Father issued two famous bulls on 9 June 1537. *Sublimis Dens* and *Veritas Ipsa* spelled out the issue in no uncertain terms. "Man is of such condition and nature that he can receive the faith of Christ and whoever has the nature of man is fitted to receive the same faith" (25). The Pope forbade any Christian to deprive Indians, or others, of their freedom, and outlawed slavery.

Although the debates were raging well before Cortés set foot in Mexico, they had little effect on the conquistadors. The papal bulls not only arrived too late to stop the excesses of the Conquest, but were hailed with a storm of protest from vested interests in New Spain. The Pope was forced to revoke some clauses of the proclamations that conflicted with earlier decrees. The Spanish Crown had set up a powerful and prestigious Council of the Indies to oversee Spain's possessions in the New World. Its members were so horrified by the bulls that they forbade their dissemination in New Spain.

The Aftermath of the Spanish Conquest

IT WAS NOT UNTIL THE EARLY 1530s that New Spain was completely subjugated by the conquistadors. While some Indian groups were easily subdued, others resisted to the death. Tens of thousands of people died in dozens of bloody encounters. Several million Indians succumbed to the ravages of such European diseases as smallpox, influenza, and measles. At the time of the Conquest, some eleven million Indians are estimated to have been living in central Mexico. Demographers Sherborne Cook and Lesley Byrd Simpson used colonial archives to calculate the population at 6,427,466 in 1540, a decline of nearly 50 percent. By 1607 the aboriginal population was less than one-fifth of that of a century earlier (see Chapter 6).

A breakup of the indigenous population was inevitable in the face of a civilization armed with overwhelming technological superiority. Both Spaniards and Aztecs acted according to their well-established cultural values and perspectives. Each made decisions that were in their best short-term interests, with little thought for the long-term consequences. Inevitably, those at a technological disadvantage came out behind in the encounter, simply because their leaders could no longer call on the huge reservoir of labor that fought their wars, built their temples, and fed the nonfarming population of the cities, a vast working force that compensated for technological inadequacies.

While the debates about the rationality of the Indian and the abuses of the *encomienda* were at their height, missionary-historian Diego Duran lamented the ravages of the Conquest: "This most fertile and rich land, together with its capital Mexico, has suffered many calamities and had declined with the loss of its grandeur and excellence and the great men who once inhabited it" (Duran 1964, 213). Even the highest-minded missionaries and officials felt betrayed by the tragic course of events. They believed Spain was giving new things to the Indians—Christianity, regal and legal authority, written literature, the Spanish language, and European notions of labor. Yet what they saw around them was discontent, exploitation, and resistance to the new order. They saw the Indians accepting the benefits of new crops, iron tools, and European dress, and expected them to accept these gifts with gratitude and to go along with radical changes in their society as well. They were puzzled and angered when the Indians resisted land takeovers and religious instruction. So they turned to the *encomienda* and forced missionary instruction and government decrees, all of which the Indians tried to evade as well.

Hernán Cortés had found himself in an impossible situation. He presided over a collapsed empire, forbidden by the Crown to grant *encomiendas,* yet forced to use the device to satisfy the greed of his unruly followers. By the mid-1550s, 130 *encomiendas* in the Basin of Mexico controlled the fate of more than 180,000 Indians. The privileged families who controlled them abused the Indians far more harshly than the Aztec nobility had done, under the flimsy pretext that they had to guard against threats of rebellion. It took most of the rest of the sixteenth century for the Crown to reassert its control over the Aztecs, and to abolish the *encomienda.*

The *encomienda* was based on forced labor, but did perpetuate many features of the trade and tribute systems of the Aztec empire. For example, the new colonial masters of Mexico respected the craftsmanship of the workers who lived on their *encomiendas,* but demands changed. The artisans who had once created gold-and-feather ornaments now became carpenters and masons, tailors and potters. Traditional craft centers continued to flourish, pre-Conquest markets remained open. But the changes in Aztec society were profound and catastrophic. The highly stratified society of earlier times became more and more homogeneous under the onslaught of colonial rule. At first the nobles fared better than the commoners. Some of Moctezuma's descendants were even granted *encomiendas.* Those who adjusted readily to Spanish culture and received a rudimentary education in missionary schools enjoyed a modest prosperity. The Conquest did enhance chances for upward mobility for a few commoners. Some enterprising domestic servants and small businessmen learned how to exploit the new system. They acquired land, engaged in profitable trading ventures, and became nobles in everything except birth. As time went on, birthright gave way to imagination and entrepreneurial drive as the road to success and wealth. The status of the nobility was undermined even further by government insistence that people be paid wages rather than donating their labor as tribute. These regulations made the ability to employ people more important than hereditary privilege.

The Spanish conquest destroyed the pre-Hispanic mythic reckoning of time, which began with a venerated primordial era when the cosmos came into being. Cycles of destruction and creation followed, which replicated the movements of planets and stars, and the cycles of life and death in nature and human life. Symbolic connections between the nobility and the primordial and venerated era lay at the very core of Aztec civilization, for its leaders claimed from Quetzalcóatl. Now the kings were eliminated, ethnic groups mixed and broken up, and the scribe who had once recorded history vanished, as did the astronomical and calendric knowledge necessary for organizing human events. No longer were ritual and oral traditions of the past efficient ways of transmitting Aztec culture from one generation to the next. But, in time, some elements of Aztec apocalyptic traditions were fused with Christian millenarianism.

Indian society was diluted even further by intermarriage with Spaniards, for a flood of immigrants followed in the conquistadors' footsteps. Most of the early Spanish settlers were men of humble birth who came to the New World to escape lives of grinding poverty at home. Yet they became the upper class of the new society, together with the educated clerics, lawyers, and high-ranking officials who came out to missionize and administer the new colony. Few Spanish women came to New Spain, so the colonists intermarried with the Indians, creating a new class of *mestizos,* who assumed all manner of social roles in Mexico. Some were indistinguishable from Spanish grandees, while others lived like Indians. The status of the Indians was as ill-defined as that of the Aztecs was well-set. The *mestizos* were at the base of the social pyramid, a homogeneous, poverty-stricken shadow of the elaborate society that had faced Cortés. Only a small number of well-connected or exceptionally able people managed to prosper on their own or succeeded in adjusting totally to the new order.

The Conquest not only decimated the Indian population and played havoc with its society; it also altered the natural environment beyond recognition. The Spaniards cut down extensive stands of timber for firewood and the building of Mexico City. Their plows penetrated deep into the Basin soil and stripped nutrients from the earth. They grew new crops—wheat, sugar cane, olives, and vines—while the Indians still preferred their traditional staples of maize and beans. The *encomiendas* maintained enormous herds of cattle and sheep that denuded the natural vegetation and changed the landscape forever. Under Spanish law, cattle had the right of common pasturage. The Indians were constantly complaining that Spanish herds were encroaching on their lands. Often this was just a preliminary to annexation of the land. Something like half the agricultural land in the Valley of Mexico passed into European hands during the first century after the Conquest.

The *encomienda* managers treated their land very differently than did the Indians. They dug their own drainage systems and filled in the Aztecs' ingenious canals. Within a few generations, the combined effects of soil erosion and altered drainage had rendered much of the Valley of Mexico useless for agriculture. Nevertheless, the Indians managed to eke out a living from the land, largely because there were many fewer of them to feed. They now planted the infertile soils with maguey cactus, from which they fermented pulque, an alcoholic drink that provided at least some refuge from the stress of their new world. All efforts to control drinking in a society that had once forbade alcohol to anyone except the old failed. So chaotic were agricultural conditions that Indians sometimes starved while Europeans grew special crops to feed their cattle and sheep.

The disintegration of the Aztec social order occurred so rapidly that missionary historians working only a generation after the Conquest had difficulty studying many details of pre-Conquest life. Aztec society fell apart while the controversies over Indian rights raged unabated in Spain. The Dominicans remained in the forefront of a tedious battle of books, pressing their arguments at court, in the university lecture hall, and from innumerable pulpits. Their wrath was directed against the settlers, and in particular against the excesses of the *encomienda*. Most eloquent of all was Bartolomé de las Casas (1474–1566), a landowner turned friar who had suffered a crisis of conscience about the treatment of the Indians in Cuba (Figure 4.3). He dedicated the rest of his life to Indian affairs with such passion that he became known as the "Apostle of the Indians." An idealist with a passion for detail, las Casas wrote manifesto after manifesto thundering against injustice and exploitation. He wrote of peaceful colonization, agriculture, gentle conversion, and rational behavior rather than the pursuit of gold and violence. In *The Only Method of Attracting All People to the True Faith* (1537), he argued that everyone on earth had been called by God to receive the faith as a free gift. Christianity, he argued, should be disseminated through peaceful means rather than by war, torture, and punishment. His opponents, many of them clerics deeply involved in secular matters and beneficiaries from the *encomienda* system, violently disagreed with him. They regarded him, not without reason, as an egotistical troublemaker.

Las Casas spent some time as the Bishop of Chiapas in Mexico, and ran into trouble with the settlers when he threatened to excommunicate them for ill-treating their Indian vassals. A storm of protest and abuse descended around his head in 1542, when he wrote *A Very Brief Account of the Destruction of the Indies*. In a torrent of indignant words, las Casas named names and cited examples. He claimed that between fifteen and twenty million Indians had perished at Spanish hands. "The reason why the Christians have killed and destroyed such infinite numbers of souls is solely because they have made gold their ultimate aim, seeking to load themselves with riches in the shortest possible time" (Hanke 1949, 25). So violent were the controversies stirred up by the *Very Brief Account* that publication

4.3   Bartolomé de las Casas by J.A. Llorente (1822)

was delayed for ten years. But within a generation, his sorry chronicle had been translated into six European languages. Las Casas's strictures were seized upon with glee by anti-Spanish propagandists, who claimed the conquistadors had slaughtered millions of Indians. This so-called Black Legend still haunts the historical literature to this day, with las Casas' opponents arguing out that it was exotic diseases rather than genocide that carried away most of the Indians. Without question, many of las Casas's claims were exaggerated, but his arguments that the Indians were not animals nor children of limited intelligence, but human beings fully capable of becoming Christians within the framework of Spanish civilization are timeless in the sense that they have not lost their validity today. They have even proved ideologically attractive to contemporary, anti-Spanish subversive movements.

Las Casas and his fellow Dominicans were powerful enough to persuade the Crown to promulgate the New Laws in 1542. These abolished *encomiendas* after the death of the current occupant, outlawed slavery for prisoners of war, and forbade ill-treatment of the Indians. In the event, the New Laws were totally ineffectual. Many provisions were revoked when the colonists pointed out that the Crown would lose a great deal of valuable tribute. Undeterred, las Casas resorted to the impressive ecclesiastical sanctions of the Catholic Church to reinforce his views. He made the colonists aware that they would be held accountable for their excesses before their bishops and confessors. Weapons like excommunication, interdict, and denial of absolution were far more effective in the sixteenth century than they are today. The *encomenderos* reacted violently by attacking the missionaries for their involvement in politics. The Church itself was deeply divided between those who supported the colonists and those who did not. The controversies culminated in the celebrated Junta de Valladolid in 1550–51. A formal court of inquiry was convened, a junta that pitted las Casas against a brilliant intellectual named Gines de Sepulveda, who believed like Aristotle that certain people were born inferior and destined for slavery.

The debate dragged on for months. Las Casas probably had the theoretical advantage in the debate, but the colonists were able to bring inexorable pressure to bear at court. The Crown chose to ignore the immense political power of the Church in the affairs of New Spain and bowed to what it thought was economic reality. The influence of the Dominicans declined gradually. The issue of the political and economic condition of the Indian assumed less and less importance at court. As the pioneer days of New Spain ended, Church and State reached an accommodation. The Indians were ignored and relegated to the role of tribute-paying citizens of the colony. Las Casas's work had proved to be of little immediate practical value, even if the influence of his old enemy, the *encomienda,* declined sharply after his death.

The Word of God

THE CHRISTIAN MISSION TO THE Aztecs began with a vengeance in 1524, when a party of twelve Franciscans arrived in Tenochtitlán. They caused a sensation among the Indians by walking barefoot all the way from Veracruz, poor, humble men quite unlike the arrogant conquistadors. They began by debating the Aztec wise men and arguing for the overwhelming superiority of Christian beliefs. "It is the doctrine of the elders that there is life because of the gods," responded the Indians, "with their sacrifice they gave us life ... And now are we to destroy the ancient order of life?" (Leon-Portilla 1963, 66). The friars pointed out eloquently that the Aztecs' gods had failed them signally and that it was time for a change. But it is questionable whether they got the better of the debate.

Once they had mastered the local dialects, the Franciscans embarked on a campaign of mass conversion. They planned an educational program to give Christian training to young nobles, the potential leaders of Indian society. At first the missionaries were successful. The Indians as a whole followed those of their younger leaders who had acquired some Christian education and abandoned their loyalty to the old gods, pagan temples, and human sacrifice. Superficially, the Indians were attracted to the elaborate rituals and colorful ceremonies of the Catholic church. Some of their own traditional practices surrounding marriage, penance, and fasting had some resemblances to Christian ritual. But the complications of belief were such that a simple transfer of spiritual allegiance was impossible. The friars were unable to communicate the deeper meanings of Christian doctrine, such as the abstract concepts of virtue and sin. Many Indians simply added the Lord to their roster of deities and considered the saints to be members of an anthropomorphic group of lesser gods.

The Indians liked and trusted the early friars, partly because they functioned within the traditional framework, and also because they lived close to their parishioners, suffering the same hardships as they did. The relationship was a logical one, for the Indians had always respected their priests. But this respect turned to hatred when zealous prelates bore down on transgressors and backsliders. Some idolaters were executed, while others were sentenced to exile and service in monasteries. Whippings were commonplace, imprisonment routine. In 1525, the church embarked on a systematic campaign to remove all signs of idolatry. Six years later the fanatical Bishop Zumarraga of Mexico boasted that he had destroyed 500 pagan shrines and 20,000 idols. The Indians gave "voluntary" contributions that built the first churches, and monasteries. The church turned to forced labor instead in the 1530s. The friars responded to criticism of their methods by arguing that they were educating people with the mental abilities of tenor twelve-year-old children.

Eventually the Church became a complex and wealthy bureaucracy whose influence on Indian society declined sharply as the people withdrew into themselves and shunned contact with Europeans. The focuses of Indian social and religious life became the small *barrio,* the local chapel, and the *cofradia,* the parishioners' association. These Indian-supported organizations provided their members with a small, intimate association of their own that provided a haven against social stress and racism. The *cofradia* became a symbol of community welfare. Each had its own patron saint, whose Christian name was sometimes a front for subtle, cherished beliefs and values that went back to earlier times. Nowhere was, nor still is, this fusion of beliefs better expressed than in countless community *fiestas,* regular celebrations of saints and holy days. The services, processions, and public feasting that accompanied them combined both Christian observance with costumes, masks, displays, and dancing that gave the Indians a sense of community and common identity. For example, the Indian preoccupation with water for crops can be discerned even today in public festivals such as the annual jaguar fights for rain that take place every May in the towns of Acatlan and Zitlala in Guerrero, Mexico. Masked fighters crack whips at one another in contests that serve as mock sacrifices for rain. Until fairly recently, people were sometimes killed in these ceremonies.

The Spaniards ruled Mexico for over three hundred years. They established a colonial form of government organized around a network of major cities surrounded by *cabeceras,* head towns ruled by former Indian rulers, and lesser settlements known as *suiegos,* themselves divided into villages and parishes. The authorities appointed *corregidors* to each small town, tax collectors who milked the local people of as much tribute and taxes as they could bear. As Spanish control of Mexico tightened, the Indians became alienated, lost their social mobility, and disengaged themselves as much as possible from European political and social life. Soon the Indians were reduced to selling their land to buy food and pay taxes. They were sometimes regrouped in smaller, more compact settlements (*congregacions*) where, theoretically, they were more accessible for religious conversion. The Indians complained with justification that they were better off on their traditional lands, where tribal and kinship ties could be cherished and fostered. Unfortunately, they lacked the political organization and unity to speak with anything like one voice, or to maintain a united front in the face of European encroachment. Rather than be herded into *congregacions,* many Indians moved into the cities, or onto the great *haciendas,* ranches that now marketed the produce that Indian farmers had once supplied to the settlers. Both the cities and *haciendas* needed large numbers of Indian laborers to function effectively. Many of these new wage earners severed their ties with their traditional homes, adding to their political and social alienation. So much Indian land was freed by the policy of *congregacion* that many communities starved. The trouble was that many Spanish immigrants were nonfarmers, so newly annexed lands often remained fallow while the Indians went hungry. The survivors of smallpox epidemics, slavery, and immunological stress were soon completely alienated from a society that did little more than organize them within the framework of a large, insensitive political unit. The Indians retreated into their own communities, taking the tatters of their beliefs and values with them. Perhaps it is well their ancestors placed limited value on life on earth and lived close to *miccatzintli,* the state of death, believing life on earth was, perhaps, only a dream.

The terrible realities of the Conquest and its aftermath saw the Spaniards gaining control over a huge Indian population largely for economic and personal gain. There was nothing idealistic about the Conquest, nor about the diseases and harsh strictures that decimated the Indian population and thrust the Aztecs into a new and unfamiliar economic, political, and spiritual world. Much of the debate that surrounded the morality of colonization and the treatment of the Native Americans was totally irrelevant to the actual course of events far across the Atlantic in Mexico. Few people actively involved with affairs in New Spain had any illusions about the nobility of the indigenous inhabitants, or believed that the Aztecs had once enjoyed a paradisiacal existence. It was left to casual travelers and to armchair philosophers back home to perpetuate the myths of noble savages living in an elusive paradise on earth that one day would be found in remote lands. It was not until the mid-eighteenth century, long after Aztec civilization was largely forgotten, that this paradisial land was located in the South Seas. It would change European perceptions of savagery for generations.

CHAPTER 5

The Land of the Rising Sun

White, which with us is a festive and cheerful color, is a sign of mourning and sadness with them, whereas they like black and mulberry as gay colors. Our vocal and instrumental music wound their ears, and they delight in their own music which truly tortures our hearing.

Jesuit missionary Alessandra Valignano, 1580,
quoted in C. R. Boxer, *The Christian Century in Japan* (1951)

As we have seen, the primary purpose of Prince Henry the Navigator's voyages of exploration down the west coast of Africa to the Cape of Good Hope and beyond was to seek a westward route to the fabled "Indies." In 1497, Portuguese navigator Vasco da Gama rounded the Cape, explored the East African coast as far north as Malindi in present-day Kenya, and enlisted the assistance of an Arab pilot to cross the Indian Ocean to Goa on the wings of the monsoon winds. The maritime gateway to Asia, the Indies, was open to European ships for the first time. Five years later, Christopher Columbus landed on San Salvador Island in the Bahamas, which he thought to be an outlying island of China. He called his tropical islands the "Indies" as well, but it soon became apparent that an entire continent lay between the trade wind routes of the Atlantic Ocean and distant Asian lands.

Europeans had known of overland routes to China since Marco Polo's day, but the journey was hazardous and beyond the capabilities of all but the boldest and most enterprising travelers. Asia itself was controlled by powerful tributary states, some of them more densely populated and, indeed, more productive, than their European counterparts, which added compelling political hazards to the equation. The ocean alternative offered boundless possibilities, without the logistical difficulties of dromedaries and restricted loads. Others followed where Vasco da Gama led, sailing along centuries-old maritime highways that used the six-monthly cycles of monsoon winds to cross from India to southeast Asia, then northward into the China Sea. These routes had been in use by Arab and Indian pilots since Roman times. Archaeologists have found imported 2,000-year-old south Indian trade pottery as far east as the island of Bali.

The Portuguese located the strategic points within the Islamic trading network that linked Africa, Arabia, India, and southeast Asia. Their relatively nimble-sailing gun-bearing ships were superior to Arab lateen-rigged *dhows*, which allowed them to seize major Islamic trading strongholds between Mombasa on the East African coast and Malacca in the heart of southeast Asia, establishing forts at their new possessions. Portuguese skippers built posts down the coast of western India and in Sri Lanka by 1518, were trading in the spice-rich southeast Asian islands by 1511, and had colonized Macao on the Canton coast by 1557. The staple of Portuguese trade was pepper, "the substance of the Indies," as the Crown put it. The Portuguese never completely dominated the spice trade, contenting themselves by controlling shipping lanes and forcing all vessels to carry a license and to pay customs dues at their trading posts. The Portuguese became an integral part of the existing trading structure.

The Dutch, in the person of the Dutch East India Company, followed soon afterward, engaging in fierce competition with the Portuguese for the lucrative spice trade. Their well-trained crews attacked Portuguese outposts, driving their rivals from Sri Lanka with its lucrative cinnamon trade in 1658, and establishing their major stronghold at Batavia on the site of modern-day Jakarta. Eventually, they gained a monopoly over the clove and nutmeg trade of the Molucca islands through agreements with local leaders. The Dutch achieved their objectives with a single-minded devotion to profit obtained by force. Their success resulted in the founding of a colony and provisioning station at the Cape of Good Hope in 1652 (see Chapter 2).

The East India Company, licensed by the British Crown, was founded in 1600. It began by challenging the Dutch for control of the spice trade, then focused its attention on India, where the Company entered into agreements with Mughal rulers, also establishing a trading post on the east coast at Madras after 1639. As the Mughals declined in the late seventeenth century, so the influence and power of the Company rose. By 1765, the East India Company effectively ruled India. It changed from being a commercial organization into a bureaucratic and military arm of the British government. The Company mobilized the vast resources of India to expand its trade with China.

For three centuries, the great European maritime powers competed with one another in Asian waters for gold, porcelain, silks, spices, and other highly lucrative commodities. They established small commercial settlements, "factories," as precarious footholds on Asian lands. Superior naval power and commercial organization allowed Europeans to control long-distance ocean trade routes. The bolder, more entrepreneurial captains encroached on the coastal carrying trade between India and China, which had been in the hands of Arab, Gujerati, Malay, and Chinese merchants for many centuries. However, their activities depended on the goodwill of local rulers and the capricious shifting sands of political alliances ashore. Europeans were unable to dominate production and commerce as they did in the Americas and Africa, the latter by virtue of their control of the slave trade. Foreigners faced enormous obstacles, among them Chinese Manchu rulers who tightly controlled trade with "red-headed barbarians." One Manchu emperor went so far as to clear a no-man's-land buffer zone between the Chinese coast and interior to prevent uncontrolled transactions between foreigners and his subjects. In response, European trading organizations created a web of commercial networks along Asian coasts, setting up specialized production centers to produce commodities such as cotton or opium to pay for Europe's newly acquired and insatiable taste for Chinese tea. The figures tell the tale. In 1664, the Dutch brought precisely two pounds, two ounces of tea to England. By 1793, the East India Company alone sold 6 million pounds, double this figure two years later. Eventually, opium became the (illegal) commodity that paid for Chinese tea. By the end of the nineteenth century, one out of every ten Chinese is thought to have become an addict.

Inevitably, the tentacles of European exploration and trading enterprise reached the shores of Japan, close offshore. Geographically isolated, with its own distinctive culture, Japan developed a unique approach to foreigners, effectively isolating itself from outside for two centuries.

The Rise of the Shogunate

THE MOUNTAINOUS 143,000 SQUARE miles of Japan were settled by hunter-gatherers during the late Ice Age, perhaps as early as 30,000 years ago (Figure 5.1). As sea levels rose during the global warming after the Ice Age, many Japanese groups congregated by estuaries, lake shores, and sheltered coasts, where they developed specialized, semi-sedentary foraging cultures, which depended heavily on fish, nuts harvests, sea mammals, and shellfish for their diet. This "Jomon" culture with its distinctive clay vessels, some of the earliest in the world, flourished for many centuries, in some areas until as late as the eighth century A.D.

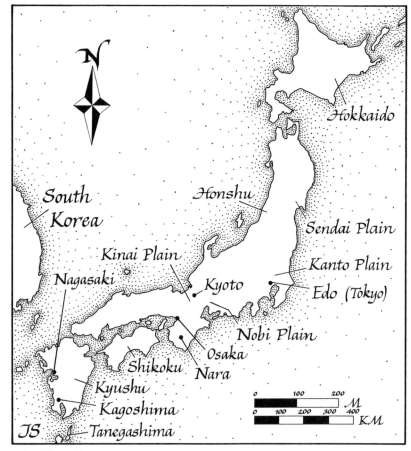

5.1   Map of Japan

Japan's abundant summer rainfall and warm climate was ideal for rice agriculture. From Kyushu in the south to about 100 miles north of Tokyo, farmers can harvest two crops a year, wheat or barley first, followed by rice. By 1000 B.C., barley and rice farming had taken hold in Kyushu, having arrived from nearby Korea. The subsequent Yayoi culture spread northward from Kyushu, displaying considerable local variation. In 221 B.C., China was united under the Qin state, whose rulers promulgated a strongly centralized form of government. A unified China under the succeeding Han dynasties extended its trading interests outward and across the Yellow Sea to Korea and Japan. Yayoi leaders from a people known as the Wa sent emissaries to the Han court in A.D. 57 and 107, bearing gifts of jade, pearls, bows and arrows, and slaves. Early Han mirrors and other artifacts in Yayoi graves testify to an increasing volume of trading activity with the mainland. Chinese records tell us Wa was a series of small polities scattered through Japan's western islands ruled from a still identified location called Yamatai, perhaps in Kyushu.

Chinese records of the late fifth century A.D. paint an incomplete picture of early Japan. At the time, Japanese society was highly decentralized, with power split among various warring clans. The most important cultural center was on the Yamato Peninsula in southern Honshu, south of the modern city of Kyoto. At the time, Nippon, (the "Land of the Rising Sun") was confined to northern Kyushi and southern Honshu. Northern Honshu was the home of the "barbarian" Ainu, people with deep roots in the remote past. The Yamato clan leader was Emperor, with at least theoretical power over all the clans. In practice, he ruled over the Yamato only. Each clan claimed descent from a specific deity (*kami*), whose cult was the core of communal life. Traditional *Shinto* ("Way of God") belief placed great emphasis on family and community, also on the doctrine that the Emperor was of divine descent, and a symbol of national unity.

In A.D. 538, a Korean ruler dispatched a Buddhist teacher to the Japanese court. The Emperor ordered one clan, the Soga, to adopt Buddhism as an experiment, to test the reaction of feudal lords. Civil war broke out at once, but more missionaries continued to arrive. In 593, Crown Prince Shotoko, an imperial regent, declared Buddhism a favored religion, and sent monks and students to China. Soon Buddhist and Confucian ideas spread widely through Japan, together with Chinese notions of politics and law. By 645, the powerful Fujiwara clan controlled the imperial court. The Fujiwara introduced the Taika Reforms, which ended landholding by clans, brought the nation under the Emperor's control, and appeased clan chieftains by appointing them to high positions in the nobility. Half a century later, the Taiho Codes of 702, introduced by the Heian clan, shaped Japanese society for five centuries. A lose confederation of clans became a highly centralized country, with provincial governors and fixed land allocations for peasants. Public education was provided for the nobility only, who were trained in Chinese ethics and values, further widening the chasm between the rulers and the ruled. Nobles never paid taxes, but peasants did, placing a heavy burden on all commoners.

By this time, Buddhism was more influential than Shinto. A new imperial capital rose at Nara, an important religious center, where wealthy nobles endowed monasteries and temples. Japanese emperors admired the powerful T'ang rulers of China and especially their Confucianist ideas, which defined the relationship between the people and government. Confucianism influenced Japanese thinking, but was changed subtly to accommodate local conditions. Confucius had preached about a natural order of society, which, in the Japanese mind, was transferred to strong notions of pyramid and hierarchy, where deference to the authority of the nobility, also to heads of families, was of fundamental importance. Confucianism also proclaimed the Emperor was descended from the gods, was a deity on earth. Under Japanese versions of this belief, he possessed the Mandate of Heaven and was the permanent head of state. Therefore those ruled by the Emperor must obey the dictates of heaven.

Throughout the eighth century, Buddhist interests became increasingly powerful, until the Fujiwara clan rose to prominence late in the century. Shrewdly, they induced royal princes to marry Fujiwara daughters, until eventually the Emperor was related to the clan on the Empress' side. The Fujiwara moved the royal capital to Kyoto and persuaded many emperors to retire early to a life of ease, leaving the affairs of government in Fujiwara regents. The central government became more powerful, expanding its rule northward and pushing the indigenous Ainu onto the island of Hokkaido. From 794 to 1185, Fujiwara regents controlled Japan. The earlier leaders were men of great ability, but the influence of the court diminished in the tenth century as corruption set in. Near-anarchy prevailed in the provinces, where a new class of military aristocrats effectively became warlords. The Heian government had modified the Taiho Codes and allowed some nobles to own landholdings of up to 1,250 acres tax free. These manors grew in size as neighboring, heavily taxed peasants turned their holdings over to the local lords, preferring service to a master to brutal taxation. The manors grew to vast size, to the point that more distant nobles presided over a patchwork of completely independent states. Inevitably, civil war between the Fujiwara and other powerful military clans broke out, culminating in a great naval battle in 1185, when Minamoto Yoritomo defeated the Taira clan and assumed control of Japan.

Yoritomo established a military government near modern Yokohama, some distance from the imperial court at Kyoto. In 1192, he visited the Emperor and persuaded his ruler to grant him the title Seii-Tai-shogun ("Barbarian-subduing supreme general"). Yoritomo acquired the title of shogun for life, a title that hitherto had only been granted temporarily at times of military emergency. He also received the privilege of appointing his own successor. Effectively, the shogun assumed all ruling power, while deferring to the Emperor, as divine monarch, in public. From 1192 to 1857, he and his successors ruled with puppet emperors by their side. Some of them ignored the Emperor completely.

Between 1186 and 1333, the foundations of Japanese feudalism came into being. Whereas China had a huge centralized bureaucracy, a need for standing armies, and for massive public irrigation and flood control works to hold the country together, Japan was isolated from outside invaders. The country was geographically more broken up, without a need for large irrigation schemes, and ruled by people who believed in a hierarchical society governed by qualifications of wealth and privilege. The large private estates throughout the countryside had swollen rapidly since the Heian period. Most of them were under the patronage of court nobles or Buddhist monasteries. The major barons carefully maintained a presence at court while estate managers and warriors (*samurai*) administered them for absentee nobles. Thousands of cultivators worked the lands of the manors under a variety of tenure systems, all of which gave them permanent rights to cultivate their acreage, a privilege denied to European serfs.

During the thirteenth century, the Hojo family acquired the shogunate through force and strategic marriages. They were harsh, incorrupt administrators, who tried to control the increasing power of landowners with their own military governors, backed by an army paid for by a special tax on the nobility. It was just as well they were strong rulers, for in 1268 the Chinese Emperor Kublai Khan sent emissaries to demand the Emperor submit to his authority. The Hojo refused to capitulate and managed to repel a massive invasion by Mongol warriors in November, 1274. A huge storm then scattered the Mongol fleet, which withdrew in confusion to Korea. The Japanese repelled a second attack, again with the help of a typhoon, in 1280, the last invasion of the islands until World War II.

The two centuries before European contact saw the emergence of powerful feudal lords (*daimyo*), many of them former military government officials. Each maintained his own army. During the fourteenth century, these barons and their samurai militia controlled the entire country. Political instability and a volatile Ashikaga shogunate led to inevitable, and constant, civil wars. Nevertheless, the country prospered. Changes in land laws increased agricultural productivity. Trade with China and Korea increased dramatically. A monetary economy replaced the age-old barter system, strengthening the position of merchants and professional guilds, who soon exercised complete control over the prices of rice and other basic food stuff. Japanese merchants exercised increasing influence in society, especially after European contact. Centuries later, they were leading players in Japan's dramatic leap from a feudal to an industrial society.

By the sixteenth century, feudal lords had turned Japan into a series of independent fiefdoms under the nominal rule of an Emperor in Kyoto. The barons maintained their own armies, squeezing their peasants with exorbitant taxation, and maintaining their authority with iron fists. There were frequent peasant revolts, often led by militant Buddhist monks. Constant warfare caused a form of political stalemate as baron intrigued against baron in a maze of plot and counterplot. The traditional weapons of war such as the horse, sword, and crossbow gave overwhelming tactical advantage to no one.

However, the arrival of the first Portuguese caravels in 1542 introduced a new factor to the military equation: firearms.

A European Toehold

IN 1542, A PORTUGUESE SHIP VOYAGING along the coast of southern China was blown far off course. The ship made landfall on the shores of Tanegashima, a small island off the southern shores of Kyushu at the south end of Japan. The caravel was laden with silks, porcelains, and other fine manufactures from the mainland. The crew carried firearms, artifacts of great interest to the local feudal lords, who immediately perceived the strategic advantage of the new weapons in a land where warriors used crossbows, and swords. Within a remarkably short time, the lethal *tanegashima teppo*, "rifles imported through Tanegashima," fostered a revolution in Japanese warfare and allowed a handful of feudal lords to dominate a land sunk in anarchy for generations.

A minor baron named Oba Nobunaga (1534–82) was the first to adopt firearms (Figure 5.2). He equipped large armies of foot soldiers with muskets, and constructed imposing forts with breastworks for cannons. Samurai cavalry were no match for Nobunaga's war machine. The once unimportant nobleman became the effective ruler of Japan in the face of powerful opposition from Buddhist interests and other warlords. His successor, and once loyal commander, Toyotomi Hideyoshi (1536–98), combined force and diplomacy to pacify Japan within a remarkably short time. Faced with the need to keep his now-vast armies busy, Hideyoshi invaded Korea in 1590. This largely unsuccessful foreign adventure resulted directly from the introduction of firearms. The Korean campaigns ended with Japanese withdrawal after Hideyoshi's death, the only overseas military initiative ever undertaken by the country's rulers until modern times.

As Nobunaga and Hideyoshi unified the country, Jesuit missionary Father Francis Xavier and two companions arrived at the port of Kagoshima on Kyushu in 1549. The local baron was anxious for more trade, so he treated the newcomers kindly, on the argument that a benign reception would attract more merchants. Xavier established a mission at Nagasaki and converted his lordly host to the Catholic faith. The Jesuits' success resulted in part from sheer persistence, and also from their active fostering of the silk and precious metal trade with the Portuguese post at Macao, an island in Canton harbor on the Chinese mainland. In 1573, Nobunaga, who regarded foreigners as petitioners allowed to stay on sufferance, permitted Christians to practice their religion in public in the capital, Kyoto. Nobunaga was no Christian, but shrewdly saw the missionaries as a counterforce to powerful and hated Buddhist factions. However, official goodwill evaporated in the face

5.2   Oba Nobunaga (courtesy of the Regents of the University of California)

of the Jesuits' overzealous missionizing and intolerance of other faiths. They offended powerful Buddhist interests, but were tolerated because of their Western technology—books, compasses, pianos, and timepieces, among others.

Hideoyoshi allowed the Jesuits considerable freedom until his enemies were subdued. In 1587, he ordered all Christian missionaries to leave Japan or face execution, while informing all Portuguese merchants they must abide by local laws. The Portuguese Viceroy in distant India wrote requesting safe conduct for Jesuit missionaries. Hideoyoshi refused, but did not enforce his order. In 1592, Spanish merchants and Franciscan friars arrived at Kyoto from the Philippines. They received the same privileges as the Jesuits, but, like the Portuguese, were prohibited from holding services in Kyoto itself. Both Franciscans and Jesuits ignored the order. Hideoyoshi was distracted by his campaigns in Korea and again did nothing.

As the Franciscans and Jesuits bickered over matters of jurisdiction, the Spanish galleon *San Filepe* took refuge from a typhoon in a harbor on Shikoku in 1590. The local baron claimed possession of the ship and its cargo. Incensed, the captain produced maps showing the vast extent of Spanish domains around the world. He threatened the lord with all the military power of the King of Spain. Missionaries, he boasted, were the forerunners of soldiers, landed to add to the possessions of the great monarch. The alarmed baron reported the interview to Hideoyoshi, who promptly executed six Franciscans and ordered all missionaries to leave his domains. They pretended to pack, but did not depart. Hideoyoshi died before he could take further action. Twelve years after his death in 1598, half-a-million Japanese were at least nominally Christians.

Hideoyoshi's successor Tokugawa Ieyasu (1542–1616) ruled from Edo, present-day Tokyo (Figure 5.3). At first, he also welcomed merchants, inviting foreign traders to his capital. Both the Portuguese and Spaniards declined on account of the distance. Ieyasu came to believe they were more interested in converts than commercial transactions. By this time, the Portuguese and Spanish stronghold over Asian trade was breaking up in the face of aggressive Dutch and English expansion. In 1600, a fleet of five Dutch vessels bound westward across the Pacific were scattered by a storm. One of them, the *Liefde*, commanded by English pilot, William Adams, sought refuge in Kyushu. Adams was a diplomatic and sensitive man, who became a close adviser to Ieyasu. He taught his hosts the arts of European shipbuilding and navigation, while warning of the dangers of expansion by foreign powers into his domains. As the Dutch opened a factory (trading post) on Hirado, an island near Nagasaki, native-built Japanese ships began sailing from Kyushu to Chinese and southeastern ports, competing openly with European merchants.

The European toehold on Japan was fragile at best. Tokugawa Ieyasu tolerated the foreigners. His successor Tokugawa Iemitsu (1622–51) was less broad-minded, perceiving Christians and converted officials in his service as potential political subversives. He stepped up persecution of missionaries, who still did not leave. By 1636, the Spanish and English had departed. Trade with the Portuguese flourished through their base at Nagasaki until 1637, when 37,000 impoverished peasants and unemployed samurai rebelled the government, protesting intolerable living conditions. They seized control of a strategic castle with the aid of Dutch ships and withstood a siege by a 100,000-soldier force for more than two months before being executed or massacred. Iemitsu suspected the rebellion had a religious basis. He now prohibited Christianity and further restricted contact with outsiders. At the same time, he forbade all Japanese to leave their homeland and halted the construction of seagoing ships. The Portuguese were banished in 1639. Only the Dutch remained, held virtually as prisoners on Deshima Island in Nagasaki Bay. A handful of Dutch ships were allowed to berth at Deshima each year.

5.3   *Tokugawa Ieyasu (courtesy of the Regents of the University of California)*

Two Centuries of Isolation

FROM 1640 TO 1854, JAPAN WAS all but isolated from the rest of the world. Seafaring ended, no colonies were established, blunting the inevitable spread of European imperialism. Japan's rulers cut off their land from international trade networks, so they could control warlords who were growing wealthy on Western trade. At the same time, they banished what they perceived as subversive faiths from their shores. For two centuries, Deshima was the only crack in the facade, a narrow window of the rapidly changing world of Western thought and technology.

A land long torn by factionalism and war now changed direction. Japanese feudalism now became highly centralized, controlled by a figurehead emperor at Kyoto, while the real power lay in the hands of shogun, the first of them Tokogawa Ieyasu. Members of the Tokogawa clan and its loyal vassals were granted land near Edo, Kyoto, and the Kanto Plain, so they could guard the capital from sudden attack. "Outside lords" resided in outlying provinces under careful supervision. Often richer than the *fudai*, the *tozama* lords were forced to spend time in Edo, to leave their wives and children as hostages, and to pay vast tribute, which often impoverished them. The government approved *tozama* marriages, so it could head off potentially dangerous alliances, also forbidding outside lords from fortifying their castles.

The Tokugawa passion for control and good order was based on the Confucian doctrine that there is a natural order to the universe. Japan's rulers set up a new ideology which defined a hierarchical order of social classes, prescribing the precise behavior expected of every member of society, whether samurai, merchant, or commoner. A strict code of conduct known as *Bushido* ("Way of the Warrior") for samurai stressed loyalty, obedience, and respect. *Bushido* was originally a feudal code of loyalty between lord and vassal. The Tokugawa modified it to create a complex ethical code that regulated behavior between all social classes, between men and women, parents and children, even older and younger siblings. *Bushido* sought to control the samurai in rigid ways, so much so that the code did not have the flexibility to change as society changed. Harsh punishments enforced codes of behavior and punished crime. The Tokugawa believed in strict retribution such as decapitation deterred criminals. Commoners could be executed for rude behavior, while a privileged samurai had the right to cut down a disrespectful peasant without question.

Centralized government brought many benefits to Japanese society, especially to merchants, who flocked to castle towns governed by prominent barons. By the end of the seventeenth century, Japan had shifted away from a centuries-old barter system based on rice to a monetary economy. The merchants became wealthy, often enriching themselves at the expense of the shogun, who lived off the land farmed by the peasants and rice allowances from the government. Japan's cities thrived, while rural areas and the shogun suffered. Some lords acquired so much rice debt that they set loose their feudal followers, causing local anarchy as the hungry raided villages and stole their rice crops. Some shogun married merchant's daughters and became wealthy. By the mid-nineteenth century, the rank of shogun was bought and sold. A new social order based on a commercialized economy had no place for warriors. The shogun became an anachronism.

At the bottom of the economic and social pyramid were the peasants, who supported the lords and their retainers through heavy taxes, administered through village headmen and a network of five-family groups called *gonin-gumi*. Like their masters, the farmers were heavily in debt to the merchants.

By 1750, they were often forced to mortgage their holdings and to engage in infanticide, being unable to support their children. Many peasants fled to the cities, or put themselves under the protection of the *tozama*, who guarded their lands jealously against outsiders.

The Tokugawa shogunate endured for two hundred years. Despite widespread suffering in the countryside, income and productivity increased. But there was widespread unrest resulting from social change and heavy debt, as the rich became richer and the poor poorer. The seeds of change were sewn under a rigid regime, which encouraged no social change whatsoever at a time when Western nations and Asian states were becoming ever more closely linked economically and politically. Many Japanese scholars knew their country was ripe for change. They devoured every Western book smuggled in by the Dutch they could lay their hands on.

The Meiji Revolution

THE END OF THE NAPOLEONIC WARS in Europe in 1815 ushered in a new era of nationalism and international competition. Rival Western nations and a newly assertive United States turned their attention anew to Asia. The Tokugawa now faced real threats from outside. During the late eighteenth century, the Russians had crossed Siberia and reached the Bering Strait. They tried to open trade with Japan, but failed, establishing settlements in the Kurile Islands and on Sakhalin Island instead. Until 1850, Western efforts aimed mainly at China, continuing three centuries of regular commerce with the emperors. California joined the Union in 1850, sparking new American interest in the far side of the Pacific Rim and in Japan. The Tokugawa continued to rebuff any friendly overtures. Shipwrecked American sailors were jailed and abused. The Anglo-Chinese opium war of 1840 was another important catalyst, for Western nations became more aggressive in pursuing trading rights.

The United States regarded an expansion of Asian trade as part of its "manifest destiny," believing Western culture and material benefits should be brought to China, Japan, and other less developed parts of the world. The country's ships also needed a strategically located coaling port, preferably in Japan, which was geographically ideal. In 1853, Commodore Perry, with a flotilla of four steamships, entered Tokyo Bay. While the Japanese had been warned by the Dutch of the impending American visit, they were startled by the clouds of steam rising from the naval vessels' smokestacks. Perry demanded that the Japanese open their ports to trade, then withdrew, promising to return in a year to receive an answer. Panic spread through Japan as the Tokugawa government realized it could not resist Western military might. Despite strong opposition from the conservative, but powerless, Emperor and his court and many barons, the shogunate signed a treaty with Perry on March 31, 1854. The agreement granted two coaling ports with trading rights at the same locations to the United States and allowed an American consul to reside in Shimoda. A thin wedge opened a narrow crack in the door. Within two years, Japan was forced to conclude equivalent treaties with Britain, Holland, and Russia.

Townsend Harris, the first American consul, arrived in 1856. It took him two years to conclude a full commercial treaty, which gave his country the right of unrestricted trade, and the privilege of residence in Osaka and Edo. Technical provisions extended the terms of the agreement to the other nations automatically. Now the door was wide open. Conservative elements in Japanese society criticized the Tokugawa mercilessly. Some barons attacked foreign ships off their coasts. Europeans were murdered on the roads. In retaliation, the British bombarded the port of Kagoshima, enraging the local daimyo. There were calls for the expulsion of all Westerners. The Tokugawa shogunate was virtually powerless and surrendered power to the Emperor on 2 November 1867.

Emperor Mutsuhito was only fourteen years old when he and his advisers assumed supreme power. His courtiers and shogun administrators were bitterly opposed to the Tokugawa regime, while at the same time resolved not to suffer China's fate. Chinese scholar-bureaucrats were profoundly conservative men, who were absolutely opposed to any Western ideas or institutions that might threaten their monopoly on learning and all forms of power. To all intents and purposes, they were powerless, as their military resources were limited and old-fashioned by Western standards. China was forced to make major economic and territorial concessions to the West.

Japan was in a different situation. The Japanese military was strong. Many of the Emperor's top officials were soldiers who had become administrators. They were ardent nationalists, who realized they could preserve Japan's cultural identity by adopting the industrial and technological know-how of the West. The strategy succeeded brilliantly during Emperor Mutsuhito's long reign, known as *Meiji* ("enlightened rule"). Between 1868 and 1912, Japan transformed itself from a feudal to a nation state. This Restoration was a deliberate act carried out by hard-nosed, practical officials, who realized the West derived its strength from industrial and military power. They also admired Western forms of constitutional government, which fostered a sense of national identity.

The *Meiji* administrators began by restoring the power and status of the emperor. They established a strong centralized government by paying daimyo to surrender their authority and assuming their debts. A ranked peerage system and pensions preserved the social status of the feudal lords. By 1871, a strong desire to preserve Japan and enormous expenditures had led to the abolition of almost all the ancient feudal estates. New laws outlawed the inequalities between traditional social classes. Commoners were now allowed to choose any occupation they wished. Two million Japanese enjoyed the privileges of samurai in 1871. In that year, the government abolished their special rights, even proscribing the shogun hairstyle and the wearing of the two samurai swords. Universal military conscription came two years later, further reducing samurai power. Sweeping economic and social changes allowed people to travel freely, encouraged industrial expansion, and forged a powerful army. Imperial officials traveled to the West, to study industrial production and learn about military tactics. Inevitably, there was social unrest, which came to a head in 1877, when the Imperial Army roundly defeated a force of rebellious samurai. This success encouraged the government to reform taxation, and to introduce modern farming methods. By the 1880s, railroads linked many parts of Japan and the close alliance of government and industry characteristic of the country was under way.

The modernization of Japan with its heavy cultural borrowing from the West seems like a deliberate break with the past. However, centuries-old Japanese cultural values lay behind the Meiji Restoration. The state formed a pyramid-like hierarchy, with the emperor at the summit. The individual was unimportant, for everyone worked toward common goals. His or her loyalty was to a kin group or other organization, duties being defined by position in that group. The effect was a constant bubbling of factionalism and competition combined with a profound conservatism that could militate against economic or social change. At times, the same cohesion and loyalty could also achieve national miracles.

By 1894, Japan had a centralized government, a constitution enshrining the basic ideals of the state which recognized the Emperor as all-powerful, sacred, and infallible. A council of advisors, *Genro* ("elder statesmen") effectively ran the country on the Emperor's behalf for the first forty years of the twentieth century. Japan's powerful army defeated both China and Russia in mainland conflicts in 1894–5 and 1904, establishing the country as a major Asian power in the early twentieth-century world.

PART II

Consequences

On what authority have you waged a detestable war against these people, who dwelt quietly and peacefully on their own land? Are these not men? Have they not rational souls?

Fray Antonio de Montesinos (1511)

CHAPTER 6

The Great Dying

I thought I'd always be that way.
That's how I was,
    but now my strength is gone.
Land that I wandered,
    that place.
Listen to me:
    forget about me.

Havasupai farewell song by Dan Hanna,
quoted in Brian Swann (ed.), *Coming to Light* (1994)

THEY CALLED IT "THE GREAT DYING," the mysterious diseases that attacked native Americans young and old, friend and foe with promiscuous impersonality. The diseases landed with the conquistadors who sailed with Columbus. Within a couple of generations, unfamiliar infectious ailments had decimated the native population of the Indies. In 1492, the population of Española (Santo Domingo) numbered about a million people. By the 1520s, only a few handfuls of Indians survived. Measles and smallpox were the main culprits, often complicated by respiratory ailments. None of the native American populations had immunities to these Old World pathogenic organisms.

The scourges of measles and smallpox spread through the Caribbean like wildfire. By an accident of history, we know that a black conquistador involved in the siege of Tenochtitlán introduced smallpox to the Mexica in 1520. An epidemic soon swept the beleaguered city. Catastrophic smallpox epidemics swept Central America again and again, decimating the Indian population. The numbers speak for themselves. In 1519, the Indian population of Central Mexico was about 11 million people. In 1540, carefully calculated estimates place the population at about 6.4 million. By 1607, less than a fifth the number of Indians inhabited the region compared with a century earlier. As many as fourteen major epidemics swept through Mesoamerica, and perhaps as many as seventeen through Peru between 1520 and 1600, reducing the population by between 79 and 92 percent.

We possess little accurate data on the extent of population decline among native American populations after European contact. Some telling figures come from prolonged demographic studies of California Indians. More than 310,000 Indians lived in California at the time of Spanish colonization in 1769. Coastal populations alone fell from about 72,000 to 18,000 by 1830. By 1900, only 20,000 California Indians survived, less than 7 percent of the pre-contact population. Much of this catastrophic decline can be attributed to the Spanish "reduction" policy, which herded thousands of hitherto well-dispersed Indians into crowded settlements near Catholic missions, where they were soon exposed to unfamiliar diseases.

Estimating Population Decline

THE ENTIRE ISSUE OF EPIDEMIC DISEASES and the native Americans is thwart with emotion, dating back to the sixteenth century, when European intellectuals and politicians accused the Spanish authorities of genocide through disease. This "Black Legend," denied indignantly by Spain, still surfaces from time to time today, as it did at the time of the Columbus Quincentennial in 1992. Herein lies one of the great controversies of anthropology: what role did infectious diseases play in the depopulation of native America?

The great University of California anthropologist Alfred Kroeber and others argued that diseases played a relatively minor role in the early decades after initial contact. However, epidemics did decimate native American populations after sustained contact. Kroeber believed that the earliest censuses of such populations reflected a total population of nine million people *before* decline took place.

In contrast, anthropologist Henry Dobyns and historical demographers Sherburne Cook and William Borah assumed that infectious diseases struck even isolated populations decades, if not centuries *before* actual physical contact between Europeans and native Americans. Thus, even the earliest post-contact estimates reflect populations reduced by as much as 95 percent from pre-Columbian levels. Dobyns has argued for an early fifteenth-century Indian population count of as high as eighteen million people, far higher than Kroeber's original estimate. He believes the documented epidemic at Tenochtitlán in 1520 was, in fact, a pandemic that spread from group to group all the way to Canada and as far south as Chile. Thus, he argues, the Inca empire encompassed at best 50 percent of the population of a decade earlier when Francisco Pizarro's conquistadors marched into the heart of their Andean kingdom. Thus, "European contact" was not a physical confrontation, but as much a process of microbial contact and subsequent depopulation, which usually occurred long before foreigners arrived in person.

Unlike Kroeber, Dobyns is never conservative in estimating indigenous populations. The very fact of depopulation before physical contact means the first censuses reflect unstable populations already adjusting to new circumstances. Dobyns and his colleagues rely on a combination of historical records and depopulation ratios derived from demographic calculations, neither of which are entirely reliable.

Archaeologist Ann Ramenovsky has evaluated the Kroeber and Dobyns' hypotheses. She points out that both new multidisciplinary approaches and much new archaeological data show beyond all reasonable doubt that constant culture change unfolded in all human societies long before European contact. For instance, University of Wisconsin archaeologist Herb Maschner has shown how coastal societies in southeastern Alaska achieved great cultural complexity long before Europeans arrived. But the degree of complexity fluctuated dramatically over the centuries, reflected in changing settlement patterns from densely concentrated villages to dispersed, often defensive settlements.

Ramenovsky has used patterns of cultural change reflected in the archaeological record to evaluate population declines independent of either ethnographic or historical records. She measured population change by using comprehensive settlement data to test a single archaeological hypothesis: "Did native Americans experience a population collapse immediately following European contact, but predating written records and sustained colonization?" She studied three regions of North America: the lower Mississippi Valley, central New York, and the middle Missouri Valley. The research proved difficult, as she had to deal with inadequate and biased archaeological samples, a lack of quantitative data on house or settlement size, and gaps in regional coverage. But she was able to show how both archaeological and historical sources document an unambiguous and precipitous decline of indigenous populations in the region in the sixteenth century—after the De Soto expedition and before the French colonization of the late seventeenth century.

The Five Nations of the Iroquois occupied the Finger Lakes region of upstate New York at the beginning of the historic period (see Chapter 13). Ramenovsky employed settlement and house roof area data to document a considerable reduction in Iroquois populations by the seventeenth century. Historical documents supported and extended the archaeological record of collapse in the sixteenth and seventeenth centuries. They chronicle drastically reorganized settlements, and, eventually, the breakdown of multi-family longhouse dwellings and the fortified communities of earlier centuries.

The Middle Missouri Valley area of the Northern Plains witnessed initial European contact in 1540, with permanent colonization three centuries later. Archaeological data from large scale river basin surveys documented major changes in indigenous settlement patterns by at least the seventeenth century, perhaps coinciding with the first appearance of European trade goods in local archaeological sites. Unfortunately, Ramenovsky's data does not reveal whether the decline took place earlier, even before foreign trade items reached the Middle Missouri.

All Ramenovsky's research tended to confirm Dobyn's theory that demographic catastrophe preceded the major influx of Europeans into North America, by decades, and in some areas by centuries. Ramenovksy estimates the pre-contact native population of North America at about twelve million people, a more conservative estimate than Dobyn's, but much higher than the estimates of Alfred Kroeber and his contemporaries.

The Causes of Depopulation

FOR REASONS STILL LITTLE UNDERSTOOD, there were no New World equivalents for European diseases. Conceivably, the parasites were killed off by arctic temperatures as tiny founder populations migrated into the Americas thousands of years ago. Furthermore, the survival of acute diseases depends on sustained contact between infected individuals, such as occurs in densely packed, sedentary settlements such as small towns and large villages. North America, and, to a certain extent, Central and South America, lacked the compact urban settlements of Europe and western Asia, where bacterial and viral diseases became fixed in city populations. Genetically, however, the relatively homogeneous native Americans were exceptionally vulnerable immunologically. The result was very high mortality rates among hitherto unexposed populations.

Epidemics spread unevenly. Much depended on the social and political conditions from one area to the next. The conquistadors swooped on the Indies in a profligate and hungry search for gold, using thousands of Indians as slaves to mine for metals and clear land for *encomiendas*. After 1494, slave trading intensified. In the early sixteenth century, tens of thousands of Indian slaves were shipped from places like Nicaragua to plantations on Caribbean islands. By 1560, at least forty thousand native Americans labored as slaves in northeast Brazil alone. Under such conditions, peoples' resistance to disease was drastically lowered.

In Mesoamerica and the Andes, the Aztecs and Incas had run their empires as giant tributary systems. Food supplies, and the circulation of commodities of all kinds, depended on highly organized systems of land use and redistribution of goods. When long-established exchange systems like those between highland and lowland Peru, collapsed with the Spanish *entrada*, many people went hungry or moved to growing colonial cities. Again, resistance to infectious disease was much reduced and tens of thousands perished.

When local conditions fostered infection, the diseases spread like wildfire, often far ahead of actual face-to-face contact between Westerner and non-Westerner. In the North American Southeast, for example, European contact began with Hernando de Soto's infamous expedition from Florida to the Mississippi River in 1540. Even then, smallpox and other diseases had spread inland from earlier, passing visitors. At the village of Talomeco in South Carolina, the conquistadors saw hundreds of bodies were stacked up in four houses. In 1583, Sir Francis Drake's seamen contracted a highly contagious fever, perhaps typhus, in the Cape Verde Islands. They attacked the Spanish settlement at Saint Augustine, Florida, and carried the virus ashore. Hundreds of Indians perished in the resulting epidemic. To the north in Virginia, Elizabethan writer Thomas Hariot observed how "within a few days of our departure from everies…townes, people began to die very fast, and many in short space" (Crosby 1972, 117).

During the following century, both exotic diseases and Western trade goods percolated far ahead of European settlement, traveling up ancient inter-village paths that had been in use for many centuries. Coastal epidemics swept inland, depopulating entire villages, sometimes 90 percent of local populations. The survivors often perished from starvation, especially if the diseases struck during periods of planting or harvest. Malaria was an earlier killer. The anopheline mosquitoes suitable for propagating malaria were present in the Americas before European contact. Once someone has been infected by malaria and acquired immunity to it, the parasite remains in their blood. Malaria parasites probably traveled to the New World in the blood of apparently healthy black slaves.

Such massive population declines were culturally devastating, especially since the diseases often attacked the youngest and oldest members of society. The elders were priceless repositories of cultural experience in societies where all knowledge was transmitted orally from one generation to the next. Such knowledge sometimes vanished within a few short weeks or months. In particular, vital genealogical and religious lore disappeared, at a time when such information would have served as a way of allowing the people to adjust to a new culture and social order. In the North American Southeast, de Soto encountered large chiefdoms, ruled by leaders presiding over quite sizable communities and many villages. The effect of the subsequent epidemics was to fragment hitherto powerful chiefdoms into much smaller-scale societies. Many people fled from their home territories, trying to escape infection, resulting in large-scale political and social disruption over wide areas.

Epidemics not only contributed to mortality rates, they also affected fertility rates and the ability of native American populations to recover from demographic crises. Many infectious diseases induce high levels of pregnancy loss and increased mortality among pregnant women. In small communities, the loss of wives and the relatively small number of potential marriage partners combined with cultural restrictions may have slowed reproduction rates. With high infant mortality and the emotional stress of catastrophic death rates, even temporary breaks in the reproduction rate may have threatened the high birth rates needed to maintain existing populations. In many areas, biological and cultural survival were the exception rather than the rule.

The Southwestern United States

THE SOUTHWEST FARED VERY DIFFERENTLY to other regions. Unlike the Southeast or the Caribbean, native peoples survived, and still constitute a significant element in the biological and cultural landscape of the region. The pattern of survival was patchy. For example, pueblo village populations south of Albuquerque disappeared before or during the great Pueblo Revolt against Spanish rule in 1680. North of Albuquerque, twelve eastern pueblos founded before 1680 still flourish. How can we account for this differing survival pattern? Why did Southwestern groups fare better than Southeastern peoples? Were exotic infectious diseases less virulent and less frequent in this arid region, where human populations were well spread out?

Spanish contact with the Southwest began with the Coronado Expedition of 1540. Coronado traveled north from New Spain in search of the legendary Seven Cities of Cibola, said to be awash in gold. The conquistadors were deeply disappointed when they found nothing more than densely occupied Zuñi pueblos. They returned empty-handed to Mexico City, having ranged over much of the Southwest and far out onto the Plains. For the next 140 years, infectious diseases more than foreigners spread through the region, decimating crowded pueblos. Catastrophic disease outbreaks are well documented for the eighteenth century onward. But what about the critical 140-year period between the Spanish *entrada* and the Pueblo Revolt? Interestingly, only two direct references to disease in the New Mexico colony are known for these decades, one overlapping with outbreaks in neighboring areas to the south, the other coinciding with four years of severe famine. However, few historians have focused specifically on disease and demography, so the record is probably incomplete.

Many of the world's most lethal human infections evolve and thrive in tropical environments. As a result, scientists believe that climate and elevation played an important role in depopulation. In Mexico, for example, Cook and Borah calculated a 26:1 population decline on the coast between 1532 and 1608, which contrasts with 13:1 among native populations on the highlands. Coastal Peru witnessed a depopulation ratio of 26:1, but above 13,000 feet (4000 m) the ratio was a mere 4:1. Coastal areas, while not always humid, experienced much more sustained contact with Spaniards than the more isolated highlands.

In New Mexico, a very different environment, Ramenovsky makes a distinction between highlands above 5,000 feet (1524 m) and lower elevations. Nearly all contemporary pueblos are in the uplands. Between 1540 and 1680, both upland and lowland populations declined, but the proportional decline (68 percent to 86 percent) is lower on higher ground.

Several factors may have contributed to the decline, among them the closer proximity of lowland villages to disease centers in Mexico. The same settlements often lay close to the main Spanish road, the Camino Real. Ramenovsky has traced the diffusion of the great smallpox epidemic of 1778–80 from the Valley of Mexico along the Camino Real into New Mexico. From there, the disease spread across the northern Plains and into the Middle Missouri. The higher elevation of the uplands may have afforded some protection against smallpox, but many Spaniards lived in close juxtaposition to native communities in towns like Santa Fe. At the same time, new Spanish agricultural methods with their reservoirs may have provided breeding grounds for malaria-carrying mosquitoes.

Depopulation in Ecuador

LINDA NEWSON OF THE UNIVERSITY OF London has studied the sixteenth-century demographic history of the Quito *Audencia* (administrative district) of Ecuador. Her study area encompassed three regions and attempted to analyze the different factors that would account for differing survival rates among native American populations in different ecological and cultural areas. The low-lying and ecologically diverse coastal zone was home to about half a million people before contact. As many as 838,600 people dwelt in the sierra region of the Andes, many of them living in kingdoms ruled by important chiefs. A fertile, diverse high altitude environment provided ample food supplies for a relatively dense population. The expanding Inca empire conquered the region about seventy years before the Spaniards arrived. The Oriente comprised the eastern flank of the Andes and the densely forested lowlands to the east, some of the richest tropical rainforest in the world. About 230,000 people lived in the Oriente before the *entrada*, mainly living in small, scattered groups. Newson believes about 1.6 million people lived in all of Ecuador before European contact.

After extensive research on historical tax and tribute records, Newson estimates that the sierra population declined from about 838,600 to 164,529 people, a depopulation ratio of about 5.1:1 (80.4 percent), comparable to figures calculated by Sherburne Cook for the neighboring Andean highlands. There were considerable differences in local decline rates, depending on geography, the severity of conquest and the exploitation of the indigenous population. The coast suffered the most severe decline, with an average depopulation ratio of 21.1:1 (95.3 percent), close to that for the Mexican coast. The greatest losses came in the Guayaquil region on the southern coast, which collapsed by a staggering ratio of 104.9:1. Guayaquil was a major port with a constant stream of visiting ships, which brought many visitors and shipments of laborers, as well as new infections. The lack of minerals and dispersed rural populations protected much of the coastal population during the sixteenth century, but sustained contact with mulattos brought population decline in later times.

The Oriente is isolated from the coastal west by the Andes. Low population densities and dispersed populations may have protected the region from many epidemics. Many diseases did not become endemic and died out, but the indirect effects of epidemics associated with high levels of adult mortality may have heightened intertribal conflict, damaged fragile subsistence systems, and reduced populations below critical thresholds. Despite major regional variations, the higher altitudes of the Oriente declined on a ratio of 3.7:1 (73.3 percent) in the sixteenth century, with a 72 percent decline at lower elevations a century later. In all, the *Audiencia* of Quito suffered an 85 percent population decline by 1600. The decline was uneven not merely because of altitude, as was the case in Peru, but because of a variable intensity of Spanish settlement, a general lack of rich gold and silver deposits, and widely separated populations in many areas.

Depopulation and the "Ethnographic Present"

CASE STUDIES ON POPULATION LOSS are proliferating, but, as Robert Dunnell points out, fundamental methodological problems await resolution. The earliest records of, say, Aztec or Tahitian society recorded by Hernán Cortés or English explorer Captain James Cook are but transitory, incomplete, and often biased snapshots of much more complex, and still little understood, human societies. Very often, our knowledge of pre-contact societies all over the world comes not from initial impressions by explorers, but from archaeological research, which measures cultural change over many centuries, even millennia. And the catastrophic population declines that either preceded or followed European contact involved not only loss of people, but constant redefinition of society as well. Thus, the notion of an ethnographic "present," a moment in time when pre-European society stood still for us to describe, is an illusion, especially in the Americas, where infectious diseases often decimated native American populations even before actual physical contact between European and Indian. For example, Hernando de Soto and his conquistadors found the Mississippi Valley teeming with dense populations in the mid-sixteenth century. A hundred years later, French explorers found the valley virtually deserted, this without prolonged European contact. Such depopulation makes a mockery of the assumption that later native American cultures were accurate reflections of earlier ones. Only a fraction of cultural knowledge and lore survived epidemics that attacked the young and old, the representatives of earlier generations and the repositories of much cultural information, and those who were destined to receive it.

Traditionally, archaeologists have relied on early travelers' accounts, and on contemporary anthropological observations to interpret what remains in the archaeological record of earlier cultures in the same region. This methodology relies on the so-called "Direct Historical Method," first pioneered in the Southwest in the early years of this century. Archaeologists worked back from the historically known to the ancient unknown. At the same time, they used ethnographic analogy, comparisons with living cultures, as a way of interpreting the material remains of earlier societies. While at least a general and well-controlled use of analogy is sometimes feasible, the effect of depopulation was to drastically reduce the biological and cultural diversity of native American societies. Today's Indian populations are the descendants of a tiny fraction of the living native Americans of the sixteenth century, decimated by a random demographic event—the introduction of infectious diseases.

These realities make the notion of continuity between pre-Columbian and more recent native American societies highly suspect except at the most platitudinous level. The survivors lived in societies that were evolving along different cultural trajectories after contact, as they became progressively more Europeanized. In the past, scholars have assumed this continuity, and thought of the transition over European contact in evolutionary terms. Today, they are beginning to assess the effects of depopulation from archaeological evidence alone, for archaeology provides the only direct information on the cultures that flourished before contact. Thus, research into such questions as to why some areas were hit harder by epidemics than others are at little more than the hypothesis stage. Were, for example, widely dispersed, less complex hunter-gatherer and village farming societies less vulnerable to epidemics than more densely populated Iroquois towns in the St. Lawrence Valley of upstate New York, or Aztec cities like Tenochtitlán, where urban populations were decimated with extraordinary rapidity? A new generation of researches, based on archaeology as much as demography, will provide definitive answers.

We have only just begun to appreciate the catastrophic short- and long-term effects of epidemic disease on indigenous American populations. But we now know enough to realize that the portraits of pre-Columbian society obtained from archaeology and ethnohistory reflect an astounding diversity and richness of native American society, which perished catastrophically and dramatically within a few generations. The destruction of biological and cultural diversity in native America is one of the harshest legacies of the clash of cultures.

CHAPTER 7

Noble Savages: The Tahitians

In the beginning there was only Ta'aroa, who had no forebears, who created himself and all other first beings and things. For countless ages Ta'aroa existed alone, floating in space and darkness within egglike shells. Finally wearying of his solitude, Ta'aroa burst out of his shells...it was only later that he made man with the help of his artisan-god, Tu.

Portion of a creation chant from the Tahitian islands,
recorded by a missionary in 1822

THE EUROPEAN NATIONS GAZED OUT on a totally different world after the sixteenth century. The knowledge of the globe brought back by travelers, missionaries, and colonists of the Age of Discovery opened up endless possibilities for new adventure and scientific exploration, and a splendid future for the centuries-old myths about paradise and the noble savage as well. The world was made up of a giant paradox. On the one hand stood the world of reality, practical politics, and soldierly deeds; on the other was a world of myth, a pervasive, but far from universal feeling that paradise did exist on earth and that savages were fundamentally good. By 1600, there were abundant descriptions of lands and peoples in Africa and the Americas. These were graphic accounts of the primitive Khoikhoi, Cortés's descriptions of the Aztecs, Peter Martyr's careful commentaries on American Indians, the copious statistics of a dramatic decline in Indian populations after the overthrow of the Aztec and Inca civilizations of Mexico and Peru. But for all these realities, the

Indian was endowed with distinctive, paradisal characteristics in the European imagination.

Peter Martyr was among those who extolled the heavenly qualities of the New World. He imbued the Indian with almost divine attributes of piety, brotherly love, and perfection, and depicted the Indian world as perhaps the last vestige of a golden age. The Indians were perceived by many to be living simple, uncomplicated lives. They were people of great physical beauty, a beauty that seemed to complement their nobility of character. Elizabethan sea captain Arthur Barlow landed in Virginia and found himself "entertained with all love and kindness, and with as much bounty, after their manner, as they could possibly give. Wee found the people most gently, loving and faithfull, void of all guile and treason, and such as lived after the manner of the golden age" (Morison 1971, 210) (Figure 7.1). Propaganda to attract settlers no doubt, but for many philosophers, nobility seemed to be inherent in non-Western peoples, a nobility that manifested itself in the form of a child-like innocence.

Although some people took Sepulveda's side and argued that the Indians were cruel, primitive people, most sixteenth- and seventeenth-century commentators admired and esteemed the Indians. The philosophers turned their eyes from Africa to the west. It was here that they found the models for their utopias and ideal states. They drew on eulogistic accounts of the Incas of Peru and other Indian societies, agreed with Bartolomé de las Casas that the Indians were people of natural, superior goodness. All the Indians needed was conversion to Christianity to become the most blessed of souls. Many European thinkers believed that the social and material beliefs and moral structure of Indian society were infinitely superior to those of their own civilization. Earlier commentators had thought it would be possible to find an actual paradise somewhere on earth. The sixteenth and seventeenth centuries saw this dream in a different light. Paradise on earth became not a nebulous dream, but the highly specific image of an ideal society. Now the search was not for a paradise, but for people who lived in the state of contentment associated with paradise, children of nature inhabiting a heaven-like country far beyond the seas.

Utopia, the ideal state, was a persistent conception of sixteenth- and seventeenth-century commentators. Most ideal states lay to the west in distant seas, the lands of El Dorado, the kingdom of gold. A host of popular works, among them Sir Thomas More's *Utopia* (1516) and Sir Francis Bacon's *New Atlantis* (1627), described such utopias, once thought to be located in the Caribbean, then America, and finally in the South Seas. The utopian image encouraged travelers to hope that there existed an ideal society on earth that could be theirs, a society where one could regain the happiness that was no longer possible in the harsh reality of Western civilization. The shortcomings

7.1 A Virginia Indian couple eating, depicted by Elizabethan artist John White in the late sixteenth century: "They are verye sober in their eating and trinkinge, and consequently verye longe lived because they do not oppresse nature... I would to God we would followe their exemple." (Courtesy of the Trustees of the British Museum)

of the Western way of life shaped the utopian outlook, a curious mixture of nostalgia for a simple lifestyle never to be regained and a hope that one might achieve such an ideal state if one only fulfilled the requirements for the simple life. Perhaps the French philosopher Michel de Montaigne (1533–1592) put it best in his *Of the Cannibals,* in which he describes the peoples of Brazil. His "cannibals" possess "the true and most profitable virtues, which we have bastardized, applying them to the pleasure of our own corrupted taste.... The laws of nature do yet commande them," he wrote. Then, in a memorable passage, he sums up his feelings: "Me seemeth that what is in these nations we see by experience, doth not only exceed all the pictures wherewith licentious Poesie hath proudly embellished the golden age, and all her quaint inventions to faine a happy condition of man, but all the conception and desire of Philosophy...Plato could not imagine a genuitie so pure and simple...nor ever believe our society might be maintained with so little art and humane combination" (Montaigne 1948, 155).

European philosophers like Montaigne might glorify the "primitives," as they were called, but their admiration and esteem was clothed in highly specific terms. Savages living in a state of nature were thought to have an idyllic life only in the sense that a group of ten-year-old children might set up an innocent and happy society among themselves. Their natural intelligence and humanity would, of course, direct a wholesome and effective social organization, but it would still be that of ten-year-old children. So civilized people might look upon the customs and societies of primitives with fondness and a kind of nostalgia, but they would never choose to live that way. Savages might represent a halcyon state of innocence and peace, but this was achieved at great cost: they lacked all the great benefits and virtues of civilization, whether economic, philosophical, or technological. This enabled Spanish missionaries to justify, for example, their harsh methods in converting the heathens: they were dealing, after all, with veritable children.

The more nostalgic and disillusioned philosophers of the Montaigne camp felt that the trappings of civilization, and indeed learning itself, were futile. Writing of the American Indian, Montaigne remarked "It is not yet full fifty yeeres that he knew neither letters, nor waight, nor measures, nor apparel nor corne, nor vines. But all was naked, simply-pure, in Nature's lap...I feare that by our contagion, we shall directly have furthered his declination, and hastened his ruine" (153). The notion that savages were beautiful, simple people who lived by plucking ripe fruit from ever-fecund trees was very attractive to philosophers weary of the daily pressures of European civilization.

The simplicity of non-Western life appealed most strongly to Europeans. This simplicity was expressed in people's nakedness, gentle behavior, and their natural friendliness and moral purity. They lived in societies where equality and a strong sense of community were paramount. Economically, these people lived in a wonderful state where everything was common property and everything came automatically to hand, as if provided by magic. The ideal society was a communal one, without division of wealth and individual property to cause social discord. Poverty, as such, was unknown. Of course there were many non-Western societies that lived in a state of quarrelsome strife, "evil" savages whose lives contrasted tragically with those "good" people. By the eighteenth century, the notion of a state of "nature," an ideal state of simplicity, was firmly entrenched in people's minds. The idea that humanity had degenerated since the Fall no longer dominated philosophical thinking. A new harmony came from a positive cult of exoticism that stressed that everything that we had lost through the corruption of civilization could be regained triumphantly, provided we gained greater insight about humanity and were prepared to ascend to a higher level of happiness. The rational, clear-thinking non-Westerner held the answer to human happiness. Soon the good savage became the ultimate criterion, a perfect example to be copied. (Note that notions of primitive communism were to feature prominently in nineteenth- and twentieth-century Marxist thought.)

The full flowering of exoticism in the eighteenth century was an expression of a new sense of self-criticism and self-analysis that led to the rejection of many aspects of a civilization that many felt was headed down a path leading in the wrong direction. The glorification of the savage deeply influenced European expansion to the west during the sixteenth and seventeenth centuries, but it did not prevent the wholesale massacres and exploitation of newly discovered societies. There was, as always, a fundamental duality between the actual physical world that was put to political and economic use and the world on which one could project all one's nostalgia and desire, dissatisfaction and idealism. This latter world was not circumscribed by harsh reality, but was infinitely variable and interpretable, capable of manipulation in any philosophical way one wished.

By the eighteenth century, literature abounded with voyages and memoirs that discussed the exotic peoples of the globe, and the nature of savagery itself. Comparisons between western society and non-Western peoples were the rule of the day, especially on the part of embittered authors like Jonathan Swift. In *Gulliver's Travels* (1726), he sets up an ideal realm, a utopia where the people have "not the least knowledge of books and literature." The Houyhnhnms have no words in their vocabulary "to express lying or falsehood." They believe that "nature teaches them to love the whole species." Gulliver has great difficulty explaining his curious custom of wearing clothes, for the Houyhnhnms "could not understand why Nature should teach us to conceal what Nature has given." The Houyhnhnm voyage is a brilliant satire on the human race. Swift's old Houyhnhnm listens to Gulliver's accounts of civilized life in perplexity; he cannot understand why people abuse nature so much.

Daniel Defoe's *Robinson Crusoe* (1719) was the masterpiece that best explored exoticism and the contrasts between European civilization and non-Western society. Defoe commemorates Crusoe as a master of technological ingenuity, while his Man Friday is a simple, rational savage who contrasts dramatically with the evil warriors who wanted to kill him. Despite Friday's lesser status as a human being and his penchant for human flesh (a vice he abandons at Crusoe's urging), he is living proof for Defoe that all humankind could survive amicably if they turned inward to their hearts rather than outward to the world. The notion persisted of a Noble Savage, a gentle yet reasonable being that sees through the superfluities of civilization. It remained for the Noble Savage to become clothed in the robes of reality.

Jean-Jacques Rousseau and Natural Humanity

"THERE EXISTS ONE BOOK, WHICH, to my taste, furnishes the happiest treatise of natural education. What then is this marvelous book? Is it Aristotle? Is it Pliny, is it Buffon? No—it is *Robinson Crusoe*," wrote famed French philosopher Jean-Jacques Rousseau (1712–1778) in 1762. If any one philosopher can be said to be associated with Romantic savagery, it was Rousseau. He was a powerful and unusual personality, whose quarrels, writings, and love for a life of rural solitude were singular even in his day. His scorn for polite society and civilization was legendary and appealed strongly to the Romantic artists of eighteenth-century Europe. Perhaps his devotion to the nobility of savagery has been overdrawn. In reality his vision of the American Indian was dry, somewhat satirical, and often grim. His real preoccupation was with humanity in its natural state.

In 1754, Rousseau published his immortal *Discours sur l'Origine et le Fondement de l'Inégalité parmi les Hommes*. He painted a picture of the savage as the "most disadvantageously disposed" of the animals. The hardy and robust savage needed few implements, and except when seeking food, was idle or asleep. In such a natural state, people had few incentives to alter their condition and were quite happy without the trappings of civilization. Give them enough to eat and savages were at peace with the world. It was not that they were good or evil; it was simply that they were governed by the "peacefulness of their passions, and their ignorance of vice." Above all they had no need of love, that terrible harbinger of strife and suffering. The savage could enjoy physical love with any woman for the purpose of reproduction: the feelings of love were an innovation of civilization. Free love governed the savage life.

To Rousseau, the most admirable feature of natural humanity was its freedom from pain and suffering, a notion that the savage was a "nonmoral but good-natured brute." But humanity did not long remain in a completely natural state. "The first expansion of the human heart were the effects of a novel situation, which united husbands and wives, fathers and children, under one roof. The habit of living together soon gave rise to the finest feelings known to humanity, conjugal love and paternal affection" (Fairchild 1928, 125–6). Rousseau was prepared to soften his image of humanity to envisage a "period of expansion of the human faculties, keeping a just mean between the indolence of the primitive state and the petulant activity of our own egoism, [which] must have been the most happy and durable of epochs" (Fairchild 1928, 126). But the rot soon set in. The beginnings of emotional feeling brought strife, envy, and other vices in their train. This bellicose state was precisely that reached by "most of the savage nations known to us." Rousseau was preoccupied with his "happy and durable epoch." As Rousseau wrote, "This state was the least subject to revolutions, and altogether the very best man could enjoy…The example of savages…seems to prove that men were meant to remain in it, that it is the real youth of the world, and that all subsequent advances have been apparently so many steps toward the perfection of the individual, but in reality towards the decrepitude of the species" (Fairchild 1928, 126).

Jean-Jacques Rousseau was a man with no illusions about humanity, whether European or non-Western. By the end of his life, he had created an image of a natural human being who was not a stupid innocent like the Noble Savage, but someone with the goodness of the savage who has used the gifts of art, science, and philosophy to blossom into a new state of strong-willed virtue and wisdom. Of course, such a person never existed, but Rousseau gained support for his vision of utopia by ennobling savages. He was not particularly enthusiastic about them himself, but his followers were. His sentimentalizing about the sensibility, eroticism, and naturalness of non-Western peoples was picked up with avidity by the writers of the Romantic movement in England.

Between 1730 and 1790, the symptoms of ardent Romanticism appeared in English and French literature. They were manifested in an interest in the fact and idea of revolution, artistic spontaneity and freedom, and the integrity of nature. Writers reacted against the corruption and injustice of European society, and seized on the idea of the Noble Savage with avidity. It was an appealing picture:

> *Happy the first of men, ere yet confin'd*
> *To smoky cities; who in sheltered groves,*
> *Warm caves, and deep-sunk vallies liv'd and lov'd*
> *By cares unwounded; what the sun and showers,*
> *And genial earth untillag'd, could produce,*
> *They gathered grateful…*

Thus a passage from Joseph Warton's "The Enthusiast," a typical effusion of the day (Fairchild 1928, 60). The literature of the Romantic movement is replete with "simple Indian swains," "dusky maidens," and "the pure pleasures of the sylvan reign." An uncritical reading of Rousseau merely strengthened the Romantic illusion. All it remained for someone to do was to find the Noble Savage in the flesh.

The Discovery of the Pacific: New Cythera

In 1513 the Spanish explorer Vasco Nuñez de Balboa stood "Silent, upon a peak in Darien" and gazed at the vast expanse of the Pacific. A new ocean came into the consciousness of the Western world. Half a century later the globe had been mapped into at least a broad resemblance of its actual shape. But there were gaps, especially in the great ocean sighted by Balboa. Ferdinand Magellan succeeded in crossing the Pacific's vast expanses in 1521, crossing from the strait named after him to the Philippines. No one had explored its inner reaches nor its southern extremities. Contemporary scientific opinion favored the existence of a great southern continent, a *Terra Australis Incognita,* to counterbalance the land masses of the northern hemisphere. Two-and-a-half centuries of arduous voyaging finally established that such a continent did not exist.

The exploration of the Pacific was a maritime exercise that depended for its success on the knowledge of unfamiliar tides, currents, and wind patterns, and on precise navigational methods. It was one thing to locate a remote tropical island, quite another to establish its exact position and to return to it again in the future. Above all the successful exploration of the Pacific depended on a combination of seamanship, leadership, and expert knowledge. The Spanish with their passion for gold and sense of divine mission, and the Dutch with a more prosaic interest in trade both made remarkable geographical discoveries. But the scientific exploration of the Pacific began in earnest with the emergence of scientific navigation and geography in the eighteenth century. This momentous century saw revolutionary changes in Western social and political life, in scientific knowledge, economic expansion, and in European knowledge of non-Western societies. Science was replacing philosophical speculation as a way of explaining the world. Eighteenth-century astronomers and scientists solved the problem of computing longitude on open water and invented the chronometer. These hard-won discoveries enabled systematic exploration of the South Seas to begin.

Expectations were high when two expeditions—one British, the other French—left Europe for the South Seas in 1766. The French had long speculated about the Pacific, about Noble Savages and the state of humankind. Their intellectuals regarded the discovery of an unknown southern continent to be among those things "useful for the human race, and curious for scholars." The South Seas were important for commerce. Furthermore, the Pacific islands were said to be the home of hairy folk with tails, people of the greatest interest to the philosophers. Author after author took up the patriotic cry: France as a nation should assume the historic role of discoverer of the Pacific. In November, 1766, Chevalier Louis Antoine de Bougainville, an elegant and talented soldier of great patriotism, sailed for the South Seas. His objective was to find and colonize the great southern continent. His ship, the *Boudeuse,* housed eleven officers, two scientists, and two hundred men.

Three months earlier, the H.M.S. *Dolphin* had sailed from Plymouth, England, under the command of Captain Samuel Wallis. His orders were to find the same continent as Bougainville. On 18 June 1766, after a miserable passage of the Strait of Magellan, the *Dolphin* sighted the island of Tahiti in the heart of Polynesia. When a dense morning mist cleared, Wallis was astonished to find himself surrounded by hundreds of canoes. The Tahitians in the canoes were as astounded as the Europeans. It took some time for Wallis to convince the islanders that he and his men came in friendship. At this signal moment of cultural confrontation, however, low comedy intervened. One of the ship's goats suddenly appeared as the first Tahitian climbed aboard, and butted him in the rear. "The appearance of this animal, so different from any he had ever seen, struck him with such terror, that he instantly leaped overboard; and all the rest, upon seeing what had happened, followed his example with the utmost precipitation" (Beaglehole 1966, 202). The Tahitians soon returned and indicated by sign language that they were at least familiar with chickens and hogs.

Eventually, Wallis managed to anchor his ship in sheltered Matavi Bay, at the east end of the island. Some friendly initial contacts evaporated when the Tahitians arrived in force with their canoes and showered the *Dolphin* with stones, under the mistaken impression that the English were attacking the island. Wallis dispersed the demonstration with his guns and destroyed fifty canoes. The warriors tried to lure sailors ashore by displaying beautiful girls on the beach, who were encouraged to "play a great many droll...tricks." Once the Tahitians realized that the visitors were only interested in trading, friendly relations were soon established. The remainder of the visit passed very pleasantly indeed. Chicken, fruit, and hogs were soon forthcoming. The Tahitians received iron nails in exchange. When the seamen discovered that the women would gladly sell their charms for the same currency, a lively trade developed. Wallis was forced to confine his men aboard, as their raids on the *Dolphin's* hardware threatened to pull the ship apart.

Wallis and his officers visited a great queen named Oborea, who entertained them in her enormous guest house. They were massaged by young girls who nearly swooned with astonishment when the surgeon removed his wig. Two landing parties explored the island. Wherever they went they were entertained by hospitable locals who offered them food and were thrilled with gifts of buttons and nails. The Europeans were delighted with the rich and fertile island and with its active and friendly inhabitants. The climate was perfect, there were no rats or snakes, and the people were incredibly healthy. Wallis considered his month's stay a visit to paradise. And an earthly paradise Tahiti became when word of the newly discovered tropical island reached London in May 1768.

The Chevalier de Bougainville anchored off Tahiti two years later on 4 April 1768, after an arduous but unsuccessful voyage in search of the elusive southern continent. The *Boudeuse* was surrounded by canoes offering fruit, but the Tahitians refused to come on board. So many canoes arrived that

Bougainville experienced some difficulty warping his ship into a safe anchorage. A large, curious, and friendly crowd followed the captain wherever he went on the island. Trade flourished. The French were able to land their sick and water ship. Like the English sailors before them, the *Boudeuse's* seamen found that a few nails would buy all the sex they wanted. Perhaps the Tahitians were somewhat less accommodating, for the nails of the *Boudeuse* were left intact. Unfortunately, however, the French left venereal disease behind them.

Bougainville had ample opportunity to admire Tahiti during his eighteen-day stay. He strolled through shady palm groves, was entertained by hospitable families, and admired the lush flora and brightly colored birds. His romantic soul was transported, and he likened the Tahitians to Greek gods. "I never saw men better made, and whose limbs were more proportionate: in order to paint Hercules or a Mars, one could nowhere find such beautiful models," he enthused (Figure 7.2). "I thought I was transported into the Garden of Eden; we crossed a turf, covered with fine fruit trees, and intersected by little rivulets, which kept up a pleasant coolness in the air, without any of those inconveniences which humidity occasions...We found companies of men and women sitting under the shade of their fruit trees...everywhere we found hospitality, ease, innocent joy, and every appearance of happiness among them" (Bougainville 1772, 225). Bougainville named his paradise *Nouvelle Cythère,* (New Cythera, after the Greek island of that name). He depicted it as a classical Arcady peopled by godlike beings gamboling in pastoral grooves.

The Tahitians seemed to be the very children of Adam and Eve. "We were stopped by an islander, of a fine figure, who lying under a tree, invited us to sit down by him on the grass. We accepted his offer: he then leaned towards us, and with a tender air he slowly sung a song, without doubt of the Anacreontic kind, to the tune of a flute, which an Indian blew...this was a charming scene..." (Bougainville 1772, 225).

Tableau after tableau, Bougainville unfolded a magnificent never-never land of Noble Savages living as close to a state of nature as one could imagine. When he arrived back in France in March 1769, accompanied by Ahuruturu, a native Tahitian who was to develop a taste for the Paris opera, the Noble Savage became the rage of European society.

Captain Cook and the Tahitians

BY THE TIME THE CHEVALIER de Bougainville returned to Paris, the British Admiralty's plans for another expedition to the Pacific were well advanced. The objectives of the new venture were both geographical and scientific. The explorers were to observe a transit of the planet Venus over the sun on 3 June 1769. Tahiti was considered a highly suitable location for witnessing the phenomenon. They were also to search for the great southern continent and to

7.2   A Tahitian beauty painted in the romantic style (courtesy of the Trustees of the National Maritime Museum, Greenwich, England)

7.3 Captain James Cook, *by Nathaniel Dance, 1776 (courtesy of the Trustees of the National Maritime Museum, Greenwich, England)*

examine the coasts of New Zealand, first sighted by Abel Tasman as long ago as 1642. The Admiralty made an inspired choice of expedition leader: an obscure officer, Lieutenant James Cook.

Cook was the son of a Yorkshire laborer. He spent his early years in the brutal world of the North Sea coal trade (Figure 7.3). In 1755, he volunteered for the Royal Navy as an able seaman. Advanced to master, he served on the Canadian coast and demonstrated extraordinary skills as a navigator and surveyor of unknown coasts. Cook's surveys of the Newfoundland coast were still in use over two centuries later. This work brought the quiet and modest Cook to the notice of the practical seamen who ran the Admiralty. They appointed him to command the *Endeavour* on half pay over the heads of dozens of more senior officers. They were never to regret their controversial decision. Cook was to make three long voyages to the Pacific between 1768 and 1779, when he was killed by the Hawaiians. European knowledge of the Pacific, and of the Tahitians, was transformed as a result of Cook's explorations.

The Admiralty gave Cook highly specific instructions about the Tahitians. He was to "endeavour by all proper means to cultivate a friendship with the Natives, presenting them such Trifles as may be acceptable to them, exchanging with them for Provisions...such of the Mercandize you have been directed to provide, as they may value, and showing them every civility and regard." He was warned to look out for treachery. "You are to be Cautious not to let yourself be surprized by them," the Admiralty enjoined (Beaglehole 1974, 148). His ship carried a crew of eighty-five and a party of civilians, including an astronomer and Joseph Banks, a young gentleman of scientific inclination who was an amateur botanist and an incurable romantic. Very much a gentleman, Banks brought a retinue of seven people with him, including two artists, a secretary, four servants, and two dogs.

The *Endeavour* left Plymouth in August 1768, and arrived in Matavi Bay, Tahiti on 13 April 1769, after a remarkably uneventful passage of eight months, most of it out of sight of land (Figure 7.4). The high mountains of the island caused a stir of excitement in the ship. "The land appeared as uneven as a piece of crumpled paper," wrote Sydney Parkinson, the artist of the expedition in a remarkably apt description. Cook conned the ship into Matavi Bay, where Wallis had anchored in 1766. The *Endeavour* lay in a sheltered berth surrounded by a beach of black sand and dense groves of palm trees. Behind the trees rose steep ridges and crests and the peak of Orofena. A few people came off to the ship with fruit. Cook landed cautiously and soon learned that most of the population had moved to the western end of the island. The ship's company built a small fort as a base for astronomical experiments. Meanwhile the Tahitians flocked to trade and socialize with the crew. Mindful of his instructions from London, Cook issued a set of "Rules" for "the better establishing a regular and uniform Trade for Provisions &c with the Inhabitants." Everyone was to "cultivate a friendship with the Natives and treat them with all imaginable humanity." All trade was to be conducted through a single member of the crew. Severe penalties were to be exacted for the loss of tools or weapons. Lastly, "No Sort of Iron, or any thing that is made of Iron or any sort of Cloth or other usefull or necessary articles are to be given in exchange for any thing

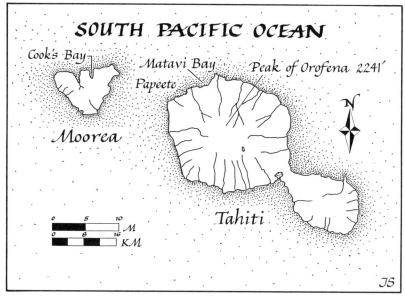

7.4   *Map of Tahiti*

but provisions" (Beaglehole 1974, 177). Cook devised these wise and sober rules to regulate trade, avoid confrontations, and maintain stable rates of exchange for the ship's finite stock of trade goods. He was acutely aware of Wallis's problems with iron nails, and was also careful to regulate contacts between his sex-starved crew and the local people. The ship's surgeon inspected every seaman for traces of venereal disease. Perhaps remembering Wallis, the Tahitians greeted the ship in a most friendly way. The only problem was that they wanted to steal everything within reach. "In this they are prodigious expert." wrote Cook. Cautious and deliberate in everything, Cook was rewarded with a far closer look at Tahitian society than his predecessors. He also spent longer on the island.

The Europeans and Tahitians had ample opportunity to examine each other closely. At first the relationship was one of unabashed curiosity on both sides, a relationship that Cook knew could end in bloodshed from one false move. On the third day of the *Endeavour*'s stay, the Tahitians were astonished when Banks shot three ducks with one blast from his musket. "Most of them fell down as though they had been shot likewise," wrote Cook in his journal. Only a few minutes later more shots rang out, this time from near the fort site. A daring islander had snatched a marine's musket. The young midshipman in charge ordered his men to open fire, which they did "with the greatest glee imaginable, as if they had been shooting at wild ducks." They killed the thief and wounded several other people. The Tahitians decamped at once. In a few

7.5 Captain Cook's ships at Moorea, depicted by John Cleveley, artist on Cook's third expedition (courtesy of the Trustees of the National Maritime Museum, Greenwich, England)

moments the entire expedition was thrown into danger. Using all their powers of persuasion, Cook and Banks succeeded in calming Tahitian fears, and peace was restored.

Cook still trod carefully. His rules were now yielding dividends. The gentlemen controlled the trade and soon learned a smattering of Polynesian. Everyone had a particular Tahitian friend, individual contacts that proved invaluable if at times embarrassing. "This might be productive of good Consequences," wrote Robert Molyneux, the sailing master. "But the women begin to have a share in our Friendship which is by no means Platonick." For four months, long after the successful observation of the transit of Venus, the *Endeavour* remained at anchor in Matavi Bay, while Cook, Banks, and the other gentlemen learned all they could about the island and its inhabitants. Much of our knowledge of Tahitian society comes from their observations.

The Tahitians

THE *ENDEAVOUR* EXPEDITION WAS UNUSUAL in that Cook came to Tahiti not on a casual visit, but for a specific scientific purpose (Figure 7.5). While he was anxious to refit his ship and obtain fresh provisions, this was no transitory visit where aborigine and European examined each other curiously, only to resume their isolated lives. The scientists had come to explore, to question, and to record. They did so with brilliant success. The sober Cook compiled records of canoes, weapons, houses, and everyday life with measured care. To him the Tahitians were just like other people—both good and bad. He was unconcerned with nobility and the Tahitians' closeness to nature. In contrast, Joseph Banks, a highly personable young man, became much closer to the islanders. He enjoyed their informal life immensely. On one occasion he took part in a funeral ceremony all decked out in Tahitian costume. He had the gift of insatiable curiosity and the priceless ability to get on with men and women, especially the latter. From the moment Banks found himself sitting next to a "very pretty girl with a fire in her eyes", he was captivated by the Tahitians, and they by him. His observations were accurate, perceptive, and yet remarkably free of illusions. The leaders of the expedition worked closely and exchanged notes freely. Untrained in fieldwork techniques and totally unfamiliar with Polynesia, they posed questions that were to become the foundation of all later work on the Tahitians. Dimly, they perceived that they were dealing with a highly complex society, one that shared few values with European culture.

The island, they soon learned, was called *Otaheite*, "It is Tahiti." And Tahiti it became from that time on. Perhaps thirty-five thousand people lived on the island, scattered in small groups around the flatter land near the coasts. "The men in general are tall, strong limb'd and well shaped, one of the tallest we saw measured Six feet 3 Inches and a half, the superior women are in every respect as large as Europeans," wrote Cook. "Their hair is almost universally black thick and strong...They have all fine white teeth and for the most part short flat noses and thick lips, yet their features are agreable and their gate graceful" (Beaglehole 1955, 123–124).

Most people were struck by the fine appearance of the Tahitians. "The natural colour of the inhabitants is olive, inclining to copper," wrote an early missionary. "Their eyes are black and sparkling; their teeth white and even; their skin soft and delicate" (Oliver 1974, 40–41). But it was the women who moved early visitors to raptures of delight. Joseph Banks was raised to heights of rhapsody: "On the island of Otaheite where love is the chief occupation, the favorite, nay, the sole luxury of the inhabitants, both the bodies and souls of the women are moulded into the utmost perfection" (Beaglehole 1962, 2:330). Later observers disagreed; they complained of flat noses and prominent eyes, and of a tendency towards obesity. "The Breasts of the young ones before they have had children are very round and beautiful, but those of the old ones hang down to their Navels," wrote one of Cook's companions on his second voyage. He added, "Their beauties have been Magnifyed" (Forster 1777, 137).

Most observers commented on the apparent idyllic simplicity of Tahitian life. The people wore the simplest of garments. They used a breechclout or an underskirt, and a length of bark cloth or plaited leaves wound around the waist, called a *pareu*. Everyone used bark cordage sandals to protect their feet against sharp coral. The most important individuals were decked out in more bark cloth and elaborate headdresses decorated with feathers. Most people wore simple turbans, caps, or wreaths.

Every early visitor commented on the custom of tattooing, a painful process executed with a sharp bone or shell fragment that drove a mixture of lamp black and candlenut oil under the skin. Joseph Banks noted: "Every one is markd thus in different parts of his body…some have ill designd figures of men, birds or dogs, but they more generaly have this figure Z…all the islanders I have seen…agree in having all their buttocks coverd with a deep black, over this most have arches drawn one over another as high as their short ribbs, which are often 1/4 of an inch broad and neatly workd on their edges with indentations &c" (Beaglehole 1962, 1:335).

Tahitian housing was as simple as their clothing. The islanders lived in thatched dwellings with flimsy or open walls and beaten earth floors. The floor was strewn with grass, which, "if not frequently removed, produced abundance of Fleas." Most people sat and slept on mats. The homestead was surrounded with a low fence; several cooking houses lay nearby. Cooking and eating utensils consisted of wooden dishes, pestles and mortars for pounding breadfruit, plantains, and taro. The people used coconut drinking cups and bottles. Chiefs enjoyed somewhat more elaborate dwellings and built much larger structures, some up to 200 feet (61 meters) long, to house large numbers of people and big war canoes. Most Tahitian dwellings were located near fresh water, their owners' gardens, and within walking distance of the ocean. "The houses or rather dwellings of these people are admirably calculated for the continual warmth of their climate," wrote Cook. "They do not build them in Towns or Villages but separate each one from the other and always in the woods…and no more ground is cleard away from each house than is just sufficient to hinder the dropping of branches from rotting the thatch…you step from the house immediately under shade and that the most beautiful! imaginable" (Beaglehole 1974, 1:128). Everything proclaimed a simple, pastoral existence.

The Tahitians never seemed to want for food. The staple food was breadfruit *(Artocarpus incisa),* harvested from productive trees that flourished on the coastal lowlands and provided plentiful shade. "These happy people can almost be said to be exempt from the curse of our forefathers; scarcely can it be said they earn their bread with the sweat of their brow when their chiefest sustenance Bread fruit is procured with no more trouble than that of climbing a tree and pulling it down" (Beaglehole 1962, 1:341). The Tahitians know at least forty varieties of breadfruit, which came into season several times a year. The breadfruit was such a reliable staple that it enabled the people to schedule social and religious activities between harvests.

The coconut provided the Tahitians with food and drink, also with cups, storage bottles, house-building materials, and even oil. The people cultivated taro *(Colocasia antiquorum)* on well-watered soils and ate a variety of wild vegetables, too. They savored the tasty flesh of the native pig, and fattened and ate dogs as well as chickens. The Tahitians relied little on hunting, but every European visitor commented on their fishing skills. The variety of marine life was extraordinary, ranging from edible tortoises, freshwater shrimps and langoustes, oysters and other mollusks, to fish of every size, from sharks to small reef species. The people also feasted off stranded whales. They used seine nets and speared lagoon fish at night, and they fished in deep water. With wood, bone, or shell fishhooks and sword grass lines, the sailing canoes headed offshore in search of birds that were following schools of albacore or dolphin.

As befitted people who spent much of their life afloat, the Tahitians were skilled boatbuilders. The largest canoes had keels made of hollowed-out logs, and topsides made of several hardwood planks, which were tightly lashed together with sennit and caulked with gum and coconut fiber (Figure 7.6). Cook said they were "the best calculated for landing in a Surf of any Vessels I ever saw, their high round sterns receives the force of the Sea in Such a manner than none ever enters the Vessel" (Beaglehole 1968, 130). The more expert Tahitian navigators thought nothing of making regular voyages under sail over open water for distances of up to two hundred miles. Cook was so impressed with their navigational skills that he and Banks carried the pilot Tupaia with them to New Zealand with the intention of bringing him back to England. Unfortunately, he died of fever in southeast Asia. Traditional Polynesian navigation techniques almost vanished until Western small boat sailors made contact with the handful of island pilots still practicing their craft in the 1960s.

The Tahitians lived in a simple, "natural" way, but their social rankings and relationships baffled both Cook and Banks. The *ari'i* were the aristocracy of the islanders, set off from everyone else by specific marriage rules. The term *ari'i* was both a form of address for chiefs and a means of identifying high office holders in society. The rest of the population was divided into *ra'atira* and *manabune,* small landowners and people who seem to have owned little property and often worked for *ari'i.* The differences between social classes were based on property, marriage, birth, occupation, and many other factors.

Tahitian society relied for its cohesiveness on social relationships—sex, relative age, kinship ties, and class level. European visitors were bemused by the many nuances of island social organization. Since the Tahitians were casual about sexual intercourse but not about having children, their society exhibited an extraordinary subtlety and flexibility. Everyone was related to specific individuals and to genealogies and descent lines that gave them relationships with people throughout the island. There were tribal *marae,* groupings of

7.6   A Tahitian fleet in review. Engraving by W. Woollett after William Hodges.

people living in a well-defined area under the rule of a tribal chief. The chief was the vital intermediary between the living people and the spirits associated with the *marae*. Such leaders had both secular and ritual duties. Like the Khoikhoi "nations," Tahitian "tribes" or "districts" were constantly merging and separating. Many tribes consisted of smaller groupings based on kinship, marriage and ever-shifting military alliances, and *marae*. Kinship ties and religious loyalties were insufficient to hold together tribal entities, so war was a major force in shaping Tahitian society. This, and human sacrifice, were the dark sides of Tahitian life in Western eyes, unpleasant realities delicately ignored by those who envied the Tahitians their idyllic life on a distant tropical island.

A chief made the decision to wage war in consultation with his relatives and other tribal leaders. "Their wars were most merciless and destructive," wrote the missionary William Ellis in 1829. "Total extermination of their enemies, with the desolation of a country, was often the avowed object of the war" (Ellis 1829, 2:486). The victors slaughtered everyone, felled breadfruit and palm trees and laid waste to the land. Most wars began after prolonged debate, elaborate rituals, and lengthy preparations. Armed with clubs, spears, rasps, and stones, the parties would engage in ferocious combat on land or sea. No quarter was given on either side. Great war canoes, twin-hulled vessels sometimes fifty to one hundred feet (fifteen to thirty meters) long with upturned sterns and raised forepeaks carried the Tahitians into their sea battles. Cook witnessed a naval review that consisted of a fleet of one hundred sixty large war canoes, each with about forty men aboard, as well as one hundred seventy smaller vessels that carried supplies, each manned by a crew of eight. Most naval battles took place inside the coral reefs. The opposing fleets lashed their canoes together in long lines, then paddled out to meet one another, with their warriors crowding the fore platforms. First they threw stones, then spears, then closed to fight hand-to-hand with great ferocity.

The Tahitians' religious beliefs permeated every aspect of their lives. Many of their deities were associated with specific tribal groups, but the cults or certain gods, especially 'Oro, were followed throughout the islands. "The sea rolled, and the tides succeeded each other for a period of nights. It was the birthright of a god, it was the night Mua Ta'aroa (First-severed); 'Oro-tana (Warrior-at-war) was the god born that night; 'Oro (Warrior), god of the air and earth; 'Oro, the manslayer; 'Oro, god of the comedians..." (Oliver 1974, 2:890). The story of 'Oro's birth was common knowledge on the islands. He was a male god, young, handsome, sexually active, and moderately prolific. 'Oro had a passion for warfare and was hungry for human lives. All Tahitians believed in 'Oro and feared him. He was a jealous god, one whom one took care to placate, hardly the deity of a simple people living close to nature.

'Oro and other Tahitian gods were worshipped at temples (also called *marae)*, sacred places where spirits and humans could interact, normally through priests *(arioi)* who acted as intermediaries. The largest *marae*, on Tahiti itself, was dominated by a rectangular stone platform with ten steps, about thirty-three feet (ten meters) high. It was at one such place that Cook saw a recently slain corpse offered to the gods (Figure 7.7). This did not deter his companions from writing about paradise in the South Seas. During the early years of European contact, powerful chiefs used human sacrifice as a means of propitiating 'Oro, also as a way of strengthening their own political power.

The reserved and inhibited Europeans who first observed the Tahitians were struck not only by their idyllic environment and simple way of life, but by the lighthearted way in which they amused themselves. "I have already painted these islanders as being great conversationalists, lively, animated, and fond of company. They sought after and found distractions and occasions for merrymaking even in those of their tasks which seemed most laborious; therefore one can almost say, in its ordinary course, their [daily] life was nothing but a holiday," wrote Jacques-Antoine Moerenhout in 1837 (Moerenhout 1837, 1:125). Their abundant leisure time was filled with simple pleasures that appealed to European sensibilities. Tahitians enjoyed boxing and wrestling,

7.7   Human sacrifice at a Tahitian marae. Captain Cook can be seen at the right.

cock fighting, and archery contests. They would surf and swim for hours. The islanders had a penchant for idle conversation and for formal oratory. "It seemed eloquence was so necessary to the chiefs that to lack it was to lack the ability to rule," wrote an observer in 1837 (125). "If one may say that eloquence was *honored*...then one should add that poetry was *a passion* with them" (125) Their chants and lyrics dealt with the deeds of gods, heroes, and chiefs. There were songs for fishing, for canoe building, and house construction. Drums, shell trumpets, rattles, and a flute blown through the nostrils provided the Tahitians with musical accompaniment.

The Tahitian dances fascinated Europeans most of all. The Tahitians danced for pleasure, in rage, during times of war, at marriages and funerals, at religious ceremonies, in competitions, and to entertain. They danced by moving not only their feet and hands, but every part of their bodies as well, shaking their hips in excellent time to drums. Some visitors were shocked by the "lascivious" Tahitian dances, many of which were explicitly sexual. "The young girls...dance a very indecent dance which they call *Timorodee* singing most indecent songs and useing most indecent actions in the practice of which they are brought up from their earliest childhood" (Beaglehole 1955, 127). The rumors of orgiastic, sexual dances titillated eighteenth-century London and Paris. But to accuse the Tahitians, as many observers did, of performing obscene dances is to do them a gross injustice. Dancing, like the dramatic performances that accompanied it, was an integral part of accepted behavior in a culture that valued social role-playing very highly.

The Tahitians regarded sex as one of life's greatest pleasures, something as essential to their well-being as eating and sleeping. Their open attitudes about sexual intercourse came as a profound shock even to relatively uninhibited eighteenth-century English gentlemen. "The great plenty of good and nourishing food, together with the fine climate, the beauty and unreserved behaviour of their females, invite them powerfully to the enjoyments and pleasures of love. They begin very early to abandon themselves to the most libidinous scenes," wrote Georg Foster (1778, 231). The austere missionaries of a generation later were duly horrified. They referred to Tahiti as "the filthy Sodom of the South Seas," and complained that the inhabitants talked of nothing but "the filthy coition of the sexes" all day.

Unlike the missionaries, European sailors delighted in Tahitian women. They found that the lower-class girls would gladly exchange their favors for iron nails and other trade goods; and Tahitian standards of privacy were quite different from the European. The Tahitians had sex whenever the opportunity presented itself, whether in their houses or in public. "Our people were daily walking in the isle without arms, either quite alone, or in little companies. They were invited to enter the houses, where the people gave them to eat; nor did the civility of their landlords stop at a slight collation, they offered them young girls..." (Bougainville 1772, 230). And the sex-starved Europeans accepted their offers. There is abundant evidence that Joseph Banks and the other gentlemen yielded to the charms of the Tahitian girls. Only Cook seems to have abstained. The memories of free love in pastoral glades only reinforced the romantic image of a tropical paradise. Small wonder that dark tales of ferocious wars and human sacrifice were conveniently set to one side.

Noble Savages?

THE *ENDEAVOUR*'s HAPPY VISIT TO Tahiti ended on 13 July, 1769, when the ship sailed from Matavi Bay surrounded by canoes full of lamenting Tahitians. Banks climbed to the topmast head and waved farewell until the canoes were out of sight. He had taken his own Tahitian along with him, a navigator named Tupaia. Banks aimed to keep him as a curiosity, "as well as some of my neighbors do lions and tygers at a greater expense than he will probably ever put me to" (Beaglehole 1962, 2:312–3). The explorers arrived back in England two years later. They brought with them thousands of plant specimens, five hundred exotic fish and over five hundred birds, as well as insects and a mass of geographical information from a new, paradisal land. Their Tahitian stories caused a sensation. Cook's biographer, the New Zealand historian J. C. Beaglehole, puts it well: "The Noble Savage entered the study and

7.8 Portrait of Omai in a classical pose by Sir Joshua Reynolds (courtesy of Mr. Charles Howard)

drawing room of Europe in naked majesty, to shake the preconceptions of morals and politics" (Beaglehole 1974, 290). Cook found himself the focus of popular attention. Banks, young, handsome, wealthy, was the fashionable hero of the hour. He entranced London with his stories of free love and the elegant Tahitian women with their natural beauty. "The scene that we saw was the truest picture of an Arcadia of which we were going to be kings that the imagination can form," he wrote (Beaglehole 1962, 1:252). He depicted the Tahitians as people with polished manners and a simple, elegant lifestyle. Contemplation of this tropical paradise was a wonderful escape from the pressures and frustrations of daily life in eighteenth-century London.

While Banks became the lion of London society, Cook quietly prepared for a second voyage to the Pacific. Meanwhile, his journals of the first voyage were handed over for publication to John Hawkesworth, a well-known literary figure of the day. It was felt that the workmanlike Cook would not do justice to the great themes of the voyage. Hawkesworth was an author of decidedly romantic persuasion who had no doubts about the Noble Savage. His book cast the Tahitians in a noble, back-to-nature light. He implied that the Tahitians never did a day's work in their lives, and were therefore incomparably happier than were Europeans. After all, their morals were quite "natural." Hawkesworth allowed his romantic imagination full play and tactfully ignored the more unattractive aspects of Tahitian society. If Cook had done his best to record unembellished facts and Banks had developed an unsentimental liking for the Tahitians, Hawkesworth had given them that popular twist of romance that made all the commercial difference, a difference reinforced by their deliciously libidinous sexual habits. Cook was infuriated by Hawkesworth's excesses, but to no avail. The Noble Savage was allowed to prance unhindered across the European imagination.

The romantic feelings of the day spilled over into the artists' depictions of the South Sea. Hawkesworth's effusions were illustrated by landscapes with a strong classical flavor, with romantic Tahitians posed in pastoral scenes. When Captain Thomas Furneaux brought a Tahitian named Omai back to London in 1774, the illusion of the Noble Savage was complete. The young Tahitian captivated high society, but soon sank into obscurity when he returned home. Omai was received with honor, introduced to the highest levels of London society, and received by the king. He sat for his portrait, depicted as a patrician gentleman in bare feet and flowing robes, posed against the background of an exotic landscape (Figure 7.8). The Noble Savage lived! Perhaps Tahiti was the utopian state that had haunted European consciousness for so long. The Tahitians in all their innocent simplicity seemed to have achieved a happiness in this world that had escaped European civilization for centuries. Many preferred to believe that the search for paradise on earth was over; indeed, the myth of the paradisal South Seas persists to this day.

CHAPTER 8

The Van Diemeners

The intimate union of the different members of a family, the sort of patriarchal life of which we had been spectators, had strongly moved us. I saw with inexpressible pleasure the realization of the happiness and simplicity of the state of nature of which I had so many times in reading felt the seductive charm.

François Peron on the Tasmanians (1811)

THE MYTH OF NOBLE SAVAGES flourished and lingered in the European mind for generations after their glorious excursions across the pages of Hawkesworth's *Voyages.* The Tahitians were still clothed in the same mythical aurora long after Omai had returned to his homeland and the harsh realities of European contact were decimating the islanders with alcohol, violence, and unfamiliar diseases. The Noble Savage served as a useful catalyst for the passionate self-scrutiny so fashionable in late eighteenth-century Europe. The myth revolved around dreams of a better world, where social equality flourished, as well as economic freedom based on division of labor and private property. This scheme was to reflect humanity's proximity to nature; the tantalizing image first focused on Europe's distant past, then shifted onto non-Western peoples like the Indians and Tahitians, who were uncorrupted and still living in a more or less paradisal state. Eventually the myth became a universal image of the nature of human existence, a form of historical philosophy that had profound lessons for people despairing of their own civilization.

The European view of the non-Western world fluctuated through the centuries and soon differed radically from that of the early days of the Age of Discovery. Captain Cook's Tahitians were considered childlike, noble, and virtuous and were held in high esteem. At other times, non-Westerners were thought brutish and violent. But just as Europeans' conceptions of other societies changed, so did their views of their own civilization. The eighteenth-century Romantics thought that civilization was clearly superior to savagery, but that their own society had serious faults. True, some Europeans lived in comfort, even luxury, but many people suffered under grinding poverty, war was an endemic condition, and the nobility enjoyed undue privilege. In contrast, the savage was noble and virtuous, untrammeled by such worries. Despite all the benefits of civilization, those who enjoyed it had lost a certain amount of innocence, just as a mature adult has no desire—nor ability—to return to the simple, carefree days of childhood. The image of civilization was tarnished, that of savagery enhanced, and as Europeans' perceptions of themselves changed, so did their views of savagery. The changes in viewpoint did not necessarily coincide; indeed, they were only vaguely connected, but Western self-images were a vital ingredient in their attitudes towards other societies.

As European explorers penetrated into the furthest corners of the Pacific, to Australia, Tasmania, and into the far interior of tropical Africa, it became harder to maintain the literary fiction of the Noble Savage, of paradisal people living at peace with nature. Expedition after expedition returned with stories of remote peoples so primitive that they seemed to be the very personification of the degradation of humanity. If these were not noble peoples, how then could one explain the differences in their culture and physical appearance? Above all, how could one raise these peoples or nations to the level of their European brothers? This idealistic viewpoint, partly scientific and partly humanistic, was one of the inspirations for the foundation of the world's first anthropological society, the Societé des Observateurs de l'Homme. The Tasmanian researches of its members were the last echo of the fiction of nobility.

The Emperor Napoleon had a passion for science and exploration. He encouraged scientific research as a way of fostering nationalism. Founded in late 1799, the Societé des Observateurs was but one of many scientific organizations founded in the early years of the French Republic. It was dedicated to self-knowledge and the advancement of humanity's perfection and happiness. The membership consisted of explorers and scientists with the broadest possible interests in humanity. Early in 1800, Captain Nicholas Baudin (1754–1803) came to the Institut National with a proposal for a grandiose expedition of scientific and geographical discovery that finally evolved into a more limited voyage to southwest Australia. The Institut turned to the Societé for help in planning the study of the Australians in their "physical, intellectual, and moral" aspects. The Societé responded with two memoranda that are a fascinating reflection on attitudes towards other societies at the time.

Joseph Marie de Gerando (Citizen Degerando) (1772–1842), philosopher, philanthropist, and publicist, contributed a set of instructions for observing savages. This fascinating document is the epitome of eighteenth-century scientific humanitarianism. By observing the most primitive societies, he remarked, it should be possible to "penetrate nature and determine its essential laws." But the key was observation, using "regular tables" to overcome the disadvantages of the transitory accounts of savages that so many explorers brought home. He attacked the bizarre, judgmental descriptions that were all too often based on a complete ignorance of local languages. He adjured, to learn a savage language meant becoming "in a manner of speaking like one among them," a "fellow citizen." One started with sign language, then passed on to simple statements of action, the culmination being abstract thought, of which even "savages cannot be utterly deprived." While learning the language, one could observe the natural environment and the physical characteristics of typical individuals, and "the savage in society." This latter included domestic life, "the state of women," modesty, love, and marriage. The observer was also to study political, civil, economic, and religious life.

Degerando posed question after question: Were the people warlike? Did they engage in trade? Did they have metals? Did their priests exert a positive influence, or did they maintain their nation "in ignorance and barbarism?" The visitor was to study oral traditions, which "cast a precious light on the mysterious history of these nations." And, to cap off the work, the observer should make every effort to bring back a family of savages to Europe, so that "we would then possess in microcosm the image of that society from which they had been carried away" (Stocking 1968, 26).

The purpose of this ambitious document was to provide data for the construction of "an exact scale of the various degrees of civilization and to assign to each the properties which characterize it" (Stocking 1968, 26). Degerando believed that the Baudin expedition would be traveling to the remotest parts of the earth, in a sense backwards into the past into an environment where it could observe prehistory in action. There was not only a scientific objective, but a philanthropic one as well: the first contacts with the savages would establish new "needs" and "desires" that would lead them eventually to civilization. "Perhaps they will become attached to us by gratitude or interest...they will call us to their midst to show them the route which will conduct them to our state. What joy! What conquest!" (27). This optimistic document was no racist manifesto. On the orders of Napoleon himself, the ships of the Baudin expedition were laden with "animals of the most useful races...grains most suitable to the temperature of their climates, the tools most necessary to man; clothes and ornaments of all kinds" (28). Europeans were to appear as benefactors and friends.

The eminent paleontologist Georges Cuvier (1769–1832) contributed the second memorandum. His anatomical researches suffered from the major disadvantage of his lack of comparative skeletal material from other societies to work with. There was not, he complained, even a single study of the skeletal differences between Negroes and whites. So his memoir stressed the need for collecting skulls. If the expedition witnessed a battle, its members must visit the "places where the dead are deposited." Above all, they were to collect bodies in "any manner whatever," boiling the bones in "solution of soda or of caustic potash" for several hours to rid them of their flesh. Cuvier was passionately interested in "race and biological differences," for these, he argued, determined cultural characteristics. His objective was science, not philanthropy, and his methods of collection barbarous; but his sole objective was the advancement of knowledge.

Baudin, Peron, and the Tasmanians

BAUDIN SAILED FOR AUSTRALIA IN October 1800. A large contingent of scientists accompanied his two ships. The expedition ran into trouble soon after arriving in the Indian Ocean. Scurvy and dysentery were rife, the scientists quarreled with the crew, and there were food and water shortages. But the expedition made anthropological history with its curiously romantic sojourn among the Tasmanians, which saw the last death throes of the eighteenth-century attitude toward savages.

Cuvier's and Degerando's memoranda were handed to a young medical student named François Peron (1775–1810), who had talked his way onto the expedition staff as a student zoologist. Peron had read Rousseau and assumed, like many of his contemporaries, that savages were healthier, stronger, and physically superior to Europeans. But balancing this, they were physically and morally insensitive, capable of withstanding unbearable pain, and cannibalistic. Peron's experiments and observations on the expedition changed his mind. He never followed the detailed instructions of Cuvier and Degerando. Instead, he used a dynamometer to measure the physical strength of Tasmanians, Australians, and others. He concluded that the scientifically measured strength of each group of subjects varied in direct proportion to their position on the ladder of civilization. At the bottom were the Tasmanians and Australians, physically weak and only periodically sexually active. The cosseted environment in which Europeans lived was a "fecund source of the sharpest, most delicate and dearest sentiments" (Peron 1816, 304). If the "disinherited children of nature gave up their ferocious and vagabond customs" and settled in villages, their social state would improve and they would enjoy much more robust temperaments. Peron was confronted by the reality of human diversity. His strictures were to be heard again and again in later decades. Peron thought of the Tasmanians in two ways, as simple, Rousseauean savages, but also as members of a weaker race, who were not using their land to its potential.

By the time Baudin's ships arrived in Tasmania—known at the time as Van Diemen's Land—the aborigines had met crews from nine major scientific expeditions and five trading ships (Figure 8.1). Visitors included the illustrious Captain James Cook, who found little appealing in what he called "an ignorant wretched race of mortals." Twelve French scientists headed by the naturalist Jacques de Labillardière had spent some weeks on the island in 1791. Labillardière had been raised on a solid diet of Rousseau. He was fascinated by the aborigines, who wore nothing more than cloaks of kangaroo hide. He watched the women dive into the chilly water for mollusks and oysters, apparently indifferent to the cold, sharks, and entangling kelp. His account of the Tasmanians is tinged with romance and reads like a surrealistic novel. The explorers arrive, bow before friendly savages, and engage in relaxed sign language as they exchange a few trinkets with their hosts. The local women are admired, white chests are stroked, and mysteriously ticking watches held to aboriginal ears. Labillardière offers a pair of brightly colored pantaloons to a young girl in exchange for her kangaroo skin. Reluctantly she agrees after Labillardière models the garment. The French gallantly assist her in donning the strange pants. The whole scene is redolent of pastoral simplicity—and unreality.

François Peron had more time to explore the countryside than did his predecessors. He was delighted to see two aborigines approaching as his boat grounded on the beach. Eventually the younger man was persuaded to approach. "His physiognomy had nothing fierce or austere," reported Peron. "His eyes were lively and expressive and his manner displayed at once both pleasure and surprise." The aborigine received Peron's embraces with complete indifference, but examined the boat and the seamen's jackets and white skins with minute care. He "expressed his astonishment by loud exclamations of surprise, and by very quick movements of the feet" (Peron 1816, 304).

Later Peron and his companions visited a Tasmanian encampment in the woods, where they found a family eating shellfish under a crude brush shelter. The aborigines offered them oysters, while the two young Frenchmen sang songs for their hosts. It must have been a strange and incongruous sight. Peron's companion was captivated by a young Tasmanian girl, who was completely unashamed of her nakedness. The Frenchmen rowed away, leaving the friendly aborigines loaded with gifts and the girl the proud possessor of a red feather.

The scientists had leisure to collect artifacts and study the Tasmanians' way of life at least superficially. They commented on their peaceful nature

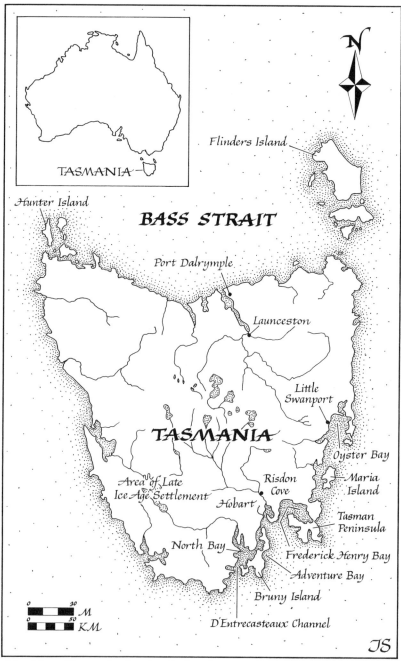

8.1   *Map of Tasmania, showing the locations mentioned in the text*

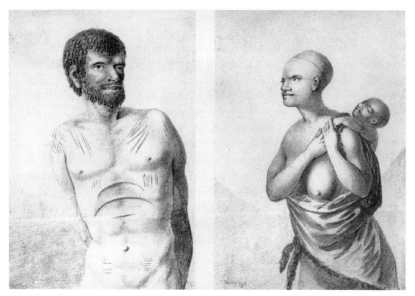

8.2   Tasmanian man and woman with child (courtesy of the Tasmanian Museum and Art Gallery)

and on their healthy appearance (Figure 8.2). Their eyes were always restless. They tattooed their bodies with raised marks. The aborigines' huts were made of brush, their drinking vessels fashioned of large seaweed leaves. They possessed only the simplest of tools, spears and innocuous clubs, and floated across sheltered bays on frail rafts of eucalyptus bark. They were friendly to strangers and enjoyed painting the faces of the scientists with red ocher or powdered charcoal. They also developed the disconcerting habit of abducting members of the expedition and stripping them from head to toe. After minutely examining their unfamiliar bodies, they would let them go unharmed.

Peron tarried in Tasmania for about six months. Unfortunately, he never published his scientific findings. His *Voyages de Decouvertes aux Terres Australes* (1807–1816) caters to a quite different audience. He lavishes Rousseauean superlatives on the Tasmanians. It is as if we were watching yet another pastoral scene among rose-covered bowers. The participants in the drama conduct themselves with the utmost delicacy and decorum. The respectful natives are treated as equals in an elegant salon. Gallantly, the gentlemen flirt with nubile young maidens. The play ends with the tearful departure of the unexpected visitors. The entranced reader is left to contemplate paradise in faraway Tasmania. "All the descriptions that I have given, are of the most rigorous exactitude," insists Peron. "This gentle confidence of the people in us, these affectionate evidences of benevolence which they never ceased to manifest towards us, the sincerity of their demonstrations, the frankness of their manners, the touching ingeniousness of their caresses, all concurred within us sentiments of the tenderest interest" (Peron 1816, 305). The Noble Savage, with all his "happiness and simplicity of the state of nature," is alive and well on this last of the eighteenth-century anthropological excursions.

François Peron may have admired the Tasmanians as "children of nature *par excellence*" and done his share of myth-making, but he had no doubt that they represented the very lowest rung of civilization, even below their Australian relatives. But like Degerando, he was an optimist about the chances of improving the Tasmanians' condition. He may have believed that they belonged to a quite different race, for they had little in common with Westerners or other humans. Their implements for hunting and fishing were cruder than anything anyone had ever seen before. Captain Nicholas Baudin perhaps best expressed the most prevailing attitude when he remarked that, while the Tasmanians were not noble savages, they were no more obnoxious than the Bretons or the Scots. At least none of them were cannibals.

In the event, Peron's observations came to naught, for he returned to find the Societé des Observateurs in eclipse. The society had collapsed in 1804. Peron's valuable collections were partially destroyed in 1814 and finally dispersed in 1829. It was three-quarters of a century before any scientist tried to write a more complete account of traditional Tasmanian society, by which time the society glimpsed by early visitors had vanished.

The Tasmanians

EVEN PERON AND HIS CONTEMPORARIES realized that the Tasmanians were among the most unsophisticated people on earth. They soon became a weird curiosity on the outermost fringes of the civilized world.

Some 3,000 to 5,000 aborigines are estimated to have been living in Van Diemen's Land in du Fresne's time. Their ancestors occupied the island, then part of the Australian continent, at least 32,000 years ago. This population was divided into about eighty different bands of 30 to 50 people, with each band consisting of a few families. Each band occupied a territory of about 200 to 300 square miles, often including some 15 to 20 miles of coastline. The Tasmanians were also grouped into nine larger social units that could be described as tribes. Each shared a common culture and distinctive language, and occupied a region of about 1,000 to 3,300 square miles.

The Tasmanians normally went around naked, except in the coldest weather, when they wore kangaroo skin cloaks. The same garment served the women for carrying infants, shellfish or vegetable foods. The men sometimes dressed their hair with red ocher, kangaroo teeth, and feathers. Men, women, and children sometimes wore flowers in their hair, too. Nakedness seemed so natural to the aborigines that they firmly resisted any attempt to clothe them in European garments. Much to the irritation of straitlaced and narrow-minded missionaries, they removed this alien clothing at the slightest provocation.

The aborigines moved through their territories in a complex pattern of seasonal movements that took advantage of seasons of shellfish and vegetable foods. The coastal bands accumulated huge piles of empty shells at favored locations, places where they returned year after year to eat mussels, oysters, and other species. Early travelers often met families moving inland with large quantities of crabs, crayfish, and mollusks that had been grilled over open fires and piled in rush baskets. It would be a mistake to assume that they ate shellfish and nothing else, but these were a vital resource in lean months and a reliable food supply for much of the year. Incredible as it may seem, the Tasmanians never ate fish. They would help the French pull in netfuls of them, but always refused the catch with contempt.

The bands of the interior relied heavily on game like the kangaroo, opossum, and wombat, often gorging themselves on major kills. "They eat voraciously, and are very little removed from the brute creation as to choice of food, entrails, and so on, sharing the same chance as the choicest parts," wrote one shocked observer (Davies 1973, 252). The aborigines would stalk lone animals or stampede groups of them with fires. The women took opossums by notching tree trunks and climbing high above the ground to pull them out of their lairs by their tails, sometimes simply shaking them into the hands of the waiting hunters beneath.

The Tasmanians snared birds and consumed small rodents and caterpillars, but scheduled their lives around the seasons of fruits, grasses, and tubers. Their favorite vegetable food was the luxuriant root of the Tara fern *(Pteris esculenta)*, which they roasted in their hearths. Like many hunter-gatherers, they seem to have concentrated on relatively few vegetable species, even if they knew of many other edible plants that could be eaten in lean times. Their diet was based on seasonal collecting and a delicate balance between different land- and seafoods. They never deliberately overexploited one food resource to the exclusion of others. Although little is known of Tasmanian beliefs, we can be sure that their traditional lore, like that of their Australian relatives, was firmly wedded to the notion of long-term balance between the people and the land.

The aborigines managed to exist comfortably for thousands of years with little more than two dozen artifacts. "Their huts are the most miserable things imaginable. A curved piece of wood is all the framework, and this is covered by some slabs of eucalyptus bark that they lift off trees" (Davies 1973, 116).

8.3 Tasmanian basket (courtesy of Jane Williams)

Each family had its own hearth, kept lighted by smoldering fire sticks that were carried from camp to camp. The men hunted with long, pliable wooden spears with fire-hardened points and whiplike "tails" that gave the missile spin in flight. A skilled hunter could propel his spear accurately for more than one hundred feet. As Marion du Fresne's men found to their cost, the aborigines could throw stones with disconcerting accuracy, even stunning birds in flight. They also carried "waddlies," a club-throwing stick that was hurled with a rapid, twirling motion to stun its victim long enough for the hunter to reach it.

The women used simple wooden spatulas to pry shellfish off rocks, and made bags and baskets of bark strips and reeds for carrying foods. Crude digging sticks, opossum-skin pouches, and abalone-shell drinking vessels were used (Figure 8.3). So simple was Tasmanian technology that they never developed the boomerang of the mainland, nor did they ever tip their spears with stone points. They used crude choppers, rudimentary knives, and a variety of stone scrapers to cut wood and prepare skins. Simple as the Tasmanians' artifacts may have been, they were certainly highly effective and well adapted to local needs. The aborigines had no need of more elaborate technology—their adaptation to their island environment was highly effective and had been so since the late Ice Age. But all this was to be destroyed within a few brief generations.

CHAPTER 9

"The Noble Savage Is a Dog!"

The true savage is neither free nor noble; he is slave to his own wants, his own passions...ignorant of agriculture, living by the chase, and improvident in success, hunger always stares him in the face, and often drives him to the dreadful alternative of cannibalism or death.

Sir John Lubbock, *Prehistoric Times* (1865)

At some future time period, not very distant as measured by centuries, the civilized races of men will almost certainly exterminate, and replace, the savage races throughout the world.

Charles Darwin, *The Descent of Man* (1871)

"*L'HOMME SAUVAGE EST UN CHIEN!*" the Emperor Napoleon is said to have remarked upon his return from his disastrous military campaign through Egypt in 1801. Europe was deep in the throes of revolution. Commentators might wax gloomy about the terrible consequences of revolutionary change for democracy, but the new political climate had profound effects on the way in which people thought about non-Western societies. The European image of civilization moved away from thoughts of paradise and its inevitable degeneration to new and vibrant feelings of optimism about the future of civilization. Westerners' conceptions of their own civilization began to improve; their self-esteem reached new heights. At the same time, savages declined in popular culture. Instead of being the sort of noble beings depicted by Rousseau and described by Labillardière and Peron, they were perceived as being ignorant, dirty, and of limited intelligence. The new European catchwords were "freedom," "progress," and "national superiority," part of the vocabulary of revolution and profound social change. Now Western supremacy, and not idyllic pastoralism, became the accepted desideratum of historical thinking, which encouraged evolutionary approaches to the human condition. The Tasmanians were caught in the midst of these changing attitudes.

By the mid- to late-nineteenth century, archaeologists and anthropologists were painting pictures of a humankind that had been marching forward inexorably for thousands of years toward the ultimate pinnacle, the glorious industrial zenith of Western civilization. Every non-Western society, however primitive or elaborate, had a place in this well-ordered scheme. And at the summit ruled the West—the monarch, as it were, of a world where the Western will to advance and civilize was the only logical rule of order and progress. This myth of inexorable progress and Western superiority was to prove as pervasive as that of paradise on earth. Exoticism lingered on in James Fenimore Cooper's lyrical evocations of the American Indian, the novels of Joseph Conrad and others about the South Seas, and even in some of the works of Rudyard Kipling. The exoticism, however, was never directed against a specific people.

The Chain of Being

THE DEMISE OF THE NOBLE SAVAGE was inevitable. Romantic notions of chivalrous Indians and well-mannered, dark-skinned peoples withered in the face of an avalanche of information about distant lands and the human societies that peopled them. Confronted with far more empirical data about other societies, the late-eighteenth-century intellectual wrestled with "the mysterious history of these nations." Why were some peoples more civilized than others? Was it not all of humanity's destiny to enjoy the fruits of civilization? By the time of the French Revolution, more and more scholars thought of civilization as the achievement of only a few "races." They had begun to ponder the European's place in the scheme of things, to try and place humankind in its rightful place among the handiworks of God. Above all, they were fascinated by the physical differences between human beings, and started to arrange animals and people into ordered hierarchies based on a wide variety of criteria.

The most widely used of all biological hierarchies was the Great Chain of Being, which systemized the whole of Creation, even the Creator Himself (Figure 9.1). The Chain had its basis in classical beliefs. It posited the placement of inanimate things at the end of a long "chain," and progressed upwards through lower forms of life and more advanced animals until it came to human beings. Humankind itself was poised midway on the chain, suspended between the beasts and the heavenly creatures who formed the uppermost ranks of the chain. A chain is a continuous linkage without gaps, so the gradations between the ranks of the great Chain were merely subtle alterations—the hierarchy was always thought of as a whole. *"Man* is part a *Brute,* part an *Angel,"* wrote scientist Edward Tyson in 1701, "and is that *Link* in the *Creation,* that joyns them both together."

The Chain of Being dramatized the Christian view of humans as creatures with divine souls, and satisfied the eighteenth century's passion for organizing the outside world. But both Linnaeus and physiologist Johann Friedrich Blumenbach (1752–1840) resisted the idea of hierarchy. Blumenbach insisted that all humans were of the same species, and distinguished varieties among them by using such characteristics as hair and skin color. Other scientists wondered why humans should not be graded by ranks on the Chain on the basis of their energy, talent, and abilities. The problem was difficult, for no one knew whether one should rank individuals or groups of people. Inevitably, some scientists turned to physiognomy as a means of ranking humans. As early as the mid-seventeenth century, the British scientist Sir William Petty had emphasized the physical differences among human beings. "There bee others more considerable, that is, between the Guiny Negroes and the Middle Europeans; and of Negroes between those of Guiny and those who live about the Cape of Good Hope [the Khoikhoi], which last are the Most beastlike of all the Souls of Men with whom our Travellers are well acquainted," he wrote in 1677 (Lansdowne 1927, 2:31).

By the late eighteenth century, physiognomic and anatomical traits were regarded as the only logical way of determining position on the Chain of Being. In the 1770s the Dutch anatomist Peter Camper pioneered the idea of the "facial angle," a measure of prognathism that enabled him to arrange the skulls in his collection in a graduated order, with the apes and Negroes at one end, the Europeans at the other. This seemed like an amusing pastime, but was in fact a far from risible experiment. Soon Khoikhoi and African Negroes were at the base of the human part of the Chain, only a short step above the bestial apes, which so many people thought they resembled. The Negroes were associated most closely with the latter in peoples' minds, because, by tragic historical coincidence, the two had been discovered in Africa at about the same time.

The rhetoric of the Chain of Being was soon applied to social relationships, especially to the position of Negroes, who so often served as slaves to whites. The famous paleontologist Georges Cuvier went so far as to place humans at the head of the animal kingdom, but argued that there were some intrinsic causes that impeded the progress of some races, even under the most favorable conditions. He stated that the Negro had never progressed beyond

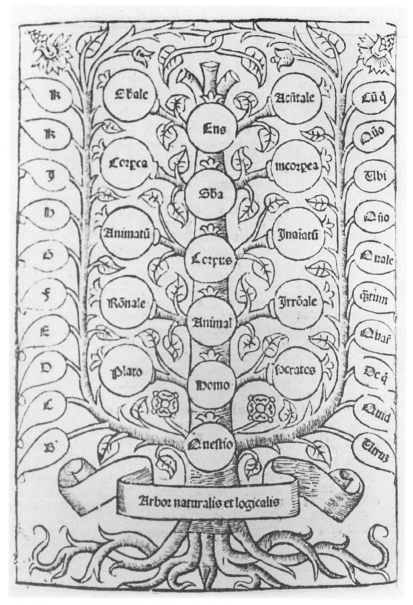

9.1 *Diagram of the Chain of Being in the form of a tree, from Raymond Lull's* De nova logica *(1512)*

unredeemable barbarism. Cuvier's arguments merely reflected commonly held views of the day. The pervasive notions of race and racial superiority that were to dominate European thinking in the nineteenth and early twentieth centuries were, to a great extent, the result of increased contact with, and experience of, dark and especially black-skinned, peoples.

Race: Monogenists and Polygenists

THE AMERICAN INDIANS AND TAHITIANS had burst upon the European consciousness between 1500 and 1770, at a time when the New World and the Pacific were still part of a mysterious realm far beyond the European landscape. At the time, "civilization" had been thought of as part of the "natural" capacity of all humankind, something that was free of all superstition, dogma, and the inhibitions of one's environment. The backwardness of some societies was explained away as "mysterious history." By the same token, any society, however primitive, had the capacity to achieve a state of civilization.

By the 1790s, it was no longer possible to conceal the biological and cultural gap between Europeans and other societies. It was all very well for revolutionaries to claim that all people were equal in potential, but some prominent social philosophers like the Comte de Saint-Simon turned to psychology and physiology to argue that blacks, because of their physical makeup, were unable to achieve the same intellectual level as Europeans, even if one gave them the same education. In other words, humankind might have shared a common ancestry in the Garden of Eden, but civilization was reserved for the white European.

The new thinking about racial superiority stemmed from many complex, and still little-understood, causes. Dozens of hitherto unknown human societies came to light during the late eighteenth century. Many more people acquired practical experience in dealing with non-Westerners. Then there was the slave trade, a major industry in late-eighteenth-century Europe. Those with a vested interest in the human trade and the colonialism that went with it played on the obvious differences between Europeans and non-Europeans, especially those of physiognomy and skin color. Clearly, no one would exploit a noble savage or enslave one, so ideas of nobility were suppressed at the expense of economic expediency.

"Race" itself was a novel concept that had to be explained. Christian dogma still had a powerful hold on European minds. While theologians were quite prepared to accept "race" as a minor factor in world history, the product of historical and environmental processes, they were insistent that all human races had originated in Adam and Eve. These *monogenists* argued for the unity of humankind. Many of them were humanitarians and philanthropists who believed in the humane treatment of other peoples. The monogenists were challenged by the *polygenists,* who stated that the physical and cultural differences among different human societies were so great that God must have created other species of humans beyond Adam. Polygenists generally took a less humanitarian line towards non-Westerners. They believed that humankind was divided into a series of unchanging races of diverse origin, whose characteristics could be defined by precise skull measurements. These cranial dimensions could be correlated with differences in mental ability and racial achievement.

The debate between the monogenists and polygenists quickly subsided at about the time when Charles Darwin's *Origin of Species* appeared in 1859. But the new racist thinking exercised a profound influence on those who pondered human diversity throughout the nineteenth century. By the time European expansion reached its height in the last three decades of the nineteenth century, most social scientists were convinced that savages had far less capacity for abstract thought than lighter-skinned peoples. They were members of lower races, races of lesser intelligence, but had the potential for improvement if given the chance. The eminent archaeologist Sir John Lubbock spoke for many scholars when he wrote that "The true savage is neither free nor noble; he is slave to his own wants, his own passions...ignorant of agriculture, living by the chase, and improvident in success, hunger always stares him in the face, and often drives him to the dreadful alternative of cannibalism or death" (1865, 87). Lubbock assumed that many non-Western societies, maladapted to a civilized world, would vanish from the face of the earth. Lubbock"s statement derived not only from the conviction of European superiority, but from a much greater awareness of hitherto unknown societies in Africa, Australia, and the Pacific.

The Tasmanians were an obvious example of a society that was still in the Stone Age. Their artifacts served as models for early archaeologists seeking to understand the crude stone axes recently discovered in European river gravels. "The Van Diemener and the South American [Fuegian Indian] are to the antiquary what the opossum and the sloth are to the zoologist," wrote Lubbock (1865, 120). The Tasmanians provided a convenient example of an alien society that lacked the mental capacity and resilience to adapt to European civilization. Given the changing intellectual climate of the early nineteenth century, it was hardly surprising that they were soon referred to as "the connecting link between man and the monkey tribes." It was inevitable, too, that they would perish in the face of European colonization.

Genocide and Colonization

THE ARRIVAL OF THE BAUDIN EXPEDITION at the Sydney convict settlement in 1802 signed the death warrant of the Tasmanians. The governor of New South

9.2 Sullivan's Cove, 1804. The first British settlers landed here, on what is now the site of Hobart. (Courtesy of the Mitchell Library, Sydney, NSW)

Wales welcomed the French, for they had an international safe conduct as a scientific enterprise. But he took immediate steps to garrison Van Diemen's Land lest Napoleon seize it. The first permanent settlers arrived in 1803, a party of twenty-one convicts, three women, and nine soldiers (Figure 9.2). A few aborigines watched them land, then vanished. The officer in charge was glad to see them disappear, for he had more than enough problems with convicts to keep him busy.

Up to this moment, the transitory visits of European ships had had little significant impact on the Tasmanians. But the newcomers were permanent residents, who carved out fields and homesteads on the banks of the River Derwent. One day in May 1804, large numbers of aborigines appeared on the heights above a new settlement at Risdon Cove on the east bank. They advanced out of the woods in a straight line, driving large herds of kangaroo in front of them. Startled by the unfamiliar houses, the Tasmanians brandished their weapons and continued to pursue their quarry into the heart of the village. The Europeans panicked. The soldiers opened fire with two cannons loaded with grapeshot. By the time the altercation ended, more than twenty aborigines were dead. The Tasmanians never approached white people openly again. The Risdon Cove settlement lay right in the path of an annual game drive that had taken place every year for centuries, even millennia. It never occurred to the aborigines that the newcomers would not realize this.

As the colonization of Van Diemen's Land took hold, incidents between aborigines and settlers became more frequent (Figure 9.3). The Tasmanians kept to remoter territory, occasionally ambushing isolated settlers by setting fire to the grass and driving them from cover like kangaroos. Gradually, the tentacles of white settlement spread inland into the heart of aboriginal tribal lands, upsetting their finely tuned adaptation to the environment. When the colony ran short of meat, hundreds of convicts and settlers fanned out into the bush to hunt down kangaroos. These bushrangers shot out the game, then became robbers and highwaymen, preying on settlers and Tasmanians alike. One former ranger boasted that he preferred killing aborigines for sport to smoking his pipe. At the same time sealers were decimating the sea mammals on the rocky coasts. The sealers needed slaves and women, and slaughtered most of the male aborigines they met. The Van Diemen's Land Company bought up huge tracts of land for sheep ranching, ending up with over half a million acres of the aborigines' territory. The Tasmanians were squeezed out into steep, inhospitable terrain and to remote coasts. Even there they were insecure, for the company had managed to gain control of the seashore and mineral rights as well.

The aborigines could only strike back at the colonists. They raided for cattle and sheep, and killed isolated farmers in revenge. So the colonists demanded that the government exterminate the pests. Missionary gentlemen argued that to take up arms against the aborigines in self-defense was entirely justified, for they had earned the awful consequences of the wrath of God. Many acts of violence were covered up under the convenient phrase, "presumed killed by blacks." Weekend hunting parties pursued the Tasmanians for sport. Matters reached a head in 1828, when the governor declared martial law. The notorious Black War culminated in a huge military operation designed to corral the surviving aborigines on offshore islands and in remote enclaves. Three regiments and over two thousand civilians swept 120 miles of rough terrain in search of what everyone thought were bloodthirsty savages. The total bag was two dead aborigines and two captives, one of whom escaped. The soldiers' quarry simply slipped quietly through the tightening cordon.

Branded as murderers and vicious beasts, the 250 or so surviving Tasmanians melted into the bush and lived in hiding. Only a few colonists cared that the aborigines were in danger of extinction. In response to their complaints, the government placed the survivors under the protection of the Crown, but the problem was how to inform the frightened aborigines. The governor had the bright idea of hanging boards bearing picture messages on trees. The paintings depicted scenes of racial harmony and a white man being hanged for murdering a Tasmanian. This was ludicrous, for no settler had ever been put to death for killing a Tasmanian.

About the only person who did anything was an eccentric bricklayer with missionary ambitions named George Augustus Robinson. Appointed as superintendent of an island encampment for captured aborigines, Robinson became a resolute supporter of their cause. He learned the rudiments of

9.3 *Governor George Arthur's proclamation to the aborigines, 1830. This bizarre document, assuring the aborigines that whites would be punished for harming them, was hung on trees in the outback. It was, of course, ineffective. (Courtesy of the Tasmanian Museum and Art Gallery)*

9.4 *Augustus Robinson and a Tasmanian band with their dogs (courtesy of the Tasmanian Museum and Art Gallery)*

aboriginal dialect from twenty-five aborigines who had been transported to his settlement, then spent months trekking through the bush contacting surviving groups (Figure 9.4). At first he was unsuccessful, but later spent weeks living among the people, sharing their nomadic life and their food. The settlers thought he was crazy, but Robinson found the aborigines to be "rational and accountable creatures," friendly and gentle people, and a far cry from the bloody savages depicted in the local newspapers. Robinson's journals are a priceless source of information on Tasmanian life.

Between 1832 and 1842, Robinson brought in the surviving aborigines, all of whom were taken to Flinders Island, forty miles off the northeastern corner of Tasmania. There they lived a tightly regimented life, enduring preaching designed to "civilize" them. Herded into crowded encampments, unable to gather their own food, and stuck on a remote island far from their age-old territories, the aborigines became completely apathetic and lost their will to fend for themselves. The authorities insisted that they wear European garments, whatever the weather. The Tasmanians sat around in wet and unfamiliar clothing and succumbed by the dozen to pneumonia. By 1838, only eighty-two aborigines were still living. Four years later, all the women were past child-bearing age. Flinders Island was closed in 1849, the remaining Tasmanians moved to a squalid encampment south of Hobart, where they died of drink, influenza, or sheer neglect. The last pure blooded Tasmanian,

9.5   *A Tasmanian (artist unknown)*

a woman named Truganini who had worked closely with Robinson, died on 8 May 1876, a scant seventy-three years after the first European colonization of Tasmania, and twelve years before the last aborigines died out on coastal islands.

Even dead, the Tasmanians were exploited and abused. By the 1870s the aborigines were grotesque curiosities (Figure 9.5). Local scientists were anxious to dissect bodies and to obtain bones for their anatomical collections. One corpse was stolen from its grave by night and the skull removed. The government buried Truganini's body in secret, but yielded to scientific pressure some years later and allowed her corpse to be exhumed. Her skeleton was displayed in the Hobart Museum until 1953, when it was removed from exhibit. Public opinion insisted she be given a state funeral on the centenary of her death.

"There is no evidence that the now extinct Tasmanians had the ability to rise," wrote the American sociologist Franklin Giddings in 1896. It was easy for the Victorians to moralize about racial superiority and to dismiss the extinction of hundreds of human societies as inevitable. Racism is now intellectually unacceptable, but this was not the case in the nineteenth century. Given the vast cultural chasm between Western civilization and peoples like the Tasmanians in the early 1800s, it is hardly surprising that many Europeans, however intelligent and disinterested, tended to think of non-Western societies as inferior, expendable beings that stood in the way of civilized progress. Only a vociferous minority believed in all sincerity that it was their divine mission to protect non-Western societies, to civilize them, and, above all, to bring them to God.

The Tasmanians came under inexorable cultural pressure long before powerful evangelical and humanitarian voices in distant Europe could be raised in their defense. Yet even these would have been in vain. Government policies might have sought to protect aborigines or grab their lands, encourage missionary activity or colonization, but in many ways these eventualities were irrelevant. Just the presence of European colonists and farmers on Tasmania, taking up age-old hunting territories and disturbing ancient ecological adaptations, was sufficient to endanger aboriginal society beyond long-term recovery. The long millennia of prehistory show that no maladaptive hunter-gatherer society lasts long. The Tasmanians survived just long enough to become a symbol of Stone Age survival, the tragically misunderstood epitome of everything frightful that primitive savagery was to become in the Victorian mind.

CHAPTER 10

The Word of God

Shall not the isles shake at the sound of thy fall, when the wounded cry, when the slaughter is made in the midst of thee?

Ezekiel 26:15

THE NOBLE SAVAGE ALWAYS RECEIVED mixed reviews, for there were many who suspected that the captivating images of romance and free love under Tahitian palms were sheer nonsense. Europeans might dream nostalgically of paradise on earth, but not even Joseph Banks nor the panegyrics of John Hawkesworth could disguise the reality that Tahitian society was far from a haven of innocence and virtuous conduct. The libidinous dances, priests who engaged in prostitution and infanticide, clear evidence of human sacrifice and vicious tribal wars—these and other obviously pagan customs shocked a large segment of British society. And apart from the ideal of nobility, some people worried about the effects of civilization on the islands.

Cook himself worried with them. During his later visits to the island, he reflected on the consequences of European contact. His sailors had contracted venereal disease from the islanders, who earlier had been infected by the French. He was concerned about the disruptions of island life caused by visiting ships and sometimes wondered whether the South Seas would have been better off unexplored by Europeans. The French intellectual Denis Diderot agreed with him. Diderot was a friend of Rousseau's, with a strong philosophical commitment to the Noble Savage. In his widely read *Supplément au Voyage de Bougainville* (1796), he argued that European civilization "with

171

10.1   *Johann Zoffany's* Death of Cook, *painted between 1789 and 1797. Two noble figures, one Cook, the other an islander, confront one another in a tragically heroic situation. The painting combines neoclassicism and naturalism. (Courtesy of the Trustees of the National Maritime Museum, Greenwich)*

crucifix in one hand and the dagger in the other" would make the Tahitians just as unhappy as Westerners were.

As familiarity succeeded initial impressions, the image of the Noble Savage living in innocence faded fast, especially among those who traveled to the South Seas. The first response to disillusionment was to depict it as classical tragedy. The artist-naturalist Johann Zoffany painted the noble figure of the dying Cook confronting a group of Hawaiian warriors as a moment of magnificent, tragic drama (Figure 10.1). When Rousseau was told of Maori cannibalism, he is said to have been amazed. "Is it possible that the good children of nature can really be so wicked?"

One reason disillusionment was slow in coming was that cultural interaction between Europeans and non-Westerners was slow and relatively superficial until after the Napoleonic wars. Each learned something of the other through trade and from lengthy visits when ships were refitted. At this point, neither Europeans nor their hosts were striving to predict or control the other's behavior. It was during this first stage of contact that many of the most enduring stereotypes of non-Westerners were planted in European minds, those of laziness, cannibalism, and primitiveness, and the most cardinal sin of all—lack of religion. This was also the period when the seeds of racist thinking were sown in Europe, to reach their full fruition during the mid- to late-nineteenth century, just when missionary endeavors also reached their height. The austere Christians who confronted the Noble Savages of Tahiti were quite prepared to concede that there had once been a Golden Age on the island. But they argued that the island was in transition from an Edenic to a darker era, one in which the Tahitians were prostituting their society on the altar of vice. So there was only one solution: convert the islanders. The evangelical missionaries who landed on Tahiti in 1797 believed that the light of religion would lead the Tahitians away from their libidinous ways.

The idea that pagan societies had no religion was, of course, completely erroneous. The Aztecs followed a cosmology and religious beliefs that, if anything, were even more sophisticated than the Catholic doctrines later thrust upon them. Like the Aztecs, the Tahitians interpreted their familiar world in terms of the deeds of non-corporeal beings and spiritual forces. Like most other societies confronted with the reality of European settlement, the islanders reworked their culture to accommodate to new conditions. They would adopt valuable innovations like iron axes or new crops, but their beliefs would remain intact until they became convinced that European expertise was rooted in something more than mere military or technological prowess. Sometimes a military defeat would cause them, like the Aztecs, to challenge the supremacy of their gods. While in an impressionable and apprehensive mood, they would come under the influence of missionaries, who urged them to alter their culture and offered strong spiritual and practical inducements for them to do so. The Tahitians were to experience the full force of evangelical fervor only a generation after contact. Much of the cataclysmic clash of cultures that took place during the nineteenth century occurred on religious grounds and was perceived by many zealous missionaries as a battle for lost souls.

The Evangelicals

SPANISH AND PORTUGUESE PRIESTS HAD borne the banner of missionary activity since the great papal bulls of the late sixteenth century. Dominicans and Franciscans had raised the Cross in the wake of the conquistadors, scourging and cajoling thousands of Mayan and Aztec Indians into the Christian fold. The exploration of the world was perceived by Prince Henry the Navigator and his Spanish neighbors not only as a commercial enterprise, but also as an opportunity to perform great deeds for the glory of God. The lengthy, agonizing debates about the morality of converting the American Indian pitted many missionaries against the pragmatic, often exploitative ambitions of conquistador and colonist in the New World. Many of the early friars, like the notorious Bishop Diego de Landa of the Yucatán, were driven zealots, who would use any measure, however draconian, to convert the heathen. The excesses of such missionaries as the Jesuits of the St. Lawrence River valley did little to improve the reputation of Catholic activities overseas in Protestant countries. Everywhere Catholic missionaries went, the universal creed of Christianity came as a challenge to the often easier-going, more flexible beliefs of non-Christian societies. Missionary activity was nothing new in the seventeenth and eighteenth centuries, but the massive explosion of Christian activity overseas coincided with the rise of Britain as a maritime power, and with the surge in evangelical piety at home.

The Noble Savage had arrived in London drawing rooms at a time of evangelical revival in Britain's middle classes. The eighteenth century was the century of inspired preachers, men like John Wesley, George Whitefield, and Henry Venn, who preached of morality and sin, of clemency and humanitarian values. Their influence was enormous, leading to reforms in popular education and the penal system, and ultimately to the abolition of the slave trade. They were men who believed that God was active in history, that Divine Providence influenced not only the rise and fall of civilizations, but even the most trivial events of daily life. They believed fervently in the power of prayer and personal intercession with the Lord. The results of this prayer were not necessarily immediate or even beneficial, for everything ran according to God's own loving judgments. This was the Lord who had created the universe and caused it to run along predictable lines.

The Evangelicals believed that God had created nature for humans to master and dominate, so that they could acquire dominion over the earth. God, they preached, was active in history. The Scriptures revealed the great narrative of his doings, from the Creation to the coming of Christ, to the triumph and spread of Christianity. Ultimately, this would lead to the Second Coming of Christ. The early Evangelicals believed that humanity's duty to God was in its overriding loyalty, a loyalty that transcended all commitments to any culture, society, or tribe. All this was alien to the societies they sought to bring into the fold of Christianity. The missionaries broke the tight bonds of the past and tried to push the societies they worked with into new and unimagined worlds. In doing this, they unleashed new and potent forces in the world. They eliminated the intensely personal and symbolic relationships between people and their environment and the forces that controlled it. Instead, they offered a simpler vision of a global brotherhood of humankind and opened up a vista of endless improvement, a world where people worked together, free, to implement the Divine Will of the Lord. Science and revolutionary change replaced the centuries-old forces of nature and historical precedent.

The sober, sin-obsessed followers of Wesley and others were concerned not only with the evils of their own society, but became increasingly preoccupied with the saving of the heathen. These unfortunate souls, cried one preacher, deserved the "emancipation from their chains of darkness and an admission into the glorious liberty of the children of God" (Stock 1898, 14). Not that the advocates of foreign missions had an easy time. A humble cobbler named William Carey rose at a Baptist meeting in 1785 to advocate preaching to the heathen. "Sit down, young man," said the chairman, "when it pleases God to convert the Heathen, he'll do it without your help, or mine" (Stock 1898, 28). Carey persisted. Six years later he published his famous *Enquiry into the Obligations of Christians to Use Means for the Conversion of the Heathen* (1792) and preached a memorable sermon at Nottingham in front of his fellow ministers that caused a sensation. Taking as his text Isaiah 54:2, "Enlarge the place of thy tent," he argued that the ministry should not only expect great things of the Lord, but should "attempt great things for God." Carey's labors bore fruit in the formation of the Baptist Missionary Society, and, three years later, in 1795, the London Missionary Society, a nonsectarian institution that was to have a profound impact on the fate of non-Western societies around the globe in the coming century. Its rolls were to include such luminaries as Samuel Marsden, who worked among the Maori, and the immortal David Livingstone, who walked across Africa. During the early nineteenth century, they made the Caribbean, Southern Africa, and the Pacific islands among the most intensively missionized parts of the world.

Two missionary organizations had been active since the early eighteenth century, the Society for Promoting Christian Knowledge and the Society for the Propagation of the Gospel in Foreign Parts. Both were in a sorry decline. Their small-scale efforts hardly satisfied the lofty ambitions of the new generation of missionaries. Obsessed with sin and the immorality of the world around them, they turned their eyes on the one island that was on everyone's lips—Tahiti. They resolved to save the Tahitians from further debauchery and error. "Amidst these enchanting scenes, savage nature still feasts on the flesh of its prisoners, appeases its gods with human sacrifices," thundered Thomas Hawkes, a founder of the London Missionary Society in a memorable sermon of 1795. "Whole societies of men and women live promiscuously, and murder every infant born amongst them" (Stock 1898, 18). Why had Omai been permitted to return to Tahiti without any religious instruction? he asked. The sermons and exhortations bore fruit and £4,000 were raised to equip a mission to Polynesia. On 10 August 1796, a large group of the devout gathered to bid farewell to thirty missionaries on the *Duff*, bound for remote Tahiti. "Jesus, at they command we launch into the deep," sang the departing preachers. They sailed for a virtually unknown world, their only sources of information the romantic writings of Hawkesworth and a few other authors.

By this time, Cook's fears had been realized. The major reef passages had been charted at least approximately and a series of anchorages on Tahiti and nearby Moorea were used by more than twenty ships between 1788 and 1808. Some were engaged in exploration, others were merchant vessels. Six of them were whaling ships, the forerunners of many more who visited Tahiti in the 1820s to refresh their crews with tropical fruit and cheap sex. Trade picked up slowly, but between 1801 and 1826, the Tahitians were the major suppliers of pork to the convict settlements in New South Wales. In return, the island-ers received hardware, tools, clothing, arms, and ammunition. Visitors to Matavi Bay were valued not for their ideas, but for the trade goods they brought—like nails and firearms—that could be assimilated into local cul-ture. A brief fashion for European clothing swept Tahiti for a few years. Then the people returned to their own cool and practical garments. Only the de-mand for metal objects remained insatiable in a culture that still lived in a technological Stone Age. The Tahitians were relatively incurious about the world outside the confines of the islands, despite the tales of returning islanders who had been as far afield as Europe, Antarctica, and Peru. Most accounts of foreign lands were received with amazement or disbelief. Sometimes return-ing travelers as well as visiting ships brought alien diseases that ran wild among the islanders. The population of Tahiti and Moorea declined from about 35,000 to around 8,000 between 1769 and 1800. Venereal disease was endemic near the favored anchorages. Many Tahitians were now addicted to strong drink. The easygoing Polynesians were only too vulnerable to Western vices.

The missionaries arrived when the Pomare lineage was the dominant po-litical force at Matavi Bay. The decades since first European contact had seen religious and political wars between various hereditary chiefs. The Pomares held their alliances together with tribute claims, threats of human sacrifice, well-timed punitive raids, and careful fostering of the cults of the war god 'Oro. The missionaries found Pomare I in firm control of Matavi Bay, and preached the gospel before him on 12 March 1797. Then they opened nego-tiations for a site for a mission station (Figure 10.2). Directors of the Society had given the missionaries strict instructions as to their conduct. They were to establish missionary communities that were "model civilized societies," on land given to them by the local people. The pioneers were to obtain full title to the mission land, guarantees of protection and undisturbed enjoyment of their religion. "The land should not be purchased but required, as a condi-tion of our remaining with them," enjoined the directors. "In negotiating with the chiefs, you will explain to them the advantages which will arise to them from our residence among them" (Typett 1971, 10). The directors assumed they were according the Tahitians a tremendous favor.

The ministers and artisans who landed from the Duff were thoroughly practical people who abhorred anything pagan and anything that even vaguely smelled of dissolution or immorality. They were mainly people from the lower strata of European society, artisans and skilled workers, often affectionately

10.2   *"Shall not the isles shake at the sound of the Fall?"* The Victorian missionary's image of Pacific island life before and after Christianity, from William Wyatt Gill's Life in the Southern Isles *(London: Religious Tract Society, 1877).*

called "godly mechanics" by their contemporaries. Most had little formal education, but were studious, driven people with a completely hands-on frame of mind. While some of them were powerful thinkers, most ran in fixed, well-oiled grooves. They were hard workers, deeply inner-directed folk with little imagination or flexibility. Above all, they believed that the virtues that served them well in British cities would help them in remote lands. The severe missionaries were the heirs of English Puritanism or Calvinism, who believed the Bible was their sole authority. Humankind had fallen from grace, and salvation could only be obtained through grace by faith, through practicing iron self-discipline and the most austere of religious rites. While their spiritual legacy was primarily Puritan, they considered themselves Evangelicals, believing that highly emotional, personal conversions were the route to grace. They did not wait for people to come to their churches. Rather, they pursued them in the fields and in villages, stressing emotional experience rather than doctrinal knowledge as the means to the Church and the Lord. The Evangelicals believed that everyone, whether white or black, European, African, or Tahitian, must be brought to the Lord. The reorientation of thought and behavior that Evangelical preachers demanded of people both at home and abroad was nothing short of revolutionary. The Methodists at home tried nothing less than to "uproot preindustrial traditions from the manufacturing districts" of England (Thompson 1966, 408). They applied the same doctrine in Polynesia.

The *Duff* missionaries arrived with the objective of redirecting Tahitian society completely. They expected the Tahitians to abandon their belief in their traditional gods, to relinquish most of their cosmology, and to survive without the various rites of passage, marriage institutions, and other customs that had bonded their communities together. They also wanted the people to cultivate European crops, to become artisans and traders, make use of Western medicines and treatments. Kinship ties were no longer important. Everyone was expected to offer total allegiance to the Church. Art, music, dress, architecture, village layout, even food, clothing, and drink were to be "redeemed" and changed to conform with established Christian norms.

From the beginning, the missionaries assumed that the Tahitians could be turned aside from their "treacherous and degenerate" way of life by sheer persistence and moral authority. The way to do this, they believed, was by civilizing the people, then converting them. Since they had to grow their own food and learn the language, this seemed a logical way to work. Mission work requires a peaceful environment to succeed, something that the Pomares' domains rarely offered. The missionaries maintained their prestige by teaching Pomare I, and his son Pomare II, to read and write and by working closely with visiting British vessels. But the Tahitians refused to listen to their preaching. In 1808–9, the domains of Pomare II were overrun by his rivals

10.3   The Cessation of Matavi, *by Robert Smirke, a painting commissioned by the London Missionary Society in 1799. The Tahitians are depicted as docile children awaiting the blessings of the Lord. Smirke made every effort to make his painting accurate. For example, Pomare and his wife are shown seated on the backs of their attendants. Had their feet touched the ground, they would have immediately owned it. (Courtesy of the Council for World Mission, London)*

(Figure 10.3). The missionaries were forced to withdraw to New South Wales in distant Australia and to abandon their work without a single convert. They departed, telling Pomare that "had Tahiti obeyed the word of the true God, Tahiti would not have rebelled, it would not have done evil to you its king" (Newberry 1980, 35).

It is doubtful these strictures had any effect on Pomare, but even then he may have recognized the political advantages of working with the missionaries, an apparently stable element in the shifting sands of Tahitian politics. Between 1811 and 1813, some eight missionary families returned, this time to the nearby island of Moorea. Fifteen missionaries were living there by 1815, an astounding density of preachers per capita far higher than in many poorer areas of London. They found themselves teaching an increasing number of people, many of them individuals of consequence in the islands. But there were no baptisms, although Pomare and others began to ask the missionaries for acceptance into the Church. The brethren were now in a much stronger position. At first they had to rely on the reluctant protection of Pomare. But he came to realize that the missionaries were a possibly valuable asset, potential providers of firearms, new technologies, and medical care. Pomare was grappling with the problems of governing a war-weary, hierarchical society where status rivalry and control of tribute and manpower were constant problems. The scourges of European diseases had decimated the people, who had turned to 'Oro and other Tahitian deities in vain. Many *marae* were falling into disrepair as the worshippers abandoned traditional rites and ceremonies. Soon there was widespread skepticism about 'Oro through the islands. Conceivably, thought Pomare, the new gods might represent a viable political solution to his woes, the missionaries being people with privileged access to the forces of heaven. Matters came to a head in November, 1815 when Pomare had returned to Matavi from exile in Moorea to mediate a series of land disputes. He took some missionaries with him. The king and his warriors were at Sunday morning worship when his enemies attacked. They grabbed their weapons and routed their attackers. Pomare regained control of his former domains, ordered the obliteration of 'Oro and his consorts, and embraced Christianity as the new religious order. Beyond question, this was partly a pragmatic political decision.

The missionaries were elated by this sudden turn of events, and claimed that Pomare's restoration to power ushered in a "Christian Era." In fact the era had begun several years before on Moorea, among people who perceived that the "God of Britain" offered long-term practical advantages in a changing political order. Pomare's restoration was probably the result of political compromise. Travelers through his domains found many of the ruler's formerly despotic powers curtailed. No longer could he give away land or demand tribute without question. The seat of political power, especially control of the land, had passed into the hands of local chiefs. Pomare's conversion filled a need within Tahitian society for a new source of leadership, and for a political and religious broker between Europeans and Tahitians. Pomare himself was baptized in 1816 and celebrated the event by building a chapel that was the largest structure in the islands, constructed, we are told, in less than three weeks. Every laborer brought a post, a pole, a rafter, or a bundle of thatching material. The church was built over a mountain stream that flowed through the congregation. Three separate sermons were preached simultaneously from three different pulpits during the consecration ceremonies. Pomare embraced his new religion with such enthusiasm that laggards were driven to church with sticks (Figure 10.4).

The last six years of Pomare's reign saw the missionaries in a unique position to alter the face of Tahitian society beyond their wildest hopes For a while they became the arbiters of correct behavior and ranked high in local society both as spiritual leaders and as providers of goods and services. They controlled the only printing press and framed the rules, setting the composition of church congregations by testing new members. When Pomare decided to

10.4   Tu-Nui-e-A'a-I-Te-Atua, Pomare II, drawn by William Ellis, c. 1819

impose a new code of law on his domains in 1819, the missionaries drafted a nineteen-section document that regulated everything from "trouble-making" to adultery and theft, prescribed penalties, and set up a justice system. Much was made of this code by the Society's backers in London, for they claimed it turned Tahiti towards the Lord. The missionaries were indeed close to the chiefs and deeply engaged in trade and economic life. Superficially, life on the island had changed dramatically. Many local people wore European clothes and no longer danced the traditional dances. Some women even cut their long hair, and on the Sabbath all work ceased. "Not a fire is lighted, neither flesh nor fruit is baked, not a tree is climbed...Religion—religion alone—is the business of these simpleminded people on the Sabbath," reported two Society emissaries in delight (Stock 1898, 144).

In reality, the missionary hold on Tahiti was a fragile one, mainly because the preachers had neglected to train local people for the ministry. The brethren firmly believed that the Tahitians had to be "civilized" before they were accepted into the Church. All too often, they gave the impression that their highest priority was the cultivation of the land, establishment of markets, and the civilizing of the island. They believed that a personal example of hard work and profit making, reinforced by a Puritan law code and perfectionist standards, would lead the people to Christ. In practice they had become the priests in local society, but they were such restrictive clerics that they left much of the indigenous priesthood on the side without a role as communicating Christians in the new order. Inevitably, the neglected Tahitian priests made trouble. The missionaries were troubled by constant backsliding and by local prophetic movements that reacted against Puritan legalisms by adopting some Christian rites and incorporating them with "dangerous "and visionary heresies."

At best the initial missionary effort was superficial. After a quarter century of mission activity, only some 2,100 of the 15,000 churchgoers on Tahiti were full communicants. The missionaries had hedged the approach to the communion table with far too many tests and probationary periods to make conversion easy. The mission stations remained separate from the mainstream of Tahitian life, places where one could learn to read and write, but bastions of Puritanism and hard work in an easy-going world. The people who stayed at the missions were often those with no secure position in Tahitian society, people cast loose by the disintegration of traditional life. To these individuals the missionaries offered land and a new social order. It was as if they were local chiefs, whose rites of baptism were a mark of social status in an unfamiliar world. In later generations, it was to be indigenous preachers who were best able to explain the new message, the notion of "fleeing to Jesus," adopting him as a patron at a time when the Tahitians were sinking towards a position of social inferiority in the new order.

The missionaries' difficulties were compounded by developments beyond their control. They would have preferred to keep the island isolated from all visitors, but could do nothing to prevent merchant vessels, especially whaling ships, from anchoring there. As many as 150 whalers a year rested up in the islands during the 1830s. Tahiti was no longer an isolated place, and by now the missionaries were not the only European residents. A floating population of escaped convicts, beachcombers, and derelicts hung around the major villages. Some became small-time traders, but most lived off the Tahitians until their limited funds gave out. Some of the escaped convicts hired themselves out as mercenaries to the local chiefs. They were paid in food and women. A decade later, the port of Papeete, nine miles west of Matavi Bay, housed American, British, and French consulates. In 1842, Herman Melville wrote, "Lying in a semicircle around the bay, the tasteful mansions of the chiefs and foreign residents impart an air of tropical elegance, heightened by the palmtrees waving here and there, and the deep-green groves of the Bread-Fruit in the background. The squalid huts of the common people are out of sight, and there is nothing to mar the prospect" (1847, 101). Fresh fruit was abundant and life away from the sleazy waterfront went on quietly enough. But there was an undercurrent of violence and drunkenness and a constant turnover of penniless flotsam from the ships that called at the port. Venereal disease was "so general as not to be deemed disreputable." By the 1840s the missionary hold on Tahiti was fragile indeed, threatened not only by overseas traders, but by the colonial ambitions of the great powers. In the end it was the French who took Tahiti under their protection in 1843, using an alleged insult to some Catholic missionaries as their excuse.

Pulled in different directions by missionaries, traders, whalers, and now the French, the Tahitians subsided into gentle apathy. Herman Melville was bitterly critical of European behavior, which is hardly surprising, since he spent some time in jail in Papeete after a shipboard dispute. He found that the inhabitants had lapsed into listlessness; even entertaining themselves was a burden. The trouble was that the missionaries had caused a cultural vacuum. There was nothing to fill the Tahitians' abundant leisure time; they were forbidden to dance, to sing their traditional songs. As a result, centuries-old crafts were forgotten, as well as ways of building large canoes. Decimated by tuberculosis, smallpox, dysentery, and venereal disease, Tahitian society was breaking down fast, the people under intense stress. When smallpox struck, the Tahitians accused the missionaries of promising them salvation and not delivering. The only salvation the Tahitians wanted was to live in peace.

For all the missionaries' preaching, the old customs were not forgotten. Melville spent some time in outlying villages on Moorea, where he found a chief willing to stage one of the "wanton" dances described by James Cook three-quarters of a century before. The young girls danced in a circle with two leaders. "Presently, raising a strange chant, they softly sway themselves, gradually quickening the movement, until at length, for a few passionate moments, with throbbing bosom, and glowing cheeks, they abandon themselves to all the spirit of the dance, apparently lost to everything around. But soon subsiding again into the same languid measure as before, the eyes swimming in their heads, they join in one wild chorus, and sink into each other's arms," wrote Melville rapturously in *Omoo* (1847, 241–2).

Another vignette of nineteenth-century Tahiti comes from the journals of the French artist Paul Gauguin. Obsessed with the dream of a tropical paradise, he arrived in Tahiti half a century after Melville, anxious to immerse himself in local life. By now the French had subdued and colonized the island. Gauguin was appalled: "The natives, having nothing, nothing at all to do, think of one thing only, drinking...Many things that are strange and picturesque existed here once, but there are no traces of them left today; everything has vanished" (Moorehead 1966, 95). His paintings depict the Tahitians as an inert, bored, and listless people. Gauguin's deep feelings about the state of the islanders can be discerned in his most famous Tahitian painting. A beautiful young girl lies naked on a bed surrounded by petals of the *tiare tahiti*. She gazes listlessly into space. Gauguin wrote one word in English on the canvas: "Nevermore" (Figure 10.5).

In 1881, the French government formally annexed Tahiti and the islands became part of France. The king of the time was pensioned off with 60,000 francs a year. In return he ceded Tahiti and other territories to France, on the condition that he retain jurisdiction over "all little matters" of justice and "all matters relative to lands." These conditions did not appear in the version of the agreement passed by the French parliament. Tahiti and Moorea bore the brunt of experiments in assimilation and land registration that gradually replaced the old nobility with white officials and policemen. The result was a torrent of litigation that engulfed the local courts, most of it concerned with land titles. Only a handful of old established noble families made the law and the courts work for them, so relatively little land was alienated in the first decades of colonial occupation. The key to social mobility for Tahitians among the two-thousand-odd European settlers was a trade or a profession and some education in English or French. Few Tahitians joined the colonial administration and all resisted total assimilation into European culture. Most accepted an overlay of Christian belief, but this was often a facade for older beliefs and superstitions.

Some intellectually inclined Tahitians dwelt on the vanished past as a way of escaping from an uncertain present. They collected oral traditions and genealogies in the face of indifference from local officials and missionaries; today, these traditions are priceless repositories of early Tahitian history. Most Europeans were under the delusion that Tahiti was now a French island, safely assimilated into the Western world. But a few perceptive visitors realized that the stamp of French culture and government was but superficial and French only in name. Some of them visited Polynesia in search of the primitive, others sought nostalgically the legendary South Seas Eden of the early explorers, but they were disappointed. As Gauguin wrote: "Nevermore."

10.5   Paul Gauguin's Nevermore *(courtesy of the Courtauld Art Institute, London)*

"A Continuous Wearing Away"

A CENTURY OF COLONIAL GOVERNANCE wrought profound changes in Tahitian society. To many people, Tahiti became a symbol for escapism from the stresses of European civilization. The island became a backdrop for the writings of imaginative novelists and travel journalists. The government became increasingly strict about admitting casual settlers. The days of the beachcomber were over. Instead the European and Asian settlers who came were soon entrenched in the islands' economic system, which depended increasingly on foreign markets. The immigrants intermarried with the Tahitians, perpetuating a tradition of interbreeding that went back to the early days of Western contact. Meantime, the indigenous Tahitian population stabilized and began to grow dramatically after a catastrophic bout with the 1918 worldwide influenza epidemic. The effects of sporadic elementary education, increasing pressures on island land, and the cash economy was altering Tahitian society slowly but profoundly.

A missionary who traveled through Tahiti's rural districts in 1926 found that the Tahitians, once landowners, had gradually allowed themselves to be relegated to a subservient place in island society, to become no more than hired labor. He blamed generations of interbreeding with Europeans and, latterly, Chinese immigrants. The half-Tahitians had retained their rights to land, yet worked closely with whites who held positions of economic power. By clever manipulation of land deals over a period of years, they could acquire considerable wealth. The native Tahitians tended to remain at the lowest levels of society.

At intervals between 1961 and 1964, psychologist Robert Levy spent many months living in two Tahitian communities, the one a rural village, the other an urban enclave of Papeete. He found that throughout the lifetime of the older members of the rural community there had been a progressive replacement of locally made products with mass-produced, imported goods purchased in local Chinese stores and in Papeete. Levy records how the older people remembered living in houses made from local materials and sitting on the floor to eat from plates made of leaves and drink from coconut shells. Some even remembered how to make fire by using the age-old fire plow or a flint.

Levy observed that Christianity was of central importance in the life of the village. The Protestant Church was the focus of much community life, for church-going and related activities structured much of the leisure time of the villagers. Church affairs were second in importance only to making a living. The pastor was an influential figure in the community, deeply involved in local political decision-making and the arbiter of family morality. He preached against drunkenness, adultery, gambling, and any form of anti-family behavior. On the surface, the stern Puritan ethic of the early missionaries, with its implicit threats of hellfire and damnation for sinners, had profoundly affected village life. This ethic had struck hard from the beginning. As early as the 1820s, missionary William Ellis reported the people were giving up such favorite entertainments as "war, pagan worship, and frivolous amusements." In the 1890s, another visitor wrote that the atmosphere was tinged by melancholy. The Tahitians were forbidden to dance, and seemed bored and listless. They were no longer happy and carefree. It was as if life had no meaning for them.

The conversion of the islanders led to a general breakdown of meaning and purpose, and then to demoralization. As time went on, meaningful new ways of life evolved that were adaptations to the new religion and accepted modes of behavior. But the shadow of Puritanism still hung over Levy's community in the 1960s; adults had few amusements except church-going, occasional movies, and drinking. These, and the usual gossip and village round, provided breaks in the quiet routine. Most adults seemed to have accepted the missionary doctrine that fun, games, and amusements were for children, not mature members of the community.

Levy returned to the community in 1970 to find even more profound changes. The last few Tahitian houses were giving way to concrete and iron-roofed dwellings; there were trucks and electrical generators in the village. Many people without land or special positions in the community had left to work in the booming economy in the city, a boom sparked by nuclear-testing programs and a flood of tourists arriving in jetliners. The village was full of children, but many spoke French rather than Tahitian. They often laughed at the old customs. They seemed to be waiting to leave as well, to acquire clothes, money, and motorcycles. Even their education was largely alien to Tahitian minds. Levy quotes one urbanized, French-speaking couple: "The children can always learn Tahitian from their friends." In fact, their friends spoke French as well. The blandishments of Western technology and a cash economy have finally undermined what a century and a half of Puritan preaching failed to—the basic values of the society, and the close-knit village households in which they flourished.

CHAPTER 11

The Fuegians

Viewing such men, one can hardly make oneself believe they are
fellow-creatures, and inhabitants of the same world. It is a common
subject of conjecture what pleasure in life some of the less gifted
animals can enjoy: how much more reasonably the same question
may be asked with respect to these barbarians.

Charles Darwin, *The Voyage of the Beagle* (1839)

THE TAHITIAN MISSION SET OUT for the South Seas at a time when powerful new political and social forces were coming into play in Western life. These were to have a major impact on Europeans' perceptions of and attitudes towards the non-Western world.

The American Declaration of Independence in 1776 focused the attention of the Western world on fundamental issues of freedom and social rights. The "self-evident" truths that all people are created equal and enjoy "certain unalienable Rights," notably "Life, Liberty and the Pursuit of Happiness," served, among other things, to highlight the terrible paradox of slavery thriving within a society dedicated to the ideals of liberty. The debate about political and social rights engulfed the Thirteen Colonies and Europe as well. Slavery and the struggle to abolish it were important components in the decades of democratic revolution that were to change the political shape of the Western world beyond recognition. Europe's ever-changing relationships with, and perceptions of, the non-Western world were inextricably bound up in the lengthy debates and controversies about the slave trade.

As early as the sixteenth century, British adventurers had been slave trading in Africa, transporting slaves to Spanish settlements in the Caribbean, and then to their own country's colonies in North America and the new sugar plantations of the West Indies. During the seventeenth and eighteenth centuries, the British elevated both the slave trade and slavery to new levels of economic and social importance. The Caribbean slave plantations produced tropical staples for European markets and are best described as proto-industrial organizations in rural settings. They consumed cheap and easily recruited labor in a fashion that was to become commonplace in nineteenth-century Europe and North America. The European nations were exporting at least 75,000 slaves from West Africa annually in the late 1780s. The profits were in the millions of dollars. Until the eighteenth century, slavery was accepted as a social way of life and few people challenged the institution.

By 1776, the whole issue of slavery came under increasing public scrutiny, partly because of growing abolitionist pressures in Britain and North America, pressures that stemmed in part from the well-known Quaker antipathy to black slavery. The Abolition Society was founded in 1787 and soon spearheaded the international drive against slavery and the slave trade. The abolitionists were determined to make slavery a major political issue. Many of them were Evangelicals and Nonconformists, people deeply committed to principles of human dignity and the word of God. The new radical ideologies of the late eighteenth century and the heady events of the American and French Revolutions added fuel to antislavery sentiments. The American radical Thomas Paine was the prophet of the new political ideology that demanded rights for all people regardless of color or rank. A lengthy parliamentary and public struggle in Britain culminated in the abolition of slavery in 1807 and in the emancipation of slaves between 1833 and 1838. These developments came about from legislative acts of Parliament, but were functions of complex social and political processes. Antislavery propaganda made the public at large far more aware of the non-Western world and stimulated the first humanitarian attempts to improve the plight of aboriginal societies in remote corners of the world.

The loss of the thirteen American colonies and the rising debate over slavery coincided with a population explosion in Britain, just as the first burst of industrial growth was beginning in Europe. The time was ripe for expanded activity overseas. The secession of the American colonies had marked the close of an epoch of trade and expansion. The decline in British fortunes was only temporary, and was followed by rapid recovery, political reform, and a renewed determination to recoup losses elsewhere in the world. Successive British governments started to look for colonies elsewhere. This contradicted an earlier theory of empire that held it desirable to own a balanced set of possessions, so that slaves, provisions, and shipping could function as an integrated commercial system to benefit the home country. Once the Napoleonic wars gave the Royal Navy mastery of the oceans, the impetus for continued exploration and colonial settlement quickened.

"The Fruitful Soil Lies Waste"

THE WORLD WAS A MUCH MORE familiar place in 1815 than it had been in Captain Cook's time. The armchair traveler and the government bureaucrat could draw on a vast store of travelers' tales to learn about remote peoples and places. Thomas Astley's *New General Collection of Voyages and Travels* appeared between 1745 and 1747, four massive volumes of carefully edited extracts from explorers' accounts that served as a vital compendium. The great sixty-five-volume *Universal History* published between 1736 and 1746 devoted nearly a third of its pages to the history of the non-Western world. The descriptions of the indigenous inhabitants of such areas as West Africa covered manners and customs, and were often far from accurate, usually burdened with ethnocentric judgments. But these and other such compendia were serious and ambitious attempts to understand other peoples with a tolerance and interest that was slowly eroded during the early nineteenth century.

These syntheses were often amplified by questionnaires sent out from the home country to people living in such regions as West Africa. The Spanish Council of the Indies had used this technique as early as 1517, when developing Indian policies for the new colonies. Questionnaires were only part of the story. A constant stream of officials, curious travelers, and scholars returned to Europe with new field information. The scientific expedition became fashionable in the late eighteenth century, promoted by such intellectual luminaries as Sir Joseph Banks of Tahiti fame. Banks, Carl Linnaeus the taxonomist, and other scientists encouraged young naturalists to travel to tropical Africa, Australia, and other distant lands. Their researches covered far more than animals and plants. Some of them studied the "natural history of man," or contemplated "human nature in simpler states." Banks and his contemporaries did far more than merely encourage individuals to study overseas. They were active in such organizations as the Association for Promoting the Discovery of the Interior Parts of Africa, founded in 1788, and the African Institution. The latter was an evangelical-humanitarian society that was one of many such pressure groups formed in the early decades of the nineteenth century as concern over slavery and the treatment of aboriginal societies intensified.

The reports of non-Western societies from European travelers and scientists were of uneven quality. Travel books always sold well, since their authors wrote to please as well as to inform. Spectacular festivals, human sacrifice, exotic marriage customs, warfare, and "piggish" eating habits were all grist for the authors' mills. The reporting often stressed those aspects of non-Western life that were most repellent to Europeans and tended to encourage notions of racial separation. The faintly libidinous was always accepted avidly, non-Western religions usually dismissed as idolatrous and pagan beyond redemption. Some of these accounts were commonly used to justify slave trade in people described as savages and little more than animals.

Despite generations of dealings with American Indians and the diverse peoples of India, Europeans as a whole were still deeply ignorant of non-Western societies, for many contacts with them had occurred on the frontiers of the known world. It was not until 1783, after the loss of the American colonies and in a spirit of general reform and rising humanitarian concern, that successive British governments found themselves forced to consider the problem of their relations with non-Western societies as an urgent priority.

This concern focused initially on West Africans because humanitarians were forced to deal with the problem of race in their efforts to reform government policy. An enormous scientific and pseudoscientific literature was used to dissect the Africans. On one side of the academic fence were writers like physician Edward Lang, who described Africans in 1774 as a "brutish, ignorant, idle, crafty, treacherous…and superstitious people." They were inferior in "faculties of mind," and had a "bestial and fetid smell." He claimed they were of a different species than Europeans, two species that had been created by God. He associated blacks with animals and went as far as to place various tribes of Africans in scale, with the Khoikhoi at the base, and the West Africans and Ethiopians nearer the top of the ladder. Much of what Lang had to say was typical planter-settler rhetoric, commonplace in colonial territories until well into this century. But Lang was regarded as a scientist, so his racist views held wide currency. His writings, and those of other polygenists, fitted well into emerging feelings of racial and cultural pride among Europeans. They were aided by widespread myths about the sexual prowess of blacks, who were claimed to have insatiable sexual appetites and excessively large penises. Only a few scientists argued that black Africans were part of a single, unified humankind.

The Africans may have suffered at the hands of the biologists, who were, after all, foundering in a sea of scientific ignorance, but they fared much better in popular literature. The Noble Savage was a notable literary fad in England during the 1760s, with pride of place going to the Tahitians and American Indians. The Africans qualified for nobility almost by default, being thought of as simple, pastoral people living close to nature. They achieved far greater nobility as the antislavery movement enlisted the sympathy and talents of literary personalities. There was, of course, no thought that Africans were equal to Europeans. After all, Christians could not depict pagans ignorant of God's word as equals unto themselves. The Africans' nobility was a literary artifice, designed to stress the artificiality of European civilization as compared to the life of a bucolic people. The antislavery movement used the device to promote the idea of "good Africans."

The humanitarians who used the convention of the Noble Savage were not so much concerned with the Africans themselves as with the lofty goal of stamping out evil in the world. The Evangelicals and Wesleyans of late-eighteenth-century Britain believed not only in the burden of personal sin, but in the responsibility of all Christians to give of their talents to relieve the suffering of their fellow humans. And they were responsible to God for the correct use of their talents. For many years, the *Church Missionary Atlas* began its African entry by describing the continent as "one universal den of desolation, misery, and crime."

The African slave trade had attracted the attention of the humanitarians since the seventeenth century. They and the abolitionists held that a lack of "commerce" had held Africa back. Its people had reached the stage of agriculture. Now they needed legitimate trade to help them advance further. European traders would come to Africa with their manufactures and export the raw materials that were there in abundance. This trade would not only reduce suffering, it would profit all concerned, and, above all, through increased prosperity, confirm the belief of both Calvinists and Evangelicals that virtue would be rewarded in this world and in the next.

A few advocates of the new trade went even further than those who merely wished to substitute one form of commerce for another. Mercantilist Malachy Postethwayt had argued in 1757 that Europeans should relocate and cultivate the land. "The fruitful soil lies waste, a very extended country, pleasant vallies, banks of the fine rivers, spacious plains, capable to cultivation to unspeakable benefit, in all probability remain, fallow and unnoticed: Why do not the *Europeans* enclose such lands for cultivation, as by their nature and situation appear proper for beneficial production?" (Curtin 1964, 70). His words foreshadowed the great expansion of Europeans into distant lands, migrations that began with the first stirrings of the Industrial Revolution and still continue to this day.

The Yahgan Indians of Tierra del Fuego

THE END OF THE NAPOLEONIC wars saw Britain ruler of the world's oceans, at the center of vast trade networks that connected Europe with every corner of the globe. This was a new, industrial world, about to be revolutionized by staggering advances in science, technology, and European knowledge and experience of human diversity. New peacetime responsibilities took Royal Navy ships to the remotest archipelagos and islands on detailed survey expeditions that lasted for years on end. Many navigational charts of the late twentieth century bear the names of obscure naval lieutenants and surveyors who

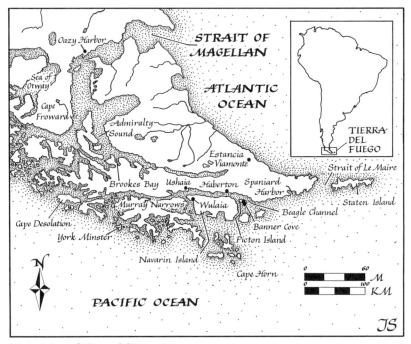

11.1   *Map of Tierra del Fuego*

braved all kinds of weather in small boats to prepare charts for the merchant vessels that followed in their wake. Armed with the sketchiest of information about the peoples they encountered, the survey captains were a pragmatic breed—hard, practical seamen with little romance in them, but often with strong religious convictions that were to lead them to extraordinary deeds. It was one of these men, Captain Robert FitzRoy of H.M.S. *Beagle,* who was to confront the Evangelicals and humanitarians with a complex spiritual and intellectual dilemma: should one try to civilize and convert people apparently so "primitive" that their existence is little better than that of animals?

Robert FitzRoy was only twenty-three years old when he was appointed commander of the *Beagle,* ordered to survey the Strait of Magellan at the southern tip of South America. But he was already an experienced seaman with a reputation for intense concentration and a talent for scientific investigation. He was also a devout Christian and an ardent Fundamentalist who believed in the absolute historical truth of Scripture.

FitzRoy reached the Strait of Magellan in April, 1829 (Figure 11.1). He immediately set out on a series of lengthy boat journeys, exploring the maze of channels that led off this little-known, hazardous waterway between the

Atlantic and Pacific. He soon came into contact with Indian tribes who appeared to live the most primitive and miserable of lives. These were "the first savages I had ever met," he wrote. FitzRoy was unimpressed and compared them to pictures of Eskimos he had seen. "Their features were bad, but peculiar, and if physiognomy can be trusted, indicated cunning, indolence, passive fortitude, deficient intellect, and want of energy," he remarked (FitzRoy 1839, pp. 23–24). He also commented on the Indians' small heads. "There were," he observed, "very few bumps for a craniologist." Soon the *Beagle* was ordered to survey the Pacific coasts of Tierra del Fuego, a mission that brought FitzRoy in touch with the Yahgan (Yamana) Indians who lived on the shores of the great strait that today bears his ship's name.

At the time of FitzRoy's visit, the Yahgan may have numbered as many as 8,000. They were short, chunky people, with slender legs and an average stature of five feet. They were among the shortest of all American Indians, the trunks of their bodies being large in proportion to their legs, no doubt an adaptation to their canoe-borne lifeway. Their dark faces and coarse hair moved the early explorers to ecstatic horror. FitzRoy himself referred to their "villainous expression of the worst description."

Considering the climate they lived in, the Yahgan wore less clothing than possibly anyone else in the world. Both men and women often went naked, the women sometimes wearing a small pubic covering (Figure 11.2). They made frequent use of sealskin or sea otter skin capes, which extended as far as the waist. The stiff and unyielding skins were tied to their chests by a thong and were worn on the windward side of the body in cold weather. Sealskin moccasins stuffed with grass kept out the cold. The Indians adorned themselves with wristlets and anklets of guanaco skin and shell or bird-bone necklaces. They decorated their faces with dot and line marks that had symbolic meaning.

The Yahgan lived in the simplest of wigwams made of pliable saplings bent into a cone (Figure 11.3). During the summer the framework was covered with grass, brush, or other convenient materials. They added a thick covering of sewn sealskins in the cold months, a covering so thick and heavy that it was often made in several pieces and carried from place to place in canoes. Two or more closely related families would live in the same winter wigwam. To keep their houses warm, the Yahgan would dig a hollow in the ground to form a large pit about two or three feet deep. The fire would be placed in the hollow, so that the heat rose towards the low roof. The inhabitants slept at a higher level, with the whole structure crouching, as it were, against the ground to keep its owners snug against the winter gales. FitzRoy remarked on the inflamed eyes of the Indians, caused by the smoke filtering inside their wigwams.

The Yahgan depended heavily on their canoes for their survival, well-made and seaworthy vessels with the great virtue of being crafted with the simplest tools. They spent so much time in these canoes that they kept fires burning

11.2   A Fuegian of the Tekeenica tribe by Conrad Martens, artist on the Beagle *expedition, from Robert FitzRoy's* Narrative of the Voyage of the *Beagle, vol. 2,* Frontispiece

11.3   Yahgan Indians by their dwelling (photograph by the French Scientific Expedition of 1884)

on a bed of clay amid ships. FitzRoy's visitors arrived with the men sitting forward between the fireplace and the spears that lay in the bow ready for immediate use against seals. The women would paddle the canoe sitting astern of the fire, while the children and dogs huddled in the stern. Each canoe carried two or more wooden paddles, spears, fishing lines, and nets, as well as baskets and that most necessary piece of equipment—a bark bailer. Most village sites lay at the head of fine, sandy beaches where canoes could be landed easily, or in sheltered, kelp-lined bays where simple runways lined with giant kelp were used to land the fragile bark craft.

The Yahgan relied very heavily on marine mammals, fishing, and shellfish for their livelihood. Their environment was diverse enough for them to have a comfortable "cushion" of foods to fall back on in times of scarcity. But the seasonality and distribution of food supplies kept them constantly on the move within their territories, returning to the same localities year after year. They levered shellfish off rocks in sheltered coves with their bare hands, occasionally using bone and wood spatulas or chisel-shaped spears. Huge shell middens accumulated at favored locations. The women would dive for underwater shells, a division of labor also found among the Tasmanians.

Like those of most other hunter-gatherers, the Yahgan's toolkit was both simple and highly portable. Their hunting and fishing technology depended heavily on the barbed spear, sling, and club, as well as the bow and arrow (Figure 11.4). An expert could stun a bird in flight with a single stone. They were expert with snares, nets, and rod fishing lines, clubbing sleeping seals with heavy sticks. The most important artifact was fire. Every group carried at least one smoldering brand with them. The women made baskets of local grasses, which were used for carrying berries and storing food. During the summers they would collect edible berries and fungi. The latter were dried on sticks and kept for winter use. Bark containers served as simple buckets and bailers, while large seashells were used as dippers and drinking vessels.

The Yahgan were organized in small bands that rarely exceeded a few families. Two or more families tended to move around together, for the heavy covers of their houses required at least two canoes to carry them. No one individual had more authority than another, although a few priest-shamans played an important part in band life. There were kinship ties that extended beyond the narrow bounds of a single community, ties that provided some restrictions on marriage customs. The Yahgan sometimes captured women from other bands and tended to change wives fairly frequently, a practice that one anthropologist has called "progressive polygamy." The Yahgan were a quarrelsome people, perennially feuding with one another over women, imagined insults, or the death of a relative. Sometimes these quarrels would erupt in individual or group fighting, conducted with spears, slings, or clubs.

Like the Khoikhoi and the Tasmanians, the Yahgan were perceived by Europeans as being without religion, when in fact they possessed a rich panoply of spiritual beliefs. Much of Yahgan religious and ritual life is lost, but their environment was peopled by numerous spirits, most of whom were malicious. The Yahgan world was ruled by a supreme being named Watauinewa, who controlled food supplies and was the agent of birth and death. The shamans acted as the intermediaries between the living and the spirit world. The Yahgan possessed a rich fount of myths and tales that provided an explanatory context for their natural environment. Their initiation ceremonies took place in large domed huts with open sides, whose interiors were adorned with painted designs. The young initiates were forced to fast, denied sleep, and instructed in food gathering and hunting. Much of this *shiehaus* ceremony consisted of singing and dancing, interspersed with ethical and religious instruction that lasted several days. Some people would go through the ceremony several times during their lifetimes. The men often participated in another ceremony in which they were instructed in tribal lore and underwent ordeals that tested their resilience in the face of suffering. One striking characteristic of the Yahgan commented upon by early visitors was their apparent indifference to European ships and their technological

11.4   Yahgan Indian lashing a spear point (photograph by the French Scientific Expedition of 1884)

wonders. Perhaps this was because they were schooled to endure food and water shortages as well as discomfort without showing emotion. Conceivably, the apparent indifference of the Yahgan to Europeans was simply the result of a reticence that stemmed from long-held custom.

The Yahgan may have developed an impressive adaptation to a harsh environment, an adaptation that had remained viable for thousands of years, but FitzRoy and his officers were shocked by their apparently miserable, pagan existence. Charles Darwin accompanied the *Beagle* to Tierra del Fuego in 1833, when the ship returned to the Indians. "Four or five men suddenly appeared on a cliff near to us; they were absolutely naked & with long streaming hair. Springing from the ground & waving their hands around their heads, they sent forth most hideous yells. Their appearance was so strange that it was scarcely like that of earthly inhabitants" (Keynes 1979, 104). He found the Indians sometimes troublesome, almost unredeemable souls with destructive weapons. Darwin expressed the sentiment of many who met them when he remarked that "in treating with savages, Europeans labor under a great disadvantage untill the cruel lesson is taught how deadly firearms are" (Keynes 1979, 105). The Fuegians presented a lofty, perhaps impossible challenge to even the most ardently evangelical of missionaries and humanitarians, a challenge that FitzRoy, among others, seized with avidity.

FitzRoy and the Fuegians

AS THE *BEAGLE* WORKED HER WAY southward in 1829, FitzRoy came across small groups of Indians who were far from friendly, and seeking knives and other utilitarian items instead of useless trinkets. They were thievish and one night stole a survey boat. FitzRoy responded by taking prisoners and destroying as many canoes as he could find. Most of his captives escaped except for three children, two of whom he managed to place with more friendly bands. The third, a girl about eight years old, was so happy on board that he kept her as a hostage for the lost boat and resolved to teach her English. FitzRoy had had time to reflect on the best way to handle the Fuegians. Language, he felt, was the key to dealing with them. Until some means could be found of communicating with the Fuegians on a daily basis, there was not the "slightest chance of their being raised one step above the low place which they then held in our estimation" (FitzRoy 1839, 26). So he decided to capture some more Indians and to train them as interpreters.

A few days later a party of Indians visited the ship in their canoes. FitzRoy chased them away from the *Beagle,* fearing with good reason that they would try and steal everything in sight. Then he went alongside one canoe and ordered one of the young men in it to get into his boat. The Indian sat down without any sign of fear. His companions paddled away without any visible emotion. Somewhat surprised by the ease of his capture, FitzRoy named his hostage York Minster after the promontory that protected the anchorage. The young man was sullen at first, but soon cheered up when he was fed well and given freedom of movement on board. He got on well with the girl, who was rapidly becoming the crew's pet. They had named her Fuegia Basket, after the strange, basketlike vessel that the stolen whaleboat's crew had improvised to make their way back to the *Beagle.* A third hostage was soon added to the bag, a young man promptly named Boat Memory.

At first FitzRoy planned to land his captives in neighboring territory, but he soon discovered the prisoners were terrified of their neighbors. Fuegia Basket screamed and hid herself when their canoes came alongside. So the devout and God-fearing FitzRoy decided that the best solution was to take the Fuegians back to England with him. They would receive a Christian education, be instructed in civilized living, and then return to their homeland to convert their fellow Indians. It was a fantastic scheme, born of the highest motives, but one that was to have terrible consequences. To round off his group of potential converts, FitzRoy purchased a fourteen-year-old boy for a large mother-of-pearl button. He was named Jemmy Button in commemoration of his price.

On his way home to England, FitzRoy had ample opportunity to study his charges. He was struck by their intelligence and potential. The men impressed him, but Fuegia Basket was, he remarked, "a displeasing specimen of uncivilized human nature." One wonders what went on in the Fuegians' minds as they saw England for the first time. We are told they were astonished by the sight of a steamship in Falmouth Harbor as it snorted and churned past the *Beagle*.

FitzRoy took extraordinary precautions to ensure that his charges were looked after carefully and protected from the danger of infectious diseases. He landed them at night, arranged for their vaccination against smallpox, and put them up at a remote country farmhouse, where they could enjoy more freedom. Meanwhile, he received assurances from the Admiralty that the Fuegians would be given passage home in due course. Despite every precaution, Boat Memory contracted smallpox and died in the naval hospital in Plymouth. FitzRoy was very upset, but pressed on with his plans to educate the remaining Fuegians. After prolonged correspondence, he made arrangements with the Church Missionary Society for their housing in the parish of Walthamstow, a London suburb. They stayed in the house of the local schoolmaster, who undertook to teach the Fuegians English and the "plainer truths of Christianity." They learned "the use of common tools," basic agriculture and animal husbandry, and elementary carpentry. Their teachers collected vocabularies and information on Fuegian customs against the day when missionary endeavors would begin in Tierra del Fuego.

From December 1830 to October 1831, the Fuegians lived quietly in Walthamstow and continued their education. They went visiting and received an audience with King William IV. The king and queen were captivated by Fuegia Basket. Queen Adelaide gave her one of her own bonnets, a ring, and a sum of money to buy clothes for her return home. The Fuegians' reaction to the audience was not recorded. They were to remain in England until 1831, when FitzRoy was again dispatched in the *Beagle,* this time on a renewed South American survey and on the famous circumnavigation that was to change the face of biological research forever.

When the *Beagle* left Plymouth in December 1831, she carried the Fuegians and a young missionary named Richard Matthews. The Church

Missionary Society was intent on starting a mission in the Fuegians' home territory. Matthews arrived on board the *Beagle* with an incredible array of crockery and household goods. Clearly, neither he nor his backers had the slightest inkling what they were getting into. FitzRoy himself probably knew, but his religious fervor caused him to sweep aside impatiently every imagined difficulty.

The *Beagle* sighted Tierra del Fuego in mid-December 1832. FitzRoy's main objective was to return his Indians to their homeland. As they neared home, York Minster announced his intention of marrying Fuegia Basket. Jemmy Button had become quite a dandy in London and was always smartly dressed in fashionable clothes. The Fuegians decided they would like to live together in Jemmy's country. FitzRoy willingly agreed, on the grounds that it would simplify his operations.

After weeks of stormy weather, FitzRoy and Darwin set out in small boats for Jemmy Button's village near Murray Narrows off the Beagle Channel (Figure 11.5). Their convoy of four boats carried the missionary and all the supplies necessary to establish his settlement. The returning Fuegians mocked some locals they encountered, calling them "large monkeys." It was astonishing how much their ideas had changed in the three years since they had left. As the party advanced up the narrows, fires were lit on every point and bands of Fuegians yelled and gestured at the boats. When FitzRoy established good relations and started trading, the Indians became importunate and pointed at everything, however large, and repeated a monotonous chant of "Yammerschooner, yammerschooner," the standard litany they used when confronted by visiting ships.

Jemmy Button guided the boats to a pretty little cove named Wulana, which his people visited regularly. The *Beagle* party was accompanied by canoes full of yelling Fuegians. FitzRoy landed Matthews at the cove and spent five days erecting wigwams for the party and unloading supplies. He marked out a boundary around the tiny settlement and dug gardens for vegetables. The curious Fuegians did nothing to hinder the work, but were inclined to pilfer anything they could. FitzRoy arranged a spectacular display of rifle firepower to impress his spectators. "At sunset they went away as usual looking very grave and talking earnestly," he reported.

The day after Jemmy's arrival, his family turned up. The long expected meeting was inauspicious. His mother barely glanced at him. His sisters ran off, while the brothers walked around and stared without saying a word. Jemmy was very upset, more so because he could only converse with his brothers in broken English, having forgotten his own language. But the women made much of Fuegia Basket. About one hundred and twenty Fuegians watched as the encampment was prepared. The fifth day they suddenly disappeared. Some of the seamen feared that a raid was imminent, so

11.5   H.M.S. *Beagle* **in Murray Narrows,** *Tierra del Fuego, by Conrad Martens*

FitzRoy left Matthews and the Fuegians alone at the settlement and anchored in a nearby cove. Everything was quiet when he returned the next day, so he set off on a survey trip to the western portions of the Beagle Channel after ensuring that Matthews had buried his most valuable possessions under the floor of his wigwam. Nine days later he returned, alarmed by the sight of several locals wearing items of European clothing. He found the encampment in a shambles. Matthews was alive and unharmed, but the garden was trampled and the place thronged with Fuegians dressed in fragments of English clothing. Three days after the boats had left, the Fuegians had arrived and manhandled Matthews as they looted his possessions. Only the valuables buried under the wigwam were intact. Jemmy had lost most of his property, but Fuegia and York Minster were unmolested. Perhaps they were in league with the looters.

Clearly, Matthews was doomed if he was left ashore, so FitzRoy reluctantly took him back to the *Beagle.* He left the Fuegians at the settlement. When he returned eleven days later, all was well. The Fuegians were still wearing their European clothes and were building canoes. Somewhat relieved, FitzRoy set off on thirteen months of arduous survey work on the Patagonian coast and in the Falkland Islands.

The *Beagle* returned to Wulaia on 4 March 1834. The settlement was deserted and there were no signs of life. Soon afterwards, three canoes approached the ship. One of them carried Jemmy Button, thin and almost naked, wearing a piece of hide round his loins. But he was as cheerful as ever and had taken a young wife. He was invited to dine on board and brought presents of otter skins and arrowheads for his friends. Apparently York Minster and Fuegia Basket had decided to return home to their own people and had persuaded Jemmy and his family to join them. As soon as they reached their friends, they abandoned Jemmy and stole all his possessions. Jemmy had returned to Wulaia, but found the large wigwams built by the seamen too drafty for comfortable living. He seemed entirely content with his lifestyle and showed no desire to return to the civilized comforts of England.

The next day, FitzRoy loaded Jemmy Button down with presents and bade him an emotional farewell. His noble experiment had failed, but, as Charles Darwin pointed out, there was a faint chance that Jemmy and his companions might one day treat a shipwrecked sailor kindly. As so many other philanthropic explorers were to find out, the objects of their attention all too often preferred to be left alone to live as they formerly had.

CHAPTER 12

Missionaries at the End of the Earth

It is sufficient that they have been taught to repeat after you certain words expressive of their entrance into the fold of Christ.

Parker Snow, *A Two Year's Cruise off Tierra del Fuego* (1857)

ROBERT FITZROY'S ADVENTURES WITH THE Fuegians coincided with the climax of the long crusade by Evangelical and Quaker philanthropists against the African slave trade. After slavery was abolished in 1833, the same crusaders led by the Quaker-born Evangelical Thomas Fowell Buxton (1786–1845) turned their attention to the treatment of the defenseless peoples of the British empire. They began with the Cape, where the treatment of the Khoikhoi and blacks was a matter of humanitarian concern in the 1820s and 1830s. In 1834, Buxton lobbied successfully for a Parliamentary Select Committee on Aborigines to investigate, among other matters "what measures ought to be adopted with respect to the Native Inhabitants of Countries where British Settlements are made, and to the Neighboring Tribes, in order to secure to them the due observance of justice and the protection of their rights; to promote the spread of Civilization among them, and to lead them to the peaceful and voluntary reception of the Christian Religion" (Stocking 1971, 369).

By 1837, the Select Committee had heard witnesses from South Africa, Canada, Australia, and New Zealand. Buxton described the voluminous testimony as "that desperate and widespread villainy, which has rendered the intercourse of the civilized and Christian man with the savage little else than one uniform system of cruelty, rapacity, and murder" (Select Committee 1836–7, 6). The Select Committee reminded the government that it had a responsibility to the societies with which its subject came into contact. "We are apt to class them under the sweeping term of savages, and perhaps in so doing, to consider ourselves as exempted from the obligations due to them as our fellow men. This assumption does not, however, alter our responsibility" (7). The committee pointed out there were no laws to prevent natives from selling their labor, nor were there restrictions on the sale of "ardent spirits" to them. The members had strong words to say about the alienation of land and illegal colonization, and called for legal indulgence towards people for "actions they have been taught to regard as praiseworthy we consider as meriting the punishment of death" (6).

A Quaker doctor named Thomas Hodgkin (1798–1866) now took up the philanthropic cudgels. Hodgkin was a famous pathologist who devoted much of his life to diagnosing and treating the disease that was later given his name. But he was an influential humanitarian and an adept organizer. He organized the supporters of the Select Committee into a more permanent body, known as the Aborigines Protection Society (APS), founded in 1838. This was perhaps the first secular, humanitarian organization to come to the defense of non-Western peoples. It undoubtedly helped moderate some of the worst excesses of colonial occupation, and continues its work to this day, having merged with the Anti-Slavery Society.

The APS had high-minded goals: "protecting the defenseless, and promoting the advancement of uncivilized tribes." Its members had no doubt that Evangelicalism abroad was the only effective way to civilize aborigines, but their real target was public opinion at home. Most people were completely ignorant about other societies and had no idea of the abuses that occurred in distant lands. So the APS resolved to collect "authentic information concerning the character, habits, and wants of the uncivilized tribes." This information it would use on the government at home and abroad, and on the public at large to change the character of European colonization overseas.

The APS may have started off life as a humanitarian organization, but many of its early activities were unashamedly what today would be called anthropological. A well-known physician named James Cowles Pritchard (1786–1848) had published a medical dissertation entitled *Researches into the Physical History of Man* in 1808, a work he successively reworked and expanded over the next forty years. This was the first systematic account of non-European society. Pritchard himself was one of the first men to argue that "it is of the greatest importance...to obtain much more extensive information than we now possess of their physical and moral characters" (Stocking 1971, 371). A committee of the APS prepared an ethnographic questionnaire that contained little relating to the Society's professed humanitarian interests.

By this time, the membership of the APS was made up of both Evangelicals and humanitarians, and of people with more scientific interests in other societies. The APS did have some success in organizing auxiliary societies among sailors likely to come in contact with aborigines. It also prepared a model "System of legislation," a program of what might be called directed cultural change "by persuasion rather than by force," but there is no evidence that this was ever put into use. There was a feeling, however, that the APS had failed in its original purpose and that the initial impetus from the report of the Select Committee was faltering. One problem was that the public at large seemed quite happy about the colonization of foreign lands. The APS, therefore, felt obliged to emphasize that it was not opposed to colonization and did not wish to maintain non-European societies "in the purity of their race...as objects of curiosity in the natural history of man." By 1843, the tensions between Evangelicals and ethnologists may have reached a head, for a group of members formed another organization, the Ethnological Society of London.

The Ethnological Society was set up "to inquire into the distinguishing characteristics, physical and moral, of the varieties of Mankind which inhabit, or have inhabited, the Earth, and to ascertain the causes of such characteristics" (Stocking 1971, 372). The members were sure that all humans were of "one blood," and that the purpose of ethnology was to tie all humankind together into a family tree. The primary means of doing so was linguistic comparisons, using language to establish connections between physically dissimilar groups. Few if any of the members had any first-hand experience of non-European societies. They spent a few winter evenings examining occasional Africans, Eskimos, and Polynesians in the flesh, most of them seamen from sailing ships in the London docks. Without question, the primary philosophical underpinning of the Ethnological Society was still religious and humanitarian, a conviction that all humankind was one and that people of other races were capable of acquiring the teachings of Christianity and the benefits of civilization. The Ethnological Society went into serious decline in the early 1850s, perhaps as a result of the Crimean War. One member believed the lack of interest was due to the deadening influence of religion.

The Evangelical and humanitarian impulses so strong in Britain were bound to have their impact on societies thousands of miles away. Throughout the nineteenth century, debates raged about the morality and strategies of missionary work, not only between colonists and church people, but between the missionaries themselves. Foremost among these debates was the issue of the "civilizing" of non-Western peoples. Should they be taught the arts of civilization before conversion or afterwards? Samuel Marsden, the New Zealand missionary, was in no doubt that "to preach the gospel without the aid of the arts will never succeed among the Heathen for any time." Others, many of them strangely obsessed with sin and Christian doctrine, disagreed violently. The Yahgan were to feel the impact of one such missionary, the strange, pathetic, and highly eccentric Allen Gardiner.

"Their Way of Thinking May Not Be the Same"

THE VISIT OF THE *BEAGLE'S* Fuegians to England aroused much public interest, especially among zealous, Evangelical Christians who were busy spreading the word of God throughout the globe. People from all walks of life were seized with such ardor for missionary endeavor that many of them lost all sense of proportion. One such fanatic was Allen Francis Gardiner, a retired naval officer and amateur missionary of unbridled enthusiasm. Where FitzRoy had merely been a Christian zealot, Gardiner was religious to the point of mental imbalance.

Allen Gardiner was born in 1794 and served with distinction in the Royal Navy in South America and the Pacific. During his service in the South Seas, Gardiner came into contact with missionaries and developed a profound interest in aboriginal peoples. He became increasingly obsessed with Christianity. In 1822, he wrote in his journal that he had been "hastening by rapid strides to the brink of eternal ruin...a great change has been wrought in my heart, and I am now enabled to derive pleasure and satisfaction in hearing and reading the Word of God" (Marsh and Stirling 1887, 12). After his retirement from the navy in 1826, Gardiner devoted the rest of his life to starting missionary projects in remote parts of the world. He set up a mission in Natal, South Africa, and tried to work in New Guinea. But his main preoccupation was with the Patagonian Indians. The influence of the Catholic Church was so powerful that all his attempts to convert them to his own Evangelical beliefs failed.

In despair, Gardiner turned to Tierra del Fuego, a part of the world that had fascinated him ever since he had heard of the *Beagle's* Fuegians. In 1841 he sailed to the Falkland Islands and chartered a schooner to take him to the archipelago. His plan was to persuade some Fuegians to accompany him back to the Falklands, where they could teach him Indian languages. After a few weeks at Oazy Harbor on the northern shore of the Strait of Magellan, Gardiner returned to England convinced he had made sufficient contacts for a mission to be established. When the harassed and overextended Church Missionary Society turned his project down, Gardiner formed the Patagonian Mission Society and tried to raise funds on his own. It was four years before he could return, accompanied by a lay preacher named Robert Hunt and enough supplies for several months. Within a few weeks, Gardiner retreated, for conditions were intolerable.

Far from being deterred by this failure, Gardiner renewed his missionary efforts with renewed fervor. After another abortive visit to Bolivia, Gardiner again sailed for Tierra del Fuego in January 1848, this time accompanied by James Erwin, a ship's carpenter, and four sailors. The party took three boats, two prefabricated huts, and six months' supplies with them. This time Gardiner landed at the southern end of the archipelago, and decided to set up a mission at Banner Cove on the north shore of Picton Island. The cove was sheltered, and wild fowl were abundant. The only problem was the Fuegians, who were hostile and aggressive. Gardiner soon realized that the mission was doomed to failure, for he did not have enough followers to guard all his possessions. The Fuegians were certain to steal the boats as soon as the ship that had brought the missionaries departed. Gardiner wisely withdrew, realizing that the only hope was a "mission vessel moored in the stream", where everything was safe from the acquisitive Fuegians.

In December 1850, Gardiner was back at Banner Cove, this time with a party of six: a surgeon, a lay preacher, James Erwin, who worshipped Gardiner, and three devout Cornish fishermen. Instead of a base ship, Gardiner took two large whalers and some tents, determined to succeed where he had failed before. At this point an element of madness creeps into the tragic story of Allen Gardiner. His new boats were no better than those he had brought before. Half of his companions were no seamen and the Fuegians were just as hostile. Banner Cove was still untenable, so Gardiner resolved to sail west up the Beagle Channel in search of Jemmy Button at Wulaia. The attempt was defeated by rough weather.

For five months, Gardiner and his colleagues hovered on the verge of starvation. They were harassed by the Indians and forced to move from cove to cove to escape them. One of the whalers was wrecked, so they converted her into a crude dwelling. All the powder and shot had been left behind on the ship that had brought them. The missionaries eked out a living and camped aimlessly, in a state of what appears to have been ecstatic resignation to their fate. Gardiner's journal is full of pious expressions of joy at being challenged by the Lord: "Blessed be my heavenly Father for the many mercies which I enjoy," he wrote, on the verge of death. The entire party died of scurvy and slow starvation. They seem to have awaited death rather than trying to sail north along the coast to the safety of Patagonia. Gardiner was the last to die on 6 September 1851. "Yet a little while, and through grace we may join the blessed throng to sing the praises of Christ throughout eternity," the last entry in his diary read (Marsh and Stirling 1887, 67). One has the unmistakable impression that he chose martyrdom rather than another pastoral failure (Figure 12.1).

The bodies of the party were found in October of the same year. News of the tragedy reached England in April 1852. Many people felt that the expedition had been an act of folly and that further missionary efforts should be abandoned forthwith. Even the London *Times*, that arbiter of public opinion,

12.1 Captain Allen Gardiner's martyrdom, as depicted by a Christian artist for a contemporary missionary tract

demanded that the Patagonian Mission Society cease operations. But Gardiner's death caused a surge of interest and concern among the pious, who paid for the equipping of an eighty-eight-ton schooner as a mission ship. She was named the *Allen Gardiner* and commanded by a dynamic, religious adventurer named Parker Snow, a thirty-seven-year-old seaman with wide experience of exploring the Arctic and other remote parts of the world as well.

Snow's instructions were to proceed to the Falkland Islands, set up a mission there, and then to go to Wulaia to persuade Jemmy Button to return to the Falklands for training as an interpreter. His problems began with the crew, for the Mission Society insisted that he sign on only devout Christians. He was infuriated by the narrow arrogance and impractical plans of his missionary colleagues. The crew would refuse to work the ship when it was time for divine service, even if there was an emergency.

Snow reached the Falklands in January 1855. It took him ten months to help the inept missionaries set up their station. It was not until the third week of October 1855, that he reached Spaniard Harbor, the scene of Gardiner's death. On 2 November, the *Allen Gardiner* was passing through Murray Narrows when she was approached by several Yahgan canoes (Figure 12.2). On impulse, Snow raised the Union Jack. Two canoes came speeding towards the ship. Snow hailed the leader: "Jemmy Button, Jemmy Button?" To his astonishment, one of the men in the canoe replied "Yes, yes, Jam-mes Button, Jam-mes Button," as he pointed to the second canoe close astern. A stout, naked man came

12.2   Fuegians in a canoe, by Conrad Martens

alongside a few moments later: "Jam-mes Button *me;* where's the ladder," he cried.

Jemmy Button was still recognizable from the portrait in FitzRoy's book. He had put on weight, but still remembered some English; indeed, he had taught it to his family. His first act was to demand clothes, which, reported Snow, made him look like "some huge baboon dressed up for the occasion." He then took tea with the captain. Snow questioned him about other visitors and learned that his was the first vessel to pass this way since the *Beagle.* He then asked Jemmy to accompany him to the Falkland Islands. Button refused at once. Although he had nostalgic memories of civilization, he had no desire to repeat the experience. Nor, he indicated, did his family. The missionaries were quite prepared to resort to trickery to obtain a few Fuegians, but Snow flatly refused to resort to such chicanery. "Savages they may be: degraded, miserable, wretched beings! But they have hearts as well as we; and *their* way of thinking may not be the same as ours on the question," he wrote (Snow 1857, 62). He was well ahead of his time in his perception of the Fuegians' delicate adaptation to their harsh environment and of the dangers of unrooting them from their homeland. The following day, the *Allen Gardiner* departed after distributing gifts to Jemmy Button and his friends. An ugly situation developed when the Indians demanded more and tried to strip Snow of his jacket. But the ship was already under way and the Indians fled to their canoes as she gained speed. The missionaries retreated to the Falklands to plan their next move.

In August 1856, the secretary of the Patagonian Mission Society, the Reverend Packenham Despard, arrived in the Falklands to take charge of the mission. Despard was a man of great resolution and energy who believed that God had a tendency to help those who helped themselves. Snow regarded Despard as an incompetent who was responsible for many of his difficulties. The two men quarreled and Snow was fired without pay. He returned to England with the help of the Falkland Islanders and published a violent attack on the missionaries. He cynically described missionary work as "a strange compound of piety and irreligion, and far from what it should be" (Snow 1857, 77). The Evangelicals ignored his strictures, which were soon forgotten.

Despard spent two years consolidating the Falklands mission before returning to Tierra del Fuego. He managed to persuade Jemmy Button, together with his wife and three children, to come back with him for six months. The missionaries were delighted, and attributed the change of heart to Divine Providence. Jemmy Button and his family proved cheerful and willing pupils, so much so that the schooner returned them to Wulaia and managed to bring another nine Indians away for training, including one of Jemmy's brothers. These students appear to have been less satisfactory, for Despard ordered them searched upon departure and upon arrival in Wulaia in November 1859, in case they made off with stolen property. The Fuegians bitterly resented these searches. In furious indignation, they tore off their clothes and jumped into waiting canoes. They did, however, leave several stolen items behind them in the process.

On his earlier visit, Despard had erected a small house for the mission at Wulaia. Garland Phillips, the missionary accompanying the nine Fuegians, now opened up the hut in an attempt to make contact with further Indians. As usual, dozens of people flocked to the schooner, among them Jemmy Button, who was furious to discover that no present had been brought for him. The Indians were importunate, constantly begging and making endless demands for gifts.

On 6 November 1859, a Sunday, the entire crew of the schooner except Albert Cole, the cook, went ashore for religious services in the hut. No one had any suspicion of danger. Everyone was unarmed. As the last of the sailors filed into the house, Cole was horrified to see dozens of Fuegians surround the hut, while others seized the oars from the boats. A few moments later the Europeans were clubbed and stoned to death as they emerged from the hut in alarm. One sailor managed to reach the shore, but was killed as he tried to swim out to the schooner. Cole swam ashore as the Indians stripped the ship of everything movable. He managed to find refuge with some relatives of Jemmy Button.

Three months later the massacre was discovered by another schooner sent to find out what had happened to the *Allen Gardiner*. Cole's account was almost incoherent, and Jemmy Button stoutly denied any knowledge of a plot to kill the missionaries. To the rescue party's astonishment, he agreed to accompany them back to the Falklands. The governor of the islands insisted on an official inquiry, at which Despard refused to give evidence. Jemmy Button's testimony threw no light on the affair. But he did point out that none of the Fuegians came to the Falklands willingly. After the inquiry, Button was returned to Wulaia. This was the last attempt to persuade him to change his way of life. The governor closed the affair by reporting to London that in his judgment the missionaries had brought the tragedy on themselves by their highhanded and insensitive treatment of the Indians.

By all accounts, this should have been the end of attempts to missionize the Yahgan. Despard himself was shattered by the massacre and asked to be relieved of his post, recommending that further attempts to convert the Fuegians be abandoned. His successor, W. H. Stirling, would have been quite content to limit his efforts to the Falklands, had it not been for the youthful enthusiasm of Despard's adopted stepson, Thomas Bridges. Young Bridges had arrived at the mission in 1856 and spent a great deal of time with the transplanted Yahgan. He had a natural facility for languages and was soon acting as the Indians' interpreter. Garland Phillips had refused to take him to Wulaia in 1859, which was probably a mistake, for Bridges might have saved the missionaries' lives. Although he had strong religious convictions, Bridges's driving force was a great liking and respect for the Indians and a passionate desire to explore Tierra del Fuego. He kept on pestering Stirling for a chance to work in the south, at the same time perfecting his Yahgan with the aid of the solitary Indian family still living at the mission. It was four years before the mission schooner approached Wulaia again, this time with Bridges aboard. The Yahgan approached cautiously. They had been expecting reprisals. When Bridges greeted the approaching canoes in their own language, the Yahgan were delighted. So successful were his efforts at rapport that Bridges returned several times in the next five years on a leisurely search for a mission site.

Bridges finally selected a bay called Ushaia (Yahgan for "inner harbor to the westward") on the northern shores of the Beagle Channel. It took four years of preparations to found the station in this remote bay. Between 1868 and 1871 Bridges built the mission house, established a flock of sheep, and returned to England to take holy orders. There he went on an extensive lecture tour and married a young woman named Mary Varder, whom he met at one of his talks. She had never traveled abroad before, yet willingly agreed to accompany her husband to one of the remotest corners of the world.

On 1 October 1871, the Bridges finally settled at Ushaia. Their only white companions were John Lewis, a carpenter, and his wife. The two couples lived in a partially completed corrugated iron and wood house. Their isolated home was surrounded by a cluster of Yahgan wigwams. Thomas Bridges had no illusions about the difficulty of maintaining the settlement at Ushaia. Although he had made great progress because of his linguistic abilities, he was well aware of the unpredictable behavior of the Indians, their sudden quarrels and the apparently trivial causes for them. He spent much of his time settling disputes and traveling in Yahgan canoes far and wide through their territory, often in vile weather. He was careful never to provoke a dispute or to threaten violence.

Within a few years, Thomas Bridges had built a mutual trust with the Indians that made the position of the Ushaia mission uniquely safe. The secret, he realized, was to live alongside the Indians, while making minimal disruptions in their traditional lifeways. Unlike his zealous compatriots in the South Seas and New Zealand, Bridges was content to observe and understand, to live patiently among his neighbors, believing that the word of God would come to them in time. His slow moving tactics hardly endeared him to his superiors in the Falklands and at home, who were preoccupied with head counts and souls saved for the Lord.

By 1884, Ushaia was a well-established mission station, a small village with four permanent British families, and a fluctuating population of occasional scientific visitors and shipwrecked mariners, directed to Ushaia by the Indians. Over a hundred Indians had abandoned their nomadic lifeway and settled permanently at Ushaia, either employed by the mission or engaged in some form of trading. Indians from miles around visited Ushaia, among them Fuegia Basket, who was curious about the missionaries. She had forgotten almost all her English and was obviously quite happy in her homeland. Bridges worried about the increasing sedentary population at Ushaia, for he feared an influx of Europeans who would introduce alcohol and new diseases into Yahgan life. He remembered an earlier measles epidemic in 1864 that had wiped out a third of the Yahgan in a few short months. The Ushaia missionaries proposed a special reserve for the local Indians, to be administered by the mission. But their narrow-minded superiors in London rejected the idea, arguing that a mission should confine its work to religious matters.

All too soon, Bridges's worst fears were realized. In September 1884, four ships of the Argentine navy arrived unexpectedly at Ushaia to establish a government outpost there. The ships' companies swarmed all over Ushaia and mixed freely with the Indians. Within three weeks the Yahgan of the Ushaia area and neighboring islands were ravaged by an epidemic of measles. Soon the Indians were dying so fast that there was a backlog of graves to be dug. Over half the Yahgan population in the region perished in the epidemic. At least half the survivors were dead within two years from the aftereffects of measles. By the 1890s, only some three hundred pure blooded Yahgan were alive, of an original population of three thousand Indians. Thirty years later, anthropologist Samuel Lothrop was told that there were fifty Yahgan on the shores of the Beagle Channel. In 1996, pureblooded Yahgan could no longer be found living in the archipelago.

The predicted catastrophe left Thomas Bridges so disillusioned with the future of the mission and disgusted with his superiors that he resigned from his post. While the Mission Society loudly proclaimed that "the Evil One" had subverted him, Bridges obtained a grant of seventy-five square miles of land at Harberton, forty miles east of Ushaia. The ranch prospered and is still in the hands of the Bridges family today. But even if Bridges's bigoted superiors had accepted the reservation plan, the Yahgan would not have been saved from their disastrous end. Their traditional way of life was totally incompatible with the new land needs of the sheep ranchers, who were beginning to settle in Tierra del Fuego at the end of the nineteenth century.

Archaeology has shown that the Yahgan's cultural adaptation to the complexities of the Fuegian environment was viable for millennia, an adaptation far more complex than any early visitor ever realized, except, perhaps, Thomas Bridges. The only reason the Yahgan lifeway collapsed was because Europeans, many of them of good intent, introduced new and maladaptive elements, such as agriculture, alien diseases, permanent settlements, and sheep herding, into their natural environment. As with the Khoikhoi, Tahitians, and so many other non-Western societies, the apparently trivial acts of one generation reaped a terrible harvest in later years.

PART III

Interconnectedness

As an inferior race… we believe… [the Indians] must give way in order to make room for a race more enlightened, and by nature and habits better fitted to perform the task of converting what is now a wilderness into productive fields and happy homes…

Anonymous British colonist,
quoted in Robin Fisher, *Contact and Conflict* (1977)

CHAPTER 13

Furs and Firearms:
The Huron of Eastern Canada

Canada...was principally a region of boreal forest, too cold to invite extensive European settlement, but rich in fur-bearing animals and laced with lakes and rivers that made the transportation of furs from the hinterland to coastal markets relatively easy. It was far easier for the white man to buy these furs from experienced Indian trappers than to hunt them for himself; hence, as long as furs remained abundant and fetched a good price on European markets, a symbiotic relationship linked the Indian hunter and the European trader.

Bruce Trigger, *The Children of Aataentsic* (1976)

By the end of the seventeenth century, European explorers, traders, missionaries, and colonists had reached most corners of the world. The maritime nations of Western Europe had taken full advantage of their superior technology and military strength to dominate vast areas of the globe. Much of the New World had been explored and colonized. The coastline of Africa had been charted. Regular trade routes joined Europe with China, India, and the Far East. Only the Pacific and extreme northern and southern latitudes were major blanks on the map. Cook and his contemporaries explored the vast wastes of the Pacific in the following century, described Tahiti and Polynesia, and probed close to the Arctic and Antarctic circles. They found no trace of the Great Southern Continent, the wealthy, mythical land that had provided the major impetus for British and French interest in the Pacific.

In North America, the late eighteenth century saw the British colonies break from the motherland and a slow acceleration of imperial expansion on a scale not seen since the days of the conquistadors in the fifteenth and sixteenth centuries. However, the American and French revolutions sowed doubts about the value, morality, and permanence of colonial empires, and at least sporadic debates about non-Western peoples that were to persist through the nineteenth century into our own times.

The ultimate impetus for this expansion was not so much spiritual as commercial. Not only individuals, but also companies and entire nations were determined to enrich themselves by overseas trade and by establishing settlements in distant lands. Western Europe's mostly self-sufficient agricultural economies were replaced by far more complex structures that fulfilled not only local needs but exported European manufactures in exchange for raw materials, tropical products, spices, textiles, and other commodities from far abroad. Inevitably there was competition and intense rivalry between individuals and nations, for the potential profits from overseas trade were enormous.

One of the most striking features of late eighteenth- and early nineteenth-century Europe was the widening of areas of international tension to include colonial possessions and foreign trade. Missionary zeal, intellectual activity, and flight from persecution were all instrumental in sending Europeans to explore distant lands. But no force was more universal than the hope of profit and a far better standard of living. And none had a stronger impact on non-Western societies whose homelands were rich sources of gold, silver, furs, and other commodities much sought by European traders. The long reach of Western trade was to affect the dynamics of non-Western societies decades before whites settled among them, sometimes even enriching their cultures before eroding and destroying them. None were more affected than the Huron Indians of what is now Ontario Province in Canada.

The Huron

IN THE EARLY SIXTEENTH CENTURY, the Huron Indians were the northernmost of the Iroquoian-speaking peoples; farmers and traders who occupied the region between Lake Ontario and Lake Huron (Figure 13.1). Their lives were to be radically transformed by the activities of newcomers who had reached the coasts of North America a short time before.

In the year 1506, Portugal levied the first tax on imported Newfoundland codfish. By this time, European fishermen had been operating for at least a generation in the Gulf of St. Lawrence in what is now Canada. In 1634, French master mariner Jacques Cartier made contact with Iroquoian Indians on the St. Lawrence. Seven years later, he landed the first colonists at Quebec. The King of France was interested not only in exploration, but in

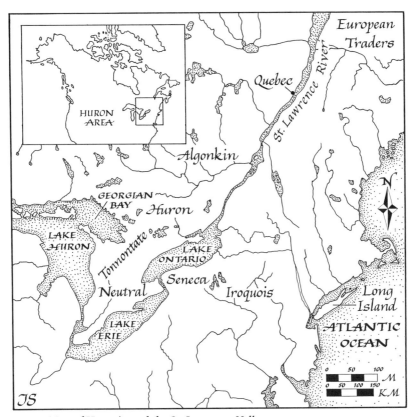

13.1   Map of Huronia and the St. Lawrence Valley

minerals and furs as well. In any event, it was furs that provided the wealth by which Indian societies hundreds of miles inland were transformed.

The name Huron comes from the French word *inure,* meaning a boar's head, and is a slang word for "rustic." The Huron actually called themselves *Wendat,* "islanders" or "dwellers on a peninsula." They were robust, tall people, who were blessed with excellent hearing and vision. Both men and women wore little more than a breechclout during the hot summers, the latter donning short skirts as well. Deer- or beaver-skin leggings and sleeves, as well as a skin cloak, protected their bodies in winter. They decorated their clothes with paint and various trimmings. Feathers, bone beads, and bead belts adorned their bodies, while oil and animal fat protected them from heat and cold. The Huron were proud of their hairstyles. The men wore their hair in all manner of arrangements, while the women kept theirs in a tress that hung down their backs.

The Huron were trained to endure hardship from birth. The French thought of them as an intelligent and content, if somewhat taciturn, people. For their part the Huron were scornful of the garrulous and emotional French, whom they described jokingly as women. These controlled and prosperous Indians lived at the southwestern corner of Georgian Bay on the lake that is now named after them. When the French first settled at Quebec, there were some twenty Huron settlements. The larger, fortified villages were built on higher ground and surrounded with wooden palisades of sharp poles, branches, and bark. Huron longhouses were generally about one hundred feet long and more than twenty feet wide, and housed several families, each with its own compartments and two to a hearth. The French complained bitterly about the Huron's noisy, smoky, and crowded houses. The Indians were oblivious to lice and dirt, belched freely while eating, and cleaned their hands on a passing dog or on their own hair.

Like their Iroquoian neighbors to the south, the Huron were maize, bean, and squash farmers (Figure 13.2). The women were the agriculturists. They also collected wild plants, while the men caught large numbers of whitefish, trout, and other lake fish, and hunted deer. The Huron lived near the northern limits of viable maize cultivation, but were able to grow sufficient surplus grain for them to trade maize as well as luxuries for fish and furs with hunter-gatherer groups to the north. This gave them a unique place in the regional economy, for they provided vital commodities to people living many miles away and augmented their own economy at the same time. Control over trade routes was an important way in which individuals could gain wealth and attain status within their tribes. The Huron regarded trade as a reciprocal act, deeply embedded in their complex network of social relations. So they cultivated good relations with friendly neighbors, forming a confederacy that protected their commerce from outsiders. Their success as traders depended on their abilities at getting on with their trading partners, especially those like the northern hunters, who had economies complementary to their own. They took considerable care to eliminate competition from rival traders. Thus, when the French arrived, the Huron simply regarded them as new, albeit powerful, trading partners. They thought it entirely logical to develop the same sort of trading alliance with the newcomers as they had enjoyed with their neighbors for centuries. It was this policy that enabled the French and Huron to trade successfully with one another for some time, without any harm being done to local society.

Gentle and controlled in their dealings with one another, the Huron took out their frustrations and hatreds on hostile neighbors and prisoners of war. Warfare was an inescapable part of Indian life. Feuds, fed by the requirement for blood revenge, agriculture, social and political organization, and religious beliefs, so affected society that war can be described as an endemic condition.

13.2   Huron Indians planting their fields, by Joseph-François Lafitau, Moeurs des sauvages amériquains *(1724); a highly inaccurate depiction copied from Theodore de Bry's famous paintings of Florida Indians, 1564–5*

Only compelling reasons like trade led to prolonged peace. The Huron's Iroquois-speaking neighbors were organized in a series of tribes, the most famous among them the Five Nations, a league made up of the Seneca, Cayuga, Onondaga, Oneida, and Mohawk. The five nations likened their territory to a vast longhouse that straddled their homelands. The Seneca were engaged in a prolonged blood feud with their Huron neighbors, where a constant state of revenge for individual killings led to warfare most summers.

Sometimes a band of warriors would besiege an enemy village, taking prisoners and lingering until reinforcements arrived. There were individual raids, too, for as with the Aztecs, prowess in war was a way to acquire status and prestige. The ultimate such achievement was to capture an enemy warrior in battle, a captive who was taken home and adopted or, more often, tortured to death. His body was dismembered and consumed in acts of ritual cannibalism. The entire act of torture was a deeply religious act, in which the people vented their hatred of the victim, and the prisoner had a last chance to prove his courage.

These, then, were the people who lived inland of the new French colony at Quebec, people whose relationships with friendly neighbors were based on reciprocal trading. This trade augmented everyone's economy, so it was inevitable that the Huron, as leaders in this centuries-old endeavor, should become the close trading partners of the French downstream. Many American Indian groups had their lifeways totally disrupted by trade with Europeans. But the Huron fared otherwise. For centuries they had traded agricultural products with their neighbors. Now they acquired new and powerful trading partners, whom they treated as equals.

The Fur Trade

THE HURON HAD NO DIRECT CONTACT with the French until the early seventeenth century. But they were aware of contacts between their eastern neighbors and French fur traders, simply because they were the conduits for furs collected and traded over a huge area of the interior. Excavations on the Draper site at Toronto International Airport chronicle some of the effects on Huron life. The Draper village was founded in the fifteenth century, before Europeans were penetrating the St. Lawrence. During the next thirty-five to fifty years, the settlement expanded from a small village of some five hundred and fifty people into a sizable town with more than two thousand inhabitants. Ten months of excavations revealed five expansions of the palisaded settlement. The Draper people added new longhouses as neighboring villages abandoned their old sites and joined the growing town. As the settlement expanded, it seems that warfare increased, for hundreds of burned and broken human bones came from the excavations. There can be little doubt that these radical changes in the Draper settlement were associated with constant warfare with Iroquoian neighbors downstream.

Why did several scattered Huron villages apparently come together into a single settlement? Undoubtedly, they were concerned with mutual protection. Warfare had always been important to the Huron, but now, with the advent of Europeans, control of trade and furs became all important. By coming together in large settlements, Huron chieftains could not only protect their interests more effectively, but they could also call up much larger numbers of warriors at short notice.

The technological changes that resulted in Huron society were probably minimal. Huron settlements had been scattered over a wide area. Now the Indians moved into larger towns, most of them strategically placed for fur trading. As the sixteenth century wore on, the Huron confederacy became larger and larger and came into increasing conflict with its Iroquoian counterpart to the south and east. At the same time the French fur traders began supplying knives, hatchets, and other weapons to their trading partners. They supplied weapons for totally pragmatic reasons, partly to stave off the threat from the vengeful and jealous Iroquoians to the south, but also to cement mutually profitable trading relationships. The fur traders also tried to make direct contact with the Huron and other interior groups. Some Huron war parties visited Quebec in about 1609. A formal alliance was concluded with the French seven years later.

Between 1609 and 1615, the Huron confederacy developed a close trading relationship with the French that kept control of the trade in the hands of traditional chiefs, yet gave every tribe in the confederacy the right to deal with the foreigners. Champlain himself visited Huron country and concluded the alliance. The Indians were happy with the treaty, for it seemed to give them license to trade freely and safely with the French, to the tune of as many as 10,000 beaver pelts annually. The French committed themselves to assist the Huron in times of war, feeling that this would help stabilize the political situation in the interior. In reality, this assistance was little more than a handful of armed Europeans who wintered among the Huron with their authorization. Traveling Frenchmen with firearms also protected Indian traders as they made their way downstream, so that direct French contact with the Huron had a considerable stabilizing effect on local warfare.

The growing European demand for furs meant that more and more Huron men were engaged in the trade. Perhaps between 200 to 500 carried furs to the St. Lawrence each year, while as many as 300 to 400 people worked in the intertribal trade. The Huron were able to expand their prehistoric trading network with apparent ease, but they seem to have done so not with European goods, but with existing agricultural products and by intensifying their own collecting activities. They never became totally dependent on European artifacts, as did some people downstream, for they continued to manufacture pottery, stone axes, and birch bark canoes. But their traders craved iron tools, arrowheads to pierce local slat armor, and metal kettles. The Huron were never able to obtain enough European goods; indeed, they stole as many as they could. Only a few missionaries and traders lived among the Indians, none of whom had the political or persuasive power to challenge established ways, even if he wanted to. The main problem the Huron had was not adjusting to Europeans, rather, it was adapting to their trade goods—and this in the absence of firearms, which were contraband.

The Feast of the Dead

THE CHANGES WROUGHT BY INDIRECT contacts with Europeans were such that Huron culture was not so much disrupted as given the opportunity to realize a fuller potential. More and more Huron settlements moved to the shores of the lake, presumably in response to the demands of the fur trade. They increased their agricultural production, too, for the non-farmers to the north would trade furs for grain. But the greatest changes were within society itself.

The fur trade enhanced the power and prestige of the chiefs, who profited from their control of the trading networks. They fulfilled social obligations by redistributing surplus imports through society as a whole. As the trade intensified, so did the social and economic distinctions between the leaders of Huron society and the rest of the confederacy population. By the 1630s, Jesuit missionaries were talking of nobles and commoners in Huron villages. But there was no major disruption of society, for those who became wealthy were those who already possessed social prestige from their traditional positions within the Huron political structure. This is not to say that there were no strains on Huron society. Undoubtedly there were, but they were not yet sufficient to cause a breakdown in traditional structures or values.

The fur trade also enriched Huron cultural life. The Huron made much more use of metal, not only for small artifacts, but also to create plaques and effigy ornaments that could be worn or sewn on clothing. Their artisans created fine bone ornaments like decorated combs, and carved human and animal effigy pipes in stone and clay. But the main impact of the wealth from the fur trade was on ceremonial life, especially on festivals like the Feast of the Dead. This ceremony was held every ten or twelve years, perhaps when large villages moved their locations. The Feast of the Dead was originally a community ritual, but assumed great importance in the early seventeenth century as a symbolic way of promoting unity among the various tribes of the confederacy.

The Feast of the Dead lasted for about ten days. The first eight were spent collecting bodies from local cemeteries for reburial (Figure 13.3). All corpses except the most recently deceased were stripped of flesh and skin and the robes in which they had been buried, which were burned. The washed and cleaned bones were wrapped in new beaver skins and placed in decorated bags. Then the families feasted and celebrated the dead. On the appointed day, processions of mourners carried the dead to the village where the ceremony was to be held. Gifts were exchanged and friendships affirmed at each settlement along the way.

Feasting and dancing continued at the host village, while a large pit some ten feet deep and fifteen feet wide was dug close by and scaffolding was erected around it. Meanwhile, the packages of bones were reopened and mourned over for the last time, then carried to the field where the empty ossuary was waiting. Each village and clan took its proper place and displayed their gifts on poles. The presents remained on view for two hours, a chance for each clan and village to show not only its piety, but also its wealth. A signal was given. Each village then hung its bone parcels on an assigned section of the scaffolding cross poles. The chiefs stood high on the platforms and announced the gifts that were given in the names of the dead. In this way, the presents were redistributed throughout the villages, while each family fulfilled its obligations within society.

13.3 The Feast of the Dead, *from Lafitau's Moeurs* des sauvages amériquains *(1724). Much of this is an eighteenth-century artist's macabre image of corpses and skeletons, but the drawing is supposedly based on Jesuit descriptions of a century earlier.*

As twilight came, the pit was lined with fifty beaver robes taken from the presents. Then the recently deceased, still-whole bodies were interred and covered with more robes. Some broken kettles and other artifacts were laid out at the bottom of the pit for the use of the dead souls. The people surrounded the pit all night. The packages of bones and grave goods were emptied into the ossuary at sunrise, while the mourners sent up a great cry of lamentation. A few men stationed in the pit mingled the bodies together with poles so that the burial was truly a communal one, not one of dozens of in-dividuals. The pit was then filled, sand and wooden poles placed at the top, and a shrine erected above all. The feast ended with the distribution of the presents and great happiness, for friendships had been renewed, social bonds strengthened, and the dead provided with a proper, honorable burial.

One cannot overestimate the importance of this ceremony to Huron so-ciety. It provided an important way of promoting unity both within the Hu-ron confederacy and with the Algonquian peoples to the north with whom they traded. The displays of wealth were impressive. The Jesuit missionaries, who worked among the Huron after 1534, counted more than 1,200 presents redistributed or buried with the dead at a feast in 1636. Many of these pre-sents were given to people from allied tribes. European goods, being prestige items, eventually made up a large part of the offerings, so much so that con-siderable quantities of them, albeit often damaged or worn-out items, were buried with the dead and removed from circulation. The result was intensi-fied competition and demand for scarce items with a high prestige value that wore out fast. The fur trade was even further intensified to meet the Indians' hunger for European imports.

Jesuits and Epidemics

BY THE LATE 1620s, THE HURON were enjoying considerable prosperity. Their social and political institutions flourished in the favorable trading environ-ment. They perceived themselves as trading partners with the French. The Indians had lived for more than a century without experiencing the negative aspects of European contact. They had no reason to believe that the situa-tion would ever change.

The political balance on the St. Lawrence was upset by the British cap-ture of Quebec in 1629. The Huron still brought furs to Quebec, but the trade soon declined. The Indians distrusted the English, who refused to police the river against marauding Iroquoians. Soon most of the tribes who had had alliances with the French came to dislike the English, whom they regarded as cowards. Once Quebec was restored to the French in 1632, the situation improved, but the Huron now came under inexorable missionary scrutiny for the first time.

Few Frenchmen lived among the Huron before 1634. Only a handful of missionaries and a few traders came to Huronia, and they were unable to change anything. This was the situation until the Society of Jesus acquired a monopoly on missionary activity among the Huron. The Jesuits had a vast experience of pastoral activity among people as far afield as China, Japan, and South America. They arrived at a time of great social change in France, of re-ligious revival and zealous concern for rechristianizing the lower classes. The zealots who championed religious revival at home were men and women who wanted to reorganize not only society at home, but societies abroad as well. The Jesuits arrived among the Huron just as such efforts were at their height.

The first missionaries to arrive among the Huron had a very utopian view of their work. They had assumed that the Indians would readily accept the Gospel and welcome the institutions of civilization. Thus, the Huron would be converted and embrace French civilization at the same time. The Jesuits were sophisticated in their thinking and quick to understand at least some of the complexities of Huron culture. They soon realized that conversion was one thing, "civilizing" the Indians quite another. Whereas earlier missionaries had planned to settle a large number of French families among the Huron, the Jesuits preferred to isolate the Indians from the evil influences of European life. Instead, they encouraged a policy of French Catholic settlement along the St. Lawrence, and as conversion proceeded, Huron Christian fur traders became the intermediaries between the Huron confederacy and markets downstream. The Jesuits took a close interest in the fur trade, for its profits provided some of the funds for their work, supplementing an annual subvention from the civil authority downstream as well as public donations. They also made use of trading canoes for transport, support, and protection on their way upstream and downstream.

The Jesuits seem to have regarded Indian culture as inferior, although they appear to have been somewhat ambivalent on this point. New missionaries were warned that they were falling into the hands of "barbarous people who care but little for your Philosophy or your Theology.... Jesus Christ is our true greatness; it is He alone and His cross that should be sought in running after these people" (Jaenen 1977, 11). In other words, the missionaries were to bring the Indians to Christ, and accommodate themselves to the realities of Huron culture. Attempts at converting and integrating the Huron into transplanted French communities had been unsuccessful, so the Jesuits planned to convert single villages, then work on the others by example. They spent their first years learning the language and trying to understand local society. They were careful to bring such exotic objects as a magnifying lodestone with them, objects that enhanced their reputation as possessors of supernatural powers. (This, of course, worked against them as well, for the Huron believed that the Jesuits could use these powers not only for good, but also for evil purposes.) The missionaries learned to be ruthless in pressing home any advantage, however minor. When a drought broke after mass, or someone was cured during a missionary visitation, they claimed it was God who had triumphed, not the tribal shamans. As in New Spain, the Catholic emphasis on the liturgy, sacraments, and colorful ceremony made the ceremonial aspects of Christianity attractive to the Indians, too. The Jesuits had infinite patience, for, as one missionary remarked in 1642, "To make a Christian out of a barbarian is not the work of a day.... A great step is gained when one has learned to know those with whom he has to deal; has penetrated their thoughts; has adapted himself to their language, their customs, and their manner of living, and when necessary, has been a Barbarian with them, in order to win them over to Jesus Christ" (Jaenen 1977, 11).

European settlement along the eastern seaboard of North America increased rapidly in the 1630s, bringing a deadly legacy with it—epidemic disease. In 1634, just as the Jesuits returned to Huron country, an epidemic of influenza or measles broke out in the St. Lawrence Valley and spread like wildfire. This affected relatively few Huron, but devastated tribes living further downstream. Few French colonists became ill, so the Indians wondered if the Europeans were using witchcraft to destroy them. Much more severe epidemics struck in 1636 and 1637, killing hundreds, if not thousands, of Huron. The Jesuits sought to exploit the situation by trying to baptize the dying. The Indians turned to their shamans and curing societies instead. When Indians died while missionaries invariably recovered from the same disease, the Jesuits claimed supernatural powers. When they insisted on conversion as a means of controlling the disease, the Huron snatched desperately at the thought that Christianity might be a curing society, one they could join while retaining their former spiritual ties. They were amazed when the Jesuits would tolerate no other faith, for their own religion was very accommodating of other beliefs. Inevitably, the Indians thought the missionaries were practicing witchcraft. Hostility towards the Jesuits increased, and they were in danger of their lives. What saved them was the fur trade. The Huron were so dependent on European trade goods that any disruption of trade by the killing of the Quebec government's official representatives was unthinkable. What they did not realize was that it really would not have mattered, for the trade was just as important to the French. Under the circumstances, the Jesuits were expendable. Furs were not.

At first, European trade goods were prestigious novelties to the Huron, but as time went on they became psychologically essential to their economy, so much so that they were unable to suspend trade with Quebec whenever they wished, as they had done in earlier years. Thus, they could no longer function with the French as equals, for their military and trading alliance had become a mechanism compelling them to accept strangely behaving missionaries in their midst. The Huron were stuck between a rock and a hard place, for they could only trade with the French. Their Iroquoian foes lay between them and the Dutch in the Hudson Valley to the south. In 1639, smallpox spread through the St. Lawrence Valley, killing thousands of Indians. The Jesuits had made considerable progress in the intervening years, but the new epidemic resurrected old hostilities against the Jesuits as traditional Indian curing societies enjoyed a new popularity.

By 1640, the Huron had lost over half their population to European diseases. Through their heavy reliance on European trade goods, they had lost their freedom of action. The new diseases attacked mostly children and old people, so the Huron found themselves with fewer young people to train as warriors to protect their villages. Many experienced artisans, shamans, counselors, and village elders perished in the epidemics, too. The loss of these people was an even more serious blow, for they were those who conducted major rituals and ceremonies, and had the most experience of dealing with the Jesuits. Many of these older people died before they could pass on the traditional lore that was such an important part of tribal life. The net result was an even greater dependence on the French, and even less will to resist the inroads of the Jesuits. As for the latter, they believed that God's divine hand was behind the epidemics that reduced the Indian population of the St. Lawrence Valley by 50 percent in less than a decade.

The drastic population decline had a serious effect on the Huron's trading activities. If the fur trade was to be maintained even at its existing level, then a much higher proportion of the labor force had to be engaged in trading and transportation of pelts, as well as the agricultural production needed to pay for them. The Huron were at a disadvantage by living upstream. Unlike the Iroquoians, and other hostile neighbors, they had to travel long distances through enemy territory to sell their pelts. Thus, they were forced to move in large parties and relied more and more on the French for their military protection. So the balance of political power tipped in favor of the Iroquoians, for the Huron were dependent on French goodwill for their safety. By this time, Iroquoians demands for European goods had reached the point where they were looking for new sources of beaver pelts outside their own territories. Unlike the Huron, who were expert traders with dozens of neighboring groups, the Iroquoians were mediocre merchants. They were, however, skillful warriors and diplomats whose only strategy for expanding trade was that of military force. The Iroquoians increased the scale of their attacks on the Huron in the mid-1640s, so that no one was safe in the fields at any season of the year. Instead of small-scale ambushes, the warriors attacked large villages where the fur pickings were larger. No longer was warfare relegated to blood feuds and minor quarrels; it became the justification for robbery on a large scale. The Huron, with their manpower scattered over wide-ranging trade routes, were ill-equipped to resist attacks mounted with firearms obtained by trade with the Dutch. This was economic warfare, desultory looting that accompanied drastic changes within Huron society at the same time.

The Dispersal of the Huron

"THE JESUITS MAY HAVE KNOWN that it was impossible, under the circumstances, to be both a good Christian and a good Huron. Nevertheless, in accordance with their own values, they placed the salvation of souls ahead of preventing divisions in Huron society" (Trigger 1972, 2:724). The missionaries' hold on Huronia was strengthened greatly with the founding of the mission settlement of Sainte-Marie in 1640 (Figure 13.4). At first the Jesuits had hoped they could encourage Huron families to settle close to the mission, beginning a process of "reduction," resettlement of the type that had been so successful (and traumatic to the Indians) in Mexico, and later in California. But the Huron were so devoted to their own villages that small Jesuit residences were established in the major settlements instead.

By now the missionaries had an impressive command of the Huron language and of Indian beliefs. They used their knowledge to play on the fears of the Indians, painting vivid pictures of hell and damnation. The missionaries lavished converts with gifts, provided them with food in times of famine, and even sold them muskets. Then they played on relatives' fears of being separated from their kinsmen after death by baptizing dying warriors. Often the entire family would convert as a result. All these strategies achieved considerable success, especially those that yielded some tangible benefits, like trading privileges. The Jesuits used these same material blandishments to encourage Indians to undergo prolonged instruction, upping the spiritual ante for baptism to new levels.

All of this caused major strains on traditional society. Some converts felt that their new religion relieved them of long-established material responsibilities, such as gift giving. As a result, they found themselves in serious trouble. Most conversions were a matter of strict self-interest; few stemmed from genuine intellectual curiosity. And few people understood the rationale behind the new religion. Concepts such as the Last Judgment and the Resurrection were completely alien to Huron culture. Many Indians were hopelessly confused when they tried to distinguish between right and wrong in Jesuit eyes. The missionaries believed Huron society worked well enough, but that it was theologically primitive. They realized Christianity was a state religion, far from appropriate for a tribal society. So they tried to alter the political makeup of Huron society.

Converts were precious to the Jesuits, so they encouraged Christian families to avoid contacts with pagans. Sainte-Marie was the center of Christian social activity, where the Christians supported and encouraged one another. This new sense of Christian identity affected Huron society at every level. Some Christians refused to be buried in village cemeteries, a decision that struck at the very core of Huron belief—the expression of community solidarity. No

13.4   Modern reconstruction of the Jesuit settlement of Sainte-Marie (courtesy of the Ministry of Tourism and Recreation, Sainte-Marie among the Huron, Midland, Ontario, Canada)

longer did serious Christians participate in traditional ceremonies. Even friendships between believer and pagan were out of the question. The more socially prominent the convert, the more serious the effect on local society. Village headmen who became Christians had to abandon their traditional duties, described by the zealous Jesuits as "obeying the Devil, presiding over hellish ceremonies, and exhorting young people to dances, feasts, and most infamous lewdness" (Trigger 1976, 2:713).

By 1645, the Christian Huron were a faction apart. The traditionalists responded by accusing them of witchcraft, especially when they refused to take part in healing rites and dream ceremonies. They used threats, promises, and bribes to persuade converts to renounce their new beliefs. Sometimes they were successful, as when the shamans pointed out what harm Christianity was doing Huron life. But many Christians were so alienated from their society that they were immune to such arguments. Some of the resistance took peculiar forms; a nativist cult claimed that a Christian Huron woman had returned from the dead to warn the people that the French tortured the deceased when they reached heaven. The story implied that non-Christians would enjoy a carefree existence after death. The growing distrust between Christian and non-Christian made political decisions more complicated and interfered with the military effectiveness of the confederacy. In their zeal to place the conversion of the heathen before all other considerations, the Jesuits sowed another seed of the Huron's eventual destruction.

In contrast to the Huron, the Iroquoians were still practicing their traditional religion and were as yet little affected by the inroads of Christianity. In 1646, the Seneca made a conscious decision to declare war on their Huron neighbors with the specific objective not of robbing them, but of dispersing them. The motives for the Seneca decision are unclear, but the strategy may have been aimed at acquiring a northern hinterland in Huron country, where the Seneca could hunt freely. Iroquoian pressure on the Huron increased sharply, precipitating a confrontation between Christians and radical traditionalists. The latter now thought of renouncing the alliance with the French, expelling the Jesuits, and allying themselves with the Iroquoians, thereby restoring their own political influence.

The confrontation became a power play between Christians and non-Christians. Unfortunately for the radicals, most Huron, whatever their beliefs, feared the Iroquoians more than the French, so the Jesuits were permitted to stay. The Jesuits rejoiced in their victory, as most of the people looked to them for leadership in the uncertain future. In any event, their secular guidance was weak and indecisive. The more conservative traditionalists felt a growing sense of apathy and resignation. Many made a personal compromise with the Iroquoians. While the Jesuits triumphed, few Huron remained who were willing, or indeed able, to provide leadership or assume responsibility for the destiny of their own society. The Iroquoians attacked in force in 1647, 1648, and 1649. The confederacy dissolved in chaos. Two Jesuits were captured in 1649 and tortured to death by warriors, some of whom were undoubtedly Huron allied to the enemy. The missionaries abandoned Sainte-Marie and burned it, retreating to the safety of an island. The winter of 1649 caused terrible suffering among the surviving Huron. The Jesuits fed all they could with imported grain, so much so that they were now called "fathers of the Huron people." Even so, many Indians died from starvation and malnutrition. Others were so weak they could not bury their dead.

By the summer of 1651, the once prosperous Huron homeland was desolate and largely uninhabited. Only one Huron tribe, the Tahontaenrat, escaped complete destruction. Individuals and families scattered in all directions. Some dispersed towards the western Great Lakes. Many others assumed new identities as members of the Five Nations and became Iroquoians themselves.

A group of about three hundred reached Quebec with Jesuit assistance, where they were settled on land near the town. Even there the Huron were harassed by the Iroquoians, for the French did little to protect them. Many of the Indians became embittered with the French. Others still cherished the hope they would return to their homeland. But in 1667 the French made peace with the Iroquoians. The surviving Huron settled at a number of villages near the north bank of the St. Lawrence, where they have survived to this day. In the eighteenth century, these Christian Huron adopted European agriculture. So strongly did they identify with their new homeland that they would show late-nineteenth-century visitors the place where their ancestors had "emerged from the soil." Both the Huron language and their clan and tribal organization vanished more than a century ago.

The dispersal of the Huron was the final chapter in a narrative of cultural change that had affected them for at least two centuries. Thus, European contact was merely a new dynamic in a process of change that had been going on for centuries. At first the Huron adjusted to changed conditions by adapting them to their own institutions. Unlike the Iroquoians, who often obtained European goods by raiding for them, the Huron took advantage of the fur trade to expand a long-established trading confederacy. Their traditional culture and ceremonial life were enriched as a result, partly because those in political and religious authority before European contact were those who benefited most from the new trade. It was not until after 1634, when the Jesuits took a hand in Huron life and European diseases had decimated the Indians, that traditional culture came apart. By excluding any Europeans other than themselves and their employees, the Jesuits were able to direct Huron society in the ways they wished. They believed every Huron converted was a soul saved from eternal damnation. Any means that achieved conversion were acceptable—including the manipulation of the fur trade and the officials that directed it from the French end.

Unfortunately, the Jesuits failed to realize that Huron religious beliefs permeated every aspect of Indian life. Huron beliefs regulated and validated every aspect of quotidian activity, however trivial. The Indians were tolerant of other faiths and rituals, so much so that they were puzzled by an intolerant religion that brooked no opposition. They were unable to muster an effective resistance to the new beliefs, because they did not understand the demands these beliefs made on them. The Jesuits realized they could only convert the Huron by making drastic changes in their traditional culture, but considered such changes to be of minimal importance when weighed against their ultimate goal—to save souls. For this goal, they would even endanger their own lives. The Jesuits cared little about the factionalism and social tension that the conversion of many Indians caused the Huron, which proved just as decimating to the Indian population as terrible epidemics and warfare. By the time the Iroquoians mounted their final attacks, the Huron were so weak that they were unable to organize a serious defense against the invaders. Furs and Christianity had proved fatal to a people who, to all intents and purposes, no longer exist as a cultural identity today.

CHAPTER 14

Northwest Coast Indians

It appears that the natives are such intelligent traders that should you be in the least lavish or inattentive in forming bargains they will so enhance the value of the furs as not only to exhaust your present stock but also to injure if not to ruin, any future adventure...

John Meares, 1797 fur trader,
quoted in Robin Fisher, *Contact and Conflict* (1977)

THE FUR TRADE WAS NOT TO bring Europeans to the northwest coasts of North America until 125 years after Huron society collapsed. The initial contact was from the Pacific, for fur traders did not cross the barrier of the Canadian Rockies until much later. The ubiquitous James Cook sighted the wooded coast of Oregon on 9 March 1777, but it was not until 29 March that he was able to approach the western shores of Vancouver Island and cast anchor in Nootka Sound, near an Indian summer village (Figure 14.1). He was to remain for a month, making repairs to his spars and taking on water. Canoe loads of Indians greeted the ships as they were towed into the sound (Figure 14.2). There were speeches and offers to trade. The local people smelled of fish, oil, and wood smoke. Their legs were bowed from constant sitting in canoes. "Their faces were bedaub'd with red & black Paint and Grease, in no regular manner, but as their fancies led them; their hair was clott'd also with dirt, & to make themselves either fine or frightful many put on the hair the down of young birds or plaited it in sea weed or thin strips of bark dyed red; the Dress of some was a loose skin thrown around their Shoulders, & which

237

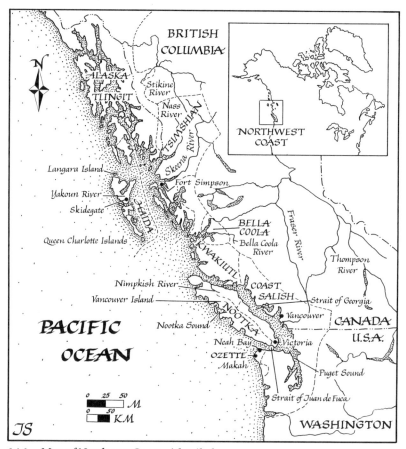

14.1   *Map of Northwest Coast with tribal areas*

was not seemingly intended to hide their private parts, which in many were exposed" (Beaglehole 1969, 302). Woven basketry hats like inverted flower-pots kept the constant rain off the Indians' faces.

Cook's ships were not the first to visit the Pacific Northwest. Sir Francis Drake may have ventured this far north, and two Spanish vessels had traded furs and carved wooden boxes with canoes off Langara Island near the Queen Charlotte Islands and Nootka Sound itself two years before. But these were only transitory contacts. The arrival of Cook's ships had amazed the Indians, who, oral traditions tell us, thought that the ships were vast fish "come alive with people." Once they realized they were crewed by human beings, they debated how to treat their visitors. The Nootka called them *mamathini* ("their houses move over the water"). They also noticed there were no women

14.2 *Nootka Indians greeting Cook (courtesy of the Trustees of the British Museum)*

among them, a trait that set them apart from other known Indian societies. In the event, the Nootka treated Cook and his men as members of a distant tribe, a potential enemy, from whom one could legitimately steal anything and whom one could kill. But their first concern was trade.

The Nootka were soon totally preoccupied with trading. The men offered dozens of furs, weapons, and bladders full of seal oil—even some human skulls and dried hands. These latter "appeared to have been lately cut off as the flesh was not reduced to an horny substance but raw" (Beaglehole 1969, 303). The Indians waved aside trinkets such as beads. All they wanted were metal objects. The Europeans' iron knives were vastly superior to the few metal tools the Indians possessed. By the time the ships left they were literally stripped of every scrap of brass, hundreds of nails, chisels—even pewter plates. Cook was forced to mount a constant guard, for the Indians stole anything of value on sight. Even his gold watch vanished from under the very eyes of the guards. Fortunately it was recovered undamaged. The seamen obtained huge piles of bear and sea otter skins in exchange for all this metal. They were to prove a superb investment for the crew.

Cook spent hours observing the trade in progress. He noticed that the local people were curiously possessive about the ships (Figure 14.3). They defied any newcomers who came to trade from elsewhere, forcing them to bargain through their chiefs. All the trading activity was accompanied by prolonged oratorical harangues, harmonious singing, and elaborate dances conducted by masked figures. Although Cook seems to have got on well with the Nootka, he commented that he had never "met with Indians who had such high notions of every thing the Country produced being their exclusive property as these; the very wood and water we took on board they at first wanted us to pay for" (Beaglehole 1969, 303). His many successors were to

14.3 Cook's ships in Nootka Sound, by John Webber (courtesy of the Trustees of the British Museum)

find the Indians efficient and expert traders, with the same strongly developed notions of property and payment for services rendered.

On 26 April 1778, the ships weighed anchor, surrounded by singing and dancing Nootka in their canoes. The Indians "importuned us much to return to them again," and provided a good supply of furs as parting gifts. The seamen put them in the hold and forgot about the pelts for more than a year, until they reached the Kamchatka Peninsula in Siberia on their long way home after Cook's death in Hawaii. When the local merchants heard that the ships carried furs, they flocked to the quayside. The prices Cook's men were offered for their furs were astounding. And these astronomical returns were exceeded in China, where the seamen received as much as $120 for a single otter pelt. The demand for skins was insatiable.

Rumors of the abundant fur markets of the Northwest Coast were confirmed with the publication of the official account of Cook's third voyage in 1784. With such fabulous prices as $120 per pelt in prospect, it was not long before fur traders were nosing into the sounds and estuaries of the Pacific Northwest. The first ships found it easy to accumulate profitable cargoes. Initially the Indians were astounded by the sight of ships so much larger than their canoes. But once their curiosity was satisfied, they fell over one another to trade with the strangers. When Captain George Dixon arrived in Cloak Bay in July, 1787, he found himself deluged with furs. The Indians were so eager to trade that they actually threw cloaks and furs on the deck of his ship without any preliminaries. Within a short half-hour, Dixon obtained over 300 furs. After a month in the Queen Charlotte Islands, he sailed away with over 1,800 on board. Other skippers did just as well, if not better. John Kendrick, master of the American ship *Columbia*, bartered 200 pelts for a chisel each in 1789—the entire transaction took just a few minutes. The pioneers' profits in China were enormous. In 1785, one skipper netted $20,000 for 560 sea otter pelts, while Dixon's earnings exceeded $54,500 on 2,500 skins. It was, wrote Nathaniel Portlock, Dixon's associate, "the most profitable and lucrative employ that the enterprising merchant can possibly engage in" (Fisher 1977, 4).

The early fur skippers soon learned the hard way that the Indians were clever and hard-nosed traders. Not for them the cheap trinkets that other peoples were more than satisfied to obtain. Carpenters to a man, the Indians used the burgeoning trade to obtain iron tools, especially chisels, knives, and axes, woodworking artifacts that were much more effective than the stone and bone tools they used before European contact. The Indians bargained long and hard, with the inevitable result that prices for furs rose sharply. The enormous profits of the early voyages were never repeated. By 1795, the going prices were over 100 percent higher than they had been three years before. But by then firearms were in wide use and there was somewhat of a glut in European trade goods.

The Indians spent little time wondering about the nature of the white strangers in large ships. They soon accepted the Europeans as fellow human beings who might have some strange customs, but who were interested in trade, as they themselves were. From the outset they treated the strangers as no more than equal partners in two-way trade. They used furs to satisfy essential needs in their own lives, especially for iron tools to replace their own less-sturdy artifacts. Once this demand had been more or less satisfied, the Indians started trading for cloth and blankets, substitutes for the furs they now exported at every opportunity. Iron tools, lengths of cloth, and blankets—all had the advantage of being commodities that were easily counted and displayed. As such they not only filled gaps in the indigenous culture, but also filled an important role in the Indians' elaborate ceremonies at which their wealth was displayed and exchanged. Of course, the fashions of the trade changed, especially in later times when people demanded firearms or alcohol, but the maritime fur trade probably played a vital role in enriching the indigenous culture of the area. In this respect, initial contact between Europeans and locals in the Pacific Northwest may have been unique compared with the experience of peoples elsewhere in the Pacific.

Pages of the early captains' journals are filled with complaints about the hard bargains driven by the Indians. They would examine every object with minute care and reject faulty merchandise without hesitation. They were impervious to flattery, knew exactly what they wanted, and had no hesitation in playing one ship off against another. The canoes would move from one ship to the next in the same anchorage, with those aboard comparing prices and refusing to hand over furs for anything but exactly the object they wanted. The first ships of the season would often hasten to pay the prevailing prices before their competitors raised them even higher.

"The Indians are sufficiently cunning to derive all possible advantage from competition, and will go from one ship to another, and back again, with assertions of offers made to them, which have no foundation in truth, and showing themselves to be as well versed in the tricks of the trade as the greatest adepts," wrote one captain (Fisher 1977, 8). This comment, coming from an experienced American trading skipper, was no mean compliment. At first, the Indians had every advantage on their side. They controlled the sources of furs, could survive very comfortably without the visitors' trade goods, and had all the time in the world to bargain. The fur traders were obliged to remain at anchor for months in the same bay, to a great extent at the mercy of the local chiefs. Most transactions were channeled through a relatively few individuals or villages. They had the patience—and the time—to wait for days to obtain their asking price. They would sit on the decks of the ships and display supreme indifference as to whether they sold their furs or not. The Indians' advantage was not to last for long and evaporated fast as soon as European and American political and colonial interests arrived on the coast.

The power wielded by those chiefs fortunate enough to control an outlet of the fur trade was enormous. The visiting captains had to treat them with deference and coddle them with lavish hospitality. A close understanding of Indian customs and one's ceremonial obligations was essential to survival in the fur trade. Particularly important were reciprocal gifts, which were exchanged to seal a transaction or which were part of the singing and dance ceremonies that accompanied any major trading activity. "A man ought to be endowed with an uncommon share of patience to trade with any of these people," wrote skipper Joseph Ingraham on a visit to the coast in 1791 (Fisher 1977, 9).

As the trade in furs became more intense, the chiefs who controlled the outlets began to barter for pelts with people further inland. One reason they were such adept traders was that they had been trading among themselves for centuries. Complicated long-distance trade routes linked people living all along the Northwest Coast and far inland. Seashells, ornaments, and basic commodities were passed from one community to the next over cumulatively enormous distances. These bartering contacts were an invaluable way of acquiring furs from inland tribes. The chiefs acquired furs by exchanging European goods with their less fortunate neighbors. As always, they drove a hard bargain, buying furs at prices that were 200 percent lower than their value on the coast. Thus, the influence of the maritime fur trade was felt throughout the Northwest Coast, even among communities far from major trade outlets. The effect was a considerable enrichment of local luxury goods as well as iron tools and clothing.

Profits declined rapidly after 1800 both because of high costs on the coast and falling prices in China. The only way to make a profit was to return to the same area again and again over a period of years and to deal honestly with the local chiefs. A high proportion of the three hundred or more ships that worked the coast returned for a second or third voyage, most of them trading with a very few Indian chiefs.

The enrichment of Northwest Coast culture that resulted from the maritime fur trade is hard for us to document, since visiting traders tended to deal with relatively few individuals, chiefs like the Maquinnas of the Nootka. The first Maquinna had probably assumed the chieftainship of the area around Nootka Sound at about the time of first European contact. He was feted and flattered by visitor after visitor, and played a key role in the abortive Spanish settlement of the area. By 1803, the Maquinna family was very wealthy. In that year they were reported to have thrown a potlatch (ceremonial display) where they gave away two hundred muskets, two hundred yards of cloth, a hundred shirts, the same number of looking glasses, and no less than seven barrels of gunpowder.

The Maquinna family was by no means unique. They and their trading colleagues up and down the coast lived in houses filled with wooden boxes stacked with European goods. These valuable assets enabled them to employ traders and hunters to acquire pelts. Their wives and slaves prepared the pelts for sale, economic activities that are thought to have had their effects on the incidence of polygamy among the higher social classes of Indian society. Those with pelts rose to social as well as economic prominence—even those families that had enjoyed no social position whatsoever before European contact. The long-term effects of the maritime fur trade on Indian society were subtle and profound.

Opinions differ as to exactly what these effects were. Many historians argue that the maritime trade had a negative effect on the coastal tribes, and that their lust for furs seriously disrupted the economic and social fabric of the coast. They theorize that European diseases like influenza and venereal infections came ashore from the ships and decimated the local populations. The introduction of firearms, this thesis continues, had a powerful and destructive effect on relations between powerful chiefs and their neighbors. The result was the virtual destruction of Indian society.

Many anthropologists have an entirely different perspective. They argue that the maritime fur trade had a stimulating effect on local culture. They point to the wealth that European ships brought to many chiefs and traders, and the stimulus that the fur trade gave local trading activities. This influx of wealth enriched local cultural traditions, especially wood carving, which played an important role in religious and ceremonial life. The Indians were selective in those aspects of European culture they acquired, as demonstrated by the goods they sought to exchange for furs. Since Europeans and Indians were not competing for the same land or minerals, nor were white people

trying to settle in the Northwest, the effects of the fur trade on Indian society were for the most part relatively beneficial.

Certainly one cannot argue that there were no negative effects on Indian
society at the end of the eighteenth century. There can be no doubt that European sailors did introduce both smallpox and venereal disease into the area
and that chiefs used firearms against their neighbors. One missionary reported in 1829 that the Haida Indians of the Queen Charlotte Islands were
decimated by European disease, but precise statistics are hard to pin down.
Although early European visitors did report seeing abandoned villages, we
cannot be sure whether these were the result of disease or of regular seasonal
movement from one settlement to another. As the demographer Norma
McArthur has pointed out with Pacific island populations, an epidemic will
have the most impact if it strikes hardest at the childbearing segment of the
population. The Northwest Coast populations would soon recover from a
temporary population loss if childbearing women were not too heavily affected. So the exact impact of European diseases on the Northwest Indians
and their culture remains unsubstantiated.

The "Privileged Ones"

AT THE TIME OF EUROPEAN contact, more than 250,000 Indians lived along
the Northwest Coast between the Columbia River and Alaska (Figure 14.4).
They relied very heavily on the ocean and coastal rivers for their livelihood.
The slopes of the great mountain ranges of the interior were covered with
great stands of spruce, cedar, and Douglas fir, trees that were found in abundance throughout the coast. It was from these forests that the Indians obtained timber for their plank canoes and wooden houses, as well as the fine
woods they used for carving totem poles, boxes, and smaller artifacts. Most
human settlement was concentrated on river banks or on the islands and
shores of the coast, where an abundance of fish and sea mammals supported
one of the richest hunter-gatherer cultures on earth.

The Pacific and the rivers that flowed into it provided whales, porpoises,
seals, sea lions, and dozens of fish species. Among these were the halibut, some
of which weighed up to a quarter of a ton. Herring, smelt, and eulachon
(candlefish) swarmed in coastal waters. No less than five species of salmon
appeared in inshore waters each year. Many communities fine-tuned their
lives to maximize the seasonal salmon runs—up to seven a year—when shoals
of migrating fish jammed the rivers as they crowded upstream to spawn. An
apocryphal settler tale claimed that during a salmon run one could walk from
one side of a river to the other on the backs of the fish—without so much as
getting one's feet wet. Shellfish, waterfowl, some game, and vegetables were also
important elements in the Indian diet. The rich and diverse coastal environment

14.4   Nootka man, by John Webber (courtesy of the British Columbia Provincial Museum, Victoria, BC)

provided over three hundred important edible animal species alone, so the people had an abundant cushion of natural resources to fall back on, in addition to the thousands of dried fish they smoked and stored during times of plenty.

With such a diversity of food supplies, even if there were occasional periods of scarcity, it is hardly surprising that the Indians developed an elaborate and complex society. They built large, durable houses, which were clustered

14.5   Inside an eighteenth-century Nootka house (courtesy of the Trustees of the British Museum)

in sizable settlements. Their dugout canoes could carry up to sixty people. Their rich artistic traditions, based on wood carving, basketry, and other skills, have become justly famous. Central and northern Northwest Coast society was organized into social classes and enjoyed a rich ceremonial life. As long as the ecological balance between human needs and available resources was maintained, Northwest Coast society could survive indefinitely, using the simplest of technology.

The damp, oceanic climate of the Northwest Coast provided the Indians with abundant natural resources to create an elaborate material culture with only the simplest of tools. The dense forests of the coastal zone were rich in easily split, straight-grained, softer woods like red and yellow cedar, fir, and spruce. The Northwest Coast carpenters possessed a wide range of tools to fell, split, and work cedar and other soft woods. They had no axes or saws, but did most of their work with adzes and chisels. Their cutting edges were made from tough, polished rocks, seashells, and horn or bone. Long before Captain Cook's time, the Indian carpenters were using iron blades—iron they probably obtained by long-distance trade with Arctic groups. Their knowledge of this invaluable metal accounted for the insatiable demand for iron from European ships. Cedarwood was so easily split into long planks that it was a logical step for the Indians to build substantial plank houses at winter villages and more important locations (Figure 14.5). Their rectangular plank houses had permanent frames, while the wall and roof planks could be removed for use elsewhere. Many families maintained house frames at several locations and simply moved their wall and roof planks from one place to the next loaded across large canoes. Each part of the house was assigned to families of

14.6   *The Haida village of Skidegate, Queen Charlotte Islands, 1884 (photograph by R. Maynard; courtesy of the British Columbia Provincial Museum, Victoria, BC)*

different rank, the spaces usually marked off by piles of wooden boxes, baskets, and other belongings. Some of their finest woodworking artistry was reserved for the canoe, a vessel that had to be not only seaworthy but a strong load carrier capable of moving hut planks, large salmon catches, or entire families and their possessions. The canoe builder was a respected specialist who could build everything from light canoes to large war craft fashioned from specially felled tree trunks and then carved and smoothed carefully. Using their steaming and carving skills, the Northwest Coast carpenters fashioned a magnificent array of wooden artifacts that ranged from large canoes and troughs to bowls, plank boxes, and dozens of smaller objects. They were not content just to make a functional box or simply to erect a rough roof beam. The Northwest Coast carpenters took great pains to make corners symmetrical and to finish off everything carefully, however large or small.

Rich decoration adorned many of the objects made by the Northwest Coast peoples, a heraldic art style that is among the most celebrated of all American Indian art forms. The Northwest Coast wood carvers emphasized themes that depicted family histories and genealogies, and incidents—both real and fictional—that led to the enhancement of the ancestors. Renowned ancestors and mythical animals and humans appear on many boxes and small objects. Perhaps the most famous art objects are the great totem poles, memorials that were once set up in front of villages, as well as commemorative posts and the portal poles attached to house fronts (Figure 14.6). Much of this art, and that on Northwest masks, was formalized—the recounting of family genealogies. But the artists were fully capable of carving magnificent, naturalistic figures and would often modify the shape of a utilitarian object, like a bowl, in order to do so.

The people lived in local groups whose internal and external relationships were determined by kinship ties that regulated the transmission of social status from one generation to the next. The local kin groups lived and worked together and considered themselves the exclusive owners of land and fishing grounds, as well as material possessions and a host of different privileges that ranged from personal names to crests, and from dance ceremonials to songs. Each autonomous local group had its own leader, and looked after its own needs for justice, peace, and war.

The local group itself was divided into "privileged ones" and commoners. There were many slaves as well, who were nothing more than chattels. One was born either a noble or a commoner, but there were precise gradations of rank among both broad classes. Everyone knew exactly what his or her individual ranking was relative to everyone else. These subtleties of rank were easily identified on ceremonial occasions, for the noblest wore the most elaborate clothes and ornaments. Those of highest rank traditionally occupied a special place in the house, often the back wall area. It was they who directed group activities.

The social distinctions provided by the ranking of noble and commoner were modified by close kinship ties that linked the highest and lowest members of society with common bonds. In this way the nobles were not a group apart, who could treat the commoners as they pleased. With so many kinship ties, everyone had a stake in the wealth and privileges of the kin group as a whole. Hereditary rank was important, but it was modified in such a way that the wealthiest and most important people had to share their wealth with others.

Wealth and social prestige were closely related; indeed, the Indians spent a great deal of time accumulating both, like people in our society. But there the resemblance ends, for Northwest Coast society regarded all wealth as the property of local kin groups as a whole rather than individuals. An individual could acquire dozens of pelts or canoes, but in the final analysis all these possessions and, more importantly, houses, lands, and prestige objects, were group property, even if the leader spoke of them as his or her own. The display and conspicuous consumption of this wealth was a primary objective of Northwest Coast life, a means of enhancing the prestige of the group among its neighbors. These displays of wealth, commonly called *potlatches,* played a vital role in Indian life, for they provided a strong unifying force between fellow kinspeople in a social environment where there was every temptation to acquire wealth for oneself.

The potlatch is perhaps the most famous of all Northwest Coast institutions. Indeed the word is synonymous with conspicuous consumption of food and goods. In its original form, the potlatch was a dignified ceremony given by a chief and his kin group, who entertained other chiefs and their groups. The term *potlatch* is a Chinook slang word that means "giving." By no means, however, did all potlatches involve feasting or the giving away of foods. They invariably marked an important event, such as the marriage of an important person, the birth of a noble heir, or the assumption of the right to a title or crest.

In the late eighteenth and much of the nineteenth centuries, potlatches were elaborately planned and staged affairs that involved formal invitations to neighboring groups. An exact protocol surrounded the arrival and seating of the guests in the potlatch house, fully as complicated as that of a diplomatic function in Washington, D.C. Important guests were seated according to rank. Speeches of welcome were recited, crests displayed. Songs and dances commemorated the privileges and ranks about to be sanctified. Some major potlatches paid tribute to a deceased chief, and offerings were made by burning food and other objects. As the new titleholder was introduced, presents were distributed to the guests. The proceedings would end with speeches of thanks, after which the holder was recognized as the official incumbent of the chieftainship or other office in question. A potlatch, therefore was far more than a party; it was an official function, whose proceedings were surrounded by a great deal of ritual and protocol. Those who attended were expected to reciprocate in the future. And when they did, they would honor the ranks that had been sanctified at earlier potlatches. Major potlatches were probably infrequent ceremonies, partly because of a shortage of goods that could be used as gifts. The pattern was to change in later times, when the influx of European trade goods caused a major redistribution of wealth within Indian society. Much of the rich ceremonial life of the Northwest Coast involved the reenactment of myths and constant reinforcement of ranks and titles, a process that involved a redistribution of wealth through society as a whole.

What the first Europeans introduced was a new element of wealth into Northwest Coast society. But European trade goods alone were insufficient to undermine Indian life. It was not until foreigners began to settle in the coastal areas that the structure of Indian society began to fall apart.

European Settlement

BY THE 1830s, THE MARITIME fur trade was dead. The sea otter was almost extinct on the Northwest Coast. The focus of the trade moved ashore, as beaver pelts replaced the otter as the staple commodity. A network of Hudson's Bay Company forts were sited in strategic places where they could interface with established Indian trading networks and communication systems. The Indians would acquire pelts, and company officials tried to buy them at the lowest possible going market price. The local people tolerated the presence of the forts because it paid them to do so, and they had always traded at these spots anyhow. Under these circumstances, the land-based fur trade had little negative effect on traditional culture.

Nevertheless, the permanent local presence of the Company had some long-term effects on Indian society. The steady flood of European trade goods became an integral part of Northwest Coast culture. The individuals who acquired great wealth were often people who in earlier times had enjoyed relatively low status. Their newly acquired wealth gave them power that was resented by other members of society, especially those with less access to trade goods. Such social changes placed stress on Indian society, even if many powerful chiefs were the major traders, since they had been associated with important trade relationships in earlier times, relationships that were now often intensified.

Some groups, notably the Haida of the Queen Charlotte Islands, began to suffer when sea otters became scarce. So they turned to other sources of income, cultivating potatoes which they sold to mainland Indians and to European trading posts. As early as 1825 the Haida were in the curio and art business, selling fine carvings and model canoes along the length of the coast. These "curiosities" were much in demand in Eastern cities and enabled the Haida to regain some of their lost wealth and prestige. The Haida were also able to cash in on their woodworking skills as a result of the increased wealth among their neighbors. Instead of languishing in neglect, Indian ceremonial life acquired a new complexity in which wood carving played an important part. The great totem poles erected with elaborate ceremony were carved with newly acquired metal tools.

The prolonged contact between Company traders and the Indians was, to a great extent, mutually beneficial. Northwest Coast culture was greatly enriched, and the Company made a handsome profit. The local people flourished, although there were reports of occasional outbreaks of smallpox, venereal disease, and measles that raised the Indian mortality rate. Northwest Coast society was undergoing cultural change, but it was not change that threatened traditional fishing grounds or the basic structure of Indian society. All this changed rapidly with an influx of European settlers into the Northwest after the Treaty of Washington established the boundaries between the United States and Canada in 1846.

In 1849 the British government granted the Hudson's Bay Company Vancouver Island, on the condition that it be developed as a colony for settler immigrants. In 1851, James Douglas, the company factor for the small settlement at Fort Victoria, became the reluctant governor of the new colony.

He took up office at a time when race relations were deteriorating badly south of the border. Hundreds of settlers were pouring into Washington State and slaughtering Indians on sight. Douglas, with many years of fur trading behind him, was deeply concerned about the Americans. He was, he said, "more suspicious of their designs, than of the wild natives of the forest." For years, he tried to avoid the same racial hatred in the colony, realizing that the unfamiliarity of the settlers with Indian customs was a potential source of serious trouble.

The colonization of Vancouver Island proceeded slowly until 1858. Early in that year Victoria was a sleepy little village with fewer than 300 inhabitants. By the end of the summer, its permanent population of settlers numbered over 3,000, with up to 6,000 people camped around the town at times. The reason was simple: gold had been discovered near the junction of the Thompson and Fraser rivers. A flood of American gold prospectors flooded into company territory. Governor Douglas did all he could to prevent bloodshed between the Indians and the miners, but was almost powerless to prevent violence in the face of the frantic lust for gold.

Douglas was well aware that drastic action was necessary, both to prevent trouble with the Indians and to stop the Americans from annexing company territory. The slow colonization of Vancouver Island had already led to difficulties with the Indians. Both the Indians and Douglas's administration realized that a new relationship was being forged between them. The Indians were beginning to feel the force of English law, which adjudicated not only crimes against the community, but internal quarrels as well. Indians felt they were now coming under closer social control. Settlers began to compete with them for land that had been theirs for centuries. Douglas negotiated eleven treaties with the Indians, under which they surrendered parcels of land in exchange for a few blankets. They were allowed to hunt on unoccupied land, but could only retain possession of land upon which their villages and houses were actually built. These treaties gave the settlers possession of most of southern Vancouver Island in perpetuity.

Perhaps the most important variable in the new situation was the settlers' attitudes to the Indians, attitudes fostered by ignorance and stereotyped American visions of Indians as hostile and treacherous. Feelings of racial superiority were much stronger in Britain and elsewhere than they had been a few decades earlier. Evolutionary doctrines were in the air, and many scientists believed that non-Western societies were merely cultures that had not evolved to the pinnacle of Victorian civilization. As a result, many settlers believed that the Indians were doomed to extinction. One visitor to the Northwest Coast argued that a "succession of races, like a rotation of crops, may be necessary to turn the earth to the best possible account" (Fisher 1977, 88). The settlers' view of the Indian was almost invariably disparaging. It was easy for them to convince themselves that there was little point in preserving the Indians' way of life.

One only has to read a sample of contemporary accounts of Indian life to get the point. The Indians enjoyed "disgusting ceremonies," were superstitious, dishonest, and incapable of a hard day's work. Settler attitudes to the Indians were founded not only in ignorance, but also in fear and insecurity. The colonists were afraid that their fragile society would collapse and that they would revert to the level of the Indians. "Going native" was a fate worse than death for many settlers, one to be avoided at all costs. The pioneers felt outnumbered and vulnerable to attack. Many of them were adjusting to completely new lives in an alien environment, alienated from their own social milieus. They were intolerant of others, and tended to believe that their own civilization was vastly superior to that of the "savages" around them. While the fur traders had worked with the local people in easy tolerance, the settlers hated Indians and competed with them. The inevitable losers were the Indians.

The fundamental conflict between the Indians and settlers was over land. Colonists everywhere acquired land. It was their means to wealth and fortune, their stake in a new country. The Indians had completely different attitudes to their territory. Their traditional hunting and fishing grounds were essential to the continuity of their culture. Every headland, every landmark had a name and a special significance to its Indian owners. To take away the Indians' land was to deprive them of their identity. But the Indians could not win. Some groups turned from hunting and gathering to agriculture, and competed with European farmers. They were unable to hunt over cleared lands. Commercial fisheries and canning operations were soon encroaching on their fishing grounds. A vast gulf of ignorance and misunderstanding separated most Indians and settlers. Most settlers felt fully justified in taking over the Indians' land, which, they argued, was going to waste because it was not cultivated. All the Indians did was hunt and fish, mere sports as opposed to the serious business of wresting a living from the soil, these arguments continued. In fact, of course, the Indians were closely adapted to their bountiful natural environment.

The period between 1860 and 1880 saw the Indian societies of the Northwest Coast falling into social and economic disorder. The acquisition of wealth was a fundamental tenet of Indian life. Their society was cemented by the social obligations that derived from economic success. When the fur trade declined, eroding the settlers' sources of wealth, the Indians found there was no way of establishing social status. The foundations of their millennia-old way of life were rapidly eroding. Traditional society went into decline. Many people moved to the vicinity of European settlements, where they eked out an existence as wage earners—if the settlers would employ them. The colonists tried to remove them en masse, under the guise of philanthropical concern about the effects of cheap whiskey on their new urban neighbors. Crowded into makeshift dwellings, many Indians contracted venereal disease. A smallpox epidemic in 1862 so alarmed the inhabitants of Victoria that the authorities evicted the Indians and burned down their shanties. As a result, smallpox spread the length of the coast and into the interior as the Indians returned to their villages. The Indians were forced to adjust to so much catastrophic disruption at once that they were powerless to adapt at all.

There was nothing the Indians could do. A few groups and individuals tried to resist the whites. Attempts at forceful resistance were put down and the ringleaders severely punished. Many people retreated deep into their home territory and removed themselves as far from the problem as they could. Gilbert Malcolm Sproat, at one time the Indian Reserve Commissioner, reported to the Ethnological Society of London in 1867 that many Indians "lived listlessly in their villages, brooding seemingly over heavy thoughts" (Fisher 1977, 117). Somewhat of an anthropologist, Sproat complained that the Indians were reluctant to give him accurate information about their customs. He theorized that the Indians had become distrustful of their old traditions, and were stunned and confused by the rapidity with which Western civilization was encroaching on them. Some groups, like the Kwakiutl of northern Vancouver Island, were under such stress that they embarked on frenzied potlatching. The wealthy would compete frantically with each other in orgies of conspicuous consumption. Food was distributed with extraordinary largesse; eulachon oil was thrown in prodigal amounts on the fire; blankets and precious coppers were consumed in the flames. Some of the most conspicuous largesse came from people with little status who had acquired wealth from contact with Europeans. That some of this potlatching was the result of pressure on traditional Indian society seems unquestionable.

As the settler population of British Columbia increased, the Indians began to feel the impact of British colonial policy directed from London. Douglas's relatively liberal policies were swept aside. The remote colony was low on the government's priorities, so the settlers took over more or less as much Indian land as they wanted. Official pressure increased even more after British Columbia became part of Canada in 1871. A decade later the government appointed Indian agents, who were responsible for the administration of Indian affairs in the province. They were supposed to advise the Indians, but were used instead to break down Indian customs. Their particular target was the potlatch, long the object of the missionaries' disapproval, and, it was thought, a major obstacle to the Westernization of the Indians. In 1884, the federal government passed a law outlawing potlatching and making the pastime a misdemeanor punishable by imprisonment. The Indians were furious and resisted the law at every turn. They pointed out to their few friends that it would be disastrous for their leaders to give up potlatching. Not only would they lose prestige and be unable to fulfill social obligations, but many people would starve. It was the one means of distributing communal wealth through society. Their entire social organization depended upon potlatching. Many Indians quietly continued to potlatch underground, and did so for many years.

As long as fur traders had dealt with them, the Indians treated religion just like every other aspect of Western culture. They adopted and rejected different aspects of it as they wished. Missionaries had been active on the coast as early as 1829, but serious pastoral efforts began in the 1850s, when Protestant Evangelicals descended on the Indians. They demanded complete rejection of all traditional beliefs. The most successful was William Duncan, a religious fanatic so obsessed with sin that he was mesmerized by the "horrid fabrication of lies" that made up the Indians' ritual life. In 1862, he moved his mission school away from the European settlement at Fort Simpson and founded a model community named Metlatlaka, where he could isolate his flock from contaminating influences. Duncan's objective was nothing less than the founding of a Victorian town.

Everyone lived in small cottages build along carefully laid-out streets. Duncan erected a huge cedarwood church complete with all the elaborate architectural features of an English edifice (Figure 14.7). He allowed more than one family to live in each house, provided they occupied different rooms. Polygamy was forbidden, clans and kinship ties were not recognized, potlatching and winter ceremonials forbidden. One concession to the Indian lifeway was made: schools were closed during the spring fishing season. The fully clothed Indians of Metlatlaka were described as being "in their right mind, and sitting at the feet of Jesus" (Fisher 1977, 134).

Since Duncan erected houses and built a large ceremonial edifice, set up symbols, and conducted rituals, he probably became the Indians' chief, both spiritual and secular leader for people whose traditional life was in ruins. The Metlatlaka experiment was copied by other missionaries and sects on a smaller scale, but with varying degrees of success. The missionaries succeeded in causing further fragmentation in Indian society. When one sect started competing with another, the Indians became even more confused. They even started their own mystical sects that were a form of resistance to Christianity, sects in which some Christian beliefs were mingled with traditional rites. Duncan's successors were the ones who waged war against the potlatch and other institutions that still held the threads of Indian society together.

A century after Cook anchored in Nootka Sound, Northwest Coast Indian culture had been reduced to a mere token of its former self. Many local people eked out a hand-to-mouth existence in urban shanty settlements, in what can only be described charitably as rural ghettoes. With their lands gone and the potlatch illegal, the two foundations of traditional life—the bounty

14.7   Indian children on the steps of Metlatlaka church, 1881 (courtesy of the American Museum of Natural History, negative no. 42304)

of the local environment and the acquisition of wealth—were removed. The Indian population had declined sharply and was to continue to fall until the 1930s. The proud tribes of a century before had been reduced to what, at best, was a peripheral role in British Columbian society. As early as the 1880s, the celebrated anthropologist Franz Boas visited the Northwest. He was disappointed in what he found, and wrote: "I hear very little about olden times."

CHAPTER 15

The Maori

...and to show us that they had eat the flesh they bit and naw'd the bone and draw'd it thro' their mouth and this in such a manner as plainly shew'd that the flesh was to them a dainty bit.

Captain James Cook, 1770

I suppose they live intirely on fish, dogs, and enemies...

Joseph Banks, 1770

THE FIRST THREE CENTURIES OF the Age of Discovery saw only a trickle of Europeans leaving their homelands to settle in remote, unfamiliar lands. The European nations had been content to skim the cream, obtaining luxuries and precious metals through barter or force while preventing their rivals from sharing in the wealth. The next stage was to set up trading stations and forts, then to annex the country and work its mines, plantations, and fields with forced labor levies or imported slaves. When the British abolished slavery in 1833, they simply turned to indentured labor as a substitute. Indentured plantation labor came not from Africa but from southern China, Java, and India, places closer to the new plantations in southeast Asia and the Pacific, and countries where millions of illiterate, landless workers could be induced to seek their fortune elsewhere. This contract system had many abuses, but it fuelled plantation agriculture in many tropical areas during the nineteenth century. The numbers of indentured emigrants were enormous. At least

16.8 million Indians are estimated to have left India to work on plantations, of whom at least 4.4 million stayed away permanently.

Until the early nineteenth century, Europeans themselves were reluctant to leave their homes to settle in such temperate places as Australia or North America. Europe's population was growing slowly. Few people were so poor or so persecuted that they wanted to uproot themselves to work in a new and unfamiliar area under the harshest of conditions. Such places were thought suitable for adventurers, criminals, derelicts, and soldiers, but not for ordinary citizens. For three centuries, only a trickle of Europeans ventured to these territories. Once there, most of them clung to the ports and shorelines where contact with home could be at least tenuously maintained. By 1800, almost two hundred years after the founding of the first permanent colony at Jamestown, Virginia, only 4.3 million whites lived in the United States. As late as 1840, fifty-two years after the start of the first penal colony in Australia, only 190,000 Europeans lived in the entire continent. New Zealand had fewer than 2,000 white inhabitants in the same year. Only with the Industrial Revolution did European emigration take off—at a breathtaking rate.

The Industrial Revolution brought dizzying changes at home. The death rate began to drop; the population burgeoned. At the time of Napoleon's defeat at Waterloo, England was a predominantly rural nation of 13 million people. By the mid-nineteenth century, the population had nearly doubled to 24 million, half of them city dwellers. Victorian Britain was a transformed nation of cities and factories, of new urban occupations and terrible poverty. The conversion from agrarian life seemed to have occurred almost overnight. Inevitably, the established social order was shaken up, leaving many people frustrated and poverty-stricken, ready to take the chance of a new life overseas. The decision to leave was made easier by the efforts of the pioneers. No longer did countries like Australia and New Zealand seem like dangerous places teeming with wild beasts. Sometimes they were painted in rosy terms as lands where a family could start again, work hard, and find a good life. The invention of the steamship made ocean travel safer and more predictable, so that one could sail to Australia and back in relative comfort at modest cost, and in discomfort for virtually nothing. Small wonder that Europe was electrified with a mania for emigration in search of a new life.

Between 1840 and 1930, at least 52 million Europeans emigrated to North America, Australia, South America, and Africa. The flood of emigration fed on itself, not only because families encouraged their relatives and friends to join them, but also because the new lands were transformed by rapid development and almost simultaneous industrialization. Countries like New Zealand were transformed almost overnight from a Stone Age economy to modern technology. To many political economists and politicians, colonization of distant lands became a creed of new and fervent belief, for the home country could do nothing but benefit by such policies. "It is by the migration of barbarous tribes that the whole earth has been peopled; by the colonizing genius of some more refined nations, that its civilization…has been affected," proclaimed political economist Herman Merivale in a lecture delivered at Oxford University (1861, 138). The effects on the non-Western societies occupying continents like New Zealand were almost invariably catastrophic.

Nieuw Zeeland

IN THE YEAR 1642, THE hardheaded directors of the Dutch East India Company had launched a search for the Great Southern Continent, for "well populated districts in favorable climates and under propitious skies." They dispatched Abel Tasman to sail south and east from Batavia to find new trading opportunities. Tasman landed briefly at the island that now bears his name, then sailed eastward until he sighted "a large land, uplifted high." He named it Nieuw Zeeland, coasted along the unknown shore, and made contact with people in canoes who called out in a "rough, loud voice" (Figure 15.1). Soon his seamen were fighting off a raiding party that killed four of his men. After twenty-three days off New Zealand, Tasman sailed off without landing at all.

No one went out of his way to explore this shadowy land more thoroughly. It remained a zigzag line of partially explored coast on European atlases until the late eighteenth century, when Captain James Cook circumnavigated the remote continent in 1769–1770, and made charts so accurate that they are of use to this day. He also had ample time to observe the people who lived there, the fierce and sophisticated Maori. New Zealand, he wrote, was abundant in good quality timber and in excellent grasses for cordage. "In short," he added prophetically, "was this Country settled by an Industrious people they would be very soon supply'd not only with the necessarys but many of the luxuries of life" (Beaglehole 1968, 276).

The Maori were completely different from the friendly Tahitians. Cook's landings were often opposed with threats, even violence. Canoe-loads of Maori would paddle out to look over the ships and to trade. All too often the people were truculent and hurled stones and threats with vehement anger. The Europeans observed numerous fortified camps, *pa,* built on strategic promontories and rocks. Their ditches, palisades, and fighting stages convinced their visitors that the Maori were warlike people. The *Endeavour's* people saw several forts that had been destroyed and burned quite recently. The sites had been carefully chosen, a "very strong and well chosen post and where a small number of resolute men might defend themselves a long time against a vast superior force, Arm'd in the manner as these People are" (Beaglehole 1968, 197) (Figure 15.2). Maori spears were such formidable weapons that only a European musket was proof against them.

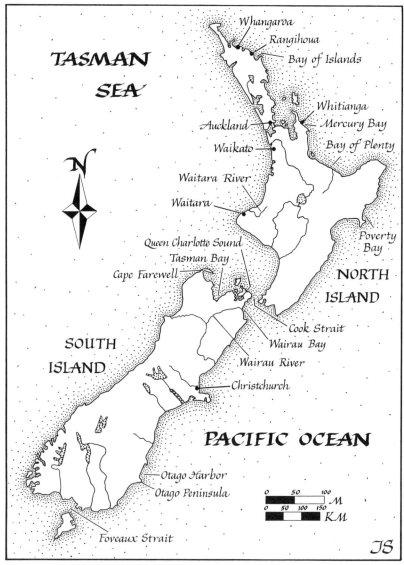

15.1   *Map of New Zealand*

Cook was convinced the Maori were cannibals. When he first heard stories of the consumption of human flesh, he maintained an open mind. Apparently some of the few Maori who came aboard the ships were fearful that the Europeans would eat them. Then, in January 1770, Cook met a group of

15.2 *The* pa *in Mercury Bay, by Sydney Parkinson (courtesy of the Trustees of the British Museum)*

Maori in Queen Charlotte Sound, across Cook Strait from the modern city of Wellington, who were cooking a dog carcass on a hearth strewn with recently butchered human bones (Figure 15.3). Next morning, the Maori brought a human bone to the ship. "And to shew us that they had eaten the flesh they bit and naw'd the bone and draw'd it thro' their mouth and this in such a manner as plainly show'd that the flesh was to them a dainty bit" (Beaglehole 1968, 236). Joseph Banks bought the preserved head of a recently eaten Maori. "I suppose they live intirely on fish, dogs and enemies," he remarked (Beaglehole 1955–67, 1:443). The Maori enjoyed a formidable reputation for cannibalism from that day on.

The Maori were just as curious about the strange visitors who possessed such superior weapons, but puzzled by Cook's unwillingness to take advantage of his powerful armament. In 1852, a European official took down Chief Te Horata te Taniwha's eyewitness account of Cook's landing at Whitianga on the east coast of North Island. He was just a boy at the time, but remembered how the old men called the ship a *tupua* ("goblin"). The oarsmen rowing to shore seemed like goblins, with eyes in the backs of their heads. How else could they see where they were going? The people stared at the white-skinned strangers, stroked their clothes, and admired their blue eyes. Some of the Maori went on board the visitor's ship, Te Horata te Taniwha among them. They tasted European food, and met Cook. He spoke but little: "All

15.3   Queen Charlotte Sound, by John Webber (courtesy of the Alexander Turnbull Library, Wellington, New Zealand)

that he did was to handle our mats…and touch the hair of our heads." His language seemed like an unintelligible hissing sound. Cook gave the young boy an iron nail, which he treasured for years.

There is a haunting similarity between this memory and those moments in other non-Western lands of first contact with Europeans. Strange beings arrive in a huge, floating village. They have white skins and a charismatic leader. "These are gods," say the priests and elders, searching the precedents of tribal lore for an explanation for these astonishing visitors. Are the strangers gods, or people? Are they friends or potential enemies? Like the Aztecs and the Tasmanians, the Maori wonder at the Europeans' white skins, strange clothes, and remarkable weapons. They are just as cautious as are the Europeans themselves, but behave towards the strangers in the same aggressive way as they would towards their own neighbors and potential enemies. The only thing both sides can do is to watch, act within the constraints of their own cultural values, and see how the situation develops.

James Cook was to visit New Zealand on four later occasions, but he added relatively little to the vast sum of knowledge collected on his first expedition. Of all the non-Western peoples he encountered, the Maori were those he seems to have respected most and treated with the most care. He felt as though he were walking on a knife-edge. The gulf of incomprehension between his men and the Maori was so great that violence could erupt at any time. The very unpredictability of the local people soon gave them a sensational reputation in Europe. Cook's companion ship on the second voyage added fuel to the horror stories in London coffeehouses. Tobias Furneaux was operating independently of his commander in the *Adventure*. He sent a ship's cutter ashore to cut wild vegetables in Palliser Bay in December 1773. The boat failed to return at dusk. The next morning a rescue party found baskets of human flesh, scattered shoes, a black servant's head, and some severed hands. There was no sign of the boat. A large crowd of Maori was dispersed with musket fire.

The French had an even more horrifying experience a year before Furneaux's crew ran into trouble. Marion du Fresne, whom we have already met in Tasmanian waters (see Chapters 1 and 7), made a landfall on North Island on 25 March 1772. After a stormy initiation, his two ships anchored in the Bay of Islands, where the crew landed the sick and cut new masts from the great trees close inshore. The local people were thievish, but friendly enough. They lavished every attention on du Fresne, so much so that he thought he was being paid royal honors. When the other officers warned him to be on the lookout, he merely scoffed at them. "How can you expect me to have a bad opinion of a people who show me so much friendship?" he cried. His confidence proved fatal. Fresne, two officers, and thirteen unarmed sailors were massacred in cold blood at Oraukawa Bay on 13 June 1772 while visiting a local chief. The very next day the Maori killed twelve more seamen who had been sent ashore to cut wood. The survivors, under Lieutenants du Clesmeur and Crozet, managed to repulse attacks on their camp. They took their revenge by burning the *pa* where their companions had been killed and leveling two more villages. Some three hundred Maori died in the retaliatory raids. Only a few fragments of clothing and some butchered bones remained of the slaughtered European victims. This tragic incident stemmed from deep suspicions on each side, from French arrogance, and unwitting yet outrageous breaking of religious taboos. The Maori exacted a terrible price for these infringements and for French carelessness.

Within a few years of Cook's brilliant circumnavigation, the coasts of New Zealand had been thoroughly explored by French and English navigators. The visitors included a galaxy of famous explorers, among them George Vancouver, Chevalier D'Entrecasteaux, and the cultured and talented Jules Sebastien Cesar Dumont d'Urville. They corrected and amplified Cook's surveys and added many details to western knowledge of the Maori. Everyone soon agreed that New Zealand was not part of the Great Southern Continent. But its 100,000 square miles of islands were covered with dense, green vegetation, a flora that was, for the most part, unfamiliar to Europeans. There were few land animals,

but the wooden countryside abounded "with a great variety of Beautiful singing Birds which made the woods echo with their different Notes which made
the greatest harmony" (Wright 1959, 4). Enormous herds of sea mammals
flourished in New Zealand waters. Nearly all European visitors agreed that this
charming land could become an agricultural paradise.

There was relatively little contact between Europeans and Maori during
the late eighteenth century. Sealing gangs were already operating in the waters off South Island by 1788, but few Maori lived in the south. The few who
did became embittered with the sealers, who succeeded in decimating the local
sea mammal populations almost completely by 1820. Some whalers and sealers may have stopped at North Island, but there was little to attract them.
Neither pigs nor potatoes, both introduced by Cook, were in sufficient supply to be traded by the Maori. By the turn of the century a few ships probably stopped at the Bay of Islands each year, but no accurate record of their
visits survives.

Some Maori shipped aboard whalers as crew. The contacts between the
New Zealanders and the whalers were probably unsatisfactory and perhaps
violent, for missionaries in Australia heard of violence and drunken brawls
from Maori seamen in Sydney. Matters came to a head in 1809, when the
Bay of Island Maori massacred the crew of a ship named the *Boyd* that
stopped to cut new masts at Whangaroa. Almost to a man, oceangoing skippers avoided the area for years.

Despite the terrible reputation of the Maori, it was inevitable that Europeans would colonize New Zealand (Figure 15.4). This was not a land of gold
and silver, nor was it a tropical paradise. The climate was more equable if
wetter than that of western Europe. But this remote territory was a place
where European farmers and artisans might reasonably be expected to make
a decent living. It was the Frenchman Dumont d'Urville, an explorer of a decidedly romantic turn of mind and phrase, who expressed these sentiments
best. He predicted there would be a day when Maori, Frenchmen, and British
would live together in harmonious civilization. "Then these shores, deserted,
or peopled only by isolated *pas,* will exhibit flourishing cities; these silent bays,
traversed now by infrequent frail canoes, will be furrowed by ships of every
size," he predicted (d'Urville, 1834–5, 2:111). Like many of his contemporaries, d'Urville believed passionately in the desirability of every human being embracing the manifest benefits of Western civilization. In the case of
the Maori, like so many other societies, even a small dose of European civilization was to prove almost fatal.

15.4 *The Maori* haka, *the war dance, by J. J. Merritt. "When they stamped, the earth shook," wrote an early settler. (Courtesy of the Rex Nan Kivell Collection, National Library of Australia)*

"A Strong, Rawboned People"

THE MAORI WERE THEMSELVES COMPARATIVE newcomers to New Zealand. Archaeologists believe that the first human inhabitants arrived in the islands from Polynesia about 1,000 years ago—the exact chronology is uncertain. The Polynesians who first settled in these southern lands found themselves confronted with an unfamiliar climate, one where such staples as bananas, breadfruit, or coconuts would not grow. Only the Andean sweet potato, *kumara,* obtained a foothold in the North Island and in the extreme northern areas of South Island. Neither pigs nor chickens survived the long canoe journey from Polynesia. The earliest settlers subsisted by hunting, fishing, and gathering, and by cultivating the sweet potato wherever this was possible. They were fortunate to be living in a forested environment where bird life was abundant, especially a flightless species known as the *moa.* The Maori

15.5 *Maori war canoes, with "the crew bidding defiance to the ship's company."*
The double canoe is under sail, while the occupants perform a war dance. A
chief stands in the stern. Drawing by Sporling. (Courtesy of the Trustees of the
British Museum. Addl. MS 23920, folio 48.1307)

had hunted the *moa* into extinction by the seventeenth century, partly
through overhunting and also by cutting down forests for sweet potato gardens. *Moa* bones were found abandoned in Maori shell mounds as early as
the 1830s and commanded high prices in the curio markets of Sydney. A *moa*
egg found with a human skeleton was sold in England in 1859 for the enormous price of £120.

Before European contact, the Maori thought their islands were the center
of the entire universe, except for a dimly remembered homeland across the
ocean named *Hawaiki*. Their priestly families retained traditional histories that
spoke of cherished ancestors who had arrived in North Island in great canoes
centuries before (Figure 15.5). Captain Cook remarked the resemblances between Maori and Polynesian culture, while archaeological research in both New
Zealand and Polynesia has revealed strong resemblances between 1,000-year-old
stone adzes, fishhooks, and other such artifacts in both areas. Most authorities
now believe the Maori came from somewhere in central Polynesia at least a
millennium ago. We are unlikely ever to have a more precise chronology, simply because the archaeological record of a tiny initial population is too sparse.

Between A.D. 1300 and 1500, classic Maori culture developed and spread
through the North Island and into those parts of the South Island where sweet
potato cultivation was possible. The emergence of classic Maori culture is

associated with more intensive cultivation of the sweet potato and the building of *pa,* the fortified villages observed by Cook and others throughout North Island. Classic Maori culture may have spread by population increases that stimulated tribal migrations and wars of conquest, as competition developed for prime agricultural land. This rich, flamboyant, and warlike culture was the one observed by Cook in 1769.

According to Cook, the Maori were "a Strong, rawboned, well made, Active People, rather above than under the common size, especially the Men; they are of a very dark brown colour, with black hair, thin, black beards, and white teeth, and such as do not disfigure their faces by tattowing, etc., have in general very good features" (Beaglehole 1968, 809). Many early observers commented on the strength and vigor of the males, who had fine teeth and thick legs, allegedly from "their constant squatting." Lieutenant Crozet observed that "The women are not so good-looking on close examination; they have generally a bad figure, are short, very thick in the waist, with voluminous mammae, coarse thighs and legs, and are of a very amorous temperament, while on the contrary the men are very indifferent in this respect" (Wright 1959, 5).

Some of the men's faces were completely tattooed with blue and black spiral patterns, and sometimes from the buttocks to the knees. They wore their black hair drawn up into a topknot (Figure 15.6). The women were tattooed on the lips and chin. Tattooing was a long and painful process, executed with a small bone chisel and a mallet that literally carved the design into the skin.

Both men and women wore simple kilts or aprons fastened with a belt that extended from waist to knees. These rattled and swished with the movement of the wearer. The Maori also donned cloaks of woven flax fiber that were tied across the shoulders. The finest cloaks took months to make, as the flax fiber was scraped with shells, then woven on cross sticks set far enough apart to accommodate the completed robe. The most valuable cloaks were edged with red-and-black thread patterns and ornamented with feather tufts or dog hair. The finest feather cloaks replicated a bird's breast in brilliant colors of red, white, blue, green, and black. Chiefs and other important personages wore feathers in their hair, sometimes whalebone or wood combs as well. Greenstone ear ornaments were much prized, as were earrings made of shark's teeth. A small amulet known as a *hei tiki* was suspended around the neck, carved in the form of a figure with folded legs. *Hei tikis* were prized heirlooms that were handed down from generation to generation.

One reason the Maori were so aggressive was because prime agricultural land for sweet potato cultivation was in short supply. *Kumara* was harvested once a year from gravelly and volcanic soils that were cleared by burning and by laborious hand labor using wooden digging sticks. The importance of sweet potato agriculture seems to have increased after the fourteenth century,

15.6 Portraits of Maori men, by Sydney Parkinson. Left, the man's hair is dressed in a topknot, with three white feathers and an ornamental comb; right, a second man wears a woven flax cloak with a bone toggle. His hair is also dressed in a topknot. (Courtesy of the Trustees of the British Museum. Addl. MS 23920, folios 54a and 55b)

perhaps after the Maori had responded to a cooler climatic change by inventing more effective ways of storing the valuable tubers. They dug large storage pits that were fumigated with fires to prevent fungus decay. A large wad of clay then replaced the hearth. In addition to large, rectangular pits up to 33 feet (10 meters) square, the Maori used smaller, bell-shaped types. The eaves of the thatched roofs of the larger pits rested on the ground around the pit. Thick layers of earth on the roof provided insulation and a constant temperature for the stored food. So important was sweet potato cultivation to the North Island Maori that all warfare ceased during the growing season.

Another vital staple was the rhizome of the fern root, or bracken fern (*Pteris aquilina var. esculenia*). The Maori called it *Te tutanga te unuhia* ("the staple that can never fail"). Fern roots were found everywhere except in the densest forests and could be collected any time of the year. The rhizomes were dug up with a digging stick and beaten with hardwood beaters to remove the tough other skin. The people also relied on a wide range of less important vegetable foods and berries that were collected in season. The Maori ate their dogs and trapped a species of Polynesian rat that had stowed away with the original settlers. Birds were a major factor in Maori diet, even after the extinction of the *moa* and other large species. They snared pigeons

15.7 *Maori fishing, by Sydney Parkinson (courtesy of the Trustees of the British Museum)*

and parrots, hunted the wingless kiwi with dogs, and even speared birds as they fed on wild berries. So effective were some snaring methods that catches of several hundred pigeons were recorded in one day. The birds were cooked and then stored in gourds in their own fat. They formed an important part of a family's wealth.

Fishing was vital to Maori well-being (Figure 15.7). The dense settlements around the sheltered Bay of Islands testify to the rich food supply that could be obtained from the Pacific. They fished from canoes with nets and hooks and lines, and speared fish in the shallows.

Many observers reported the Maori sometimes turned to human flesh when it was available in the form of prisoners of war and slaves. According to Maori author Sir Peter Buck (*Te Rangi Hiroa*), slaves and other people were killed and eaten on special occasions such as a marriage or a funeral. While cannibalism may have begun as a need to consume more meat, it eventually acquired a definite role in Maori life. It was often practiced more for its ritual significance than for dietary reasons. Maori warriors would eat the heart and eyes of the first enemy slain in battle. To eat a portion of your enemy's body was the ultimate insult.

Maori material culture was based on conveniently available natural resources. Most Maori houses were about 18 to 20 feet (5.5 to 6 meters) long, and about 10 feet (3 meters) across, with a roof about 6 feet (1.8 meters) high.

Slender sticks formed the house frame. Both walls and roof were covered with dense layers of dried grass to protect the inhabitants from the cold. The family slept on mats inside the house, with a central fireplace. The *whare whakairo,* or carved meeting house, was the largest and most imposing structure in Maori villages. These carved houses were 60 or more feet (18 meters) in length, as much as 33 feet (10 meters) wide, and 24 feet (7.3 meters) high. The building of a *whare* began with the erection of the carved ridge posts. It projected in front of the *whare* to shelter the veranda. The thick wall posts were shaped like slabs carved with ancestral human figures. Dressed and painted timber rafters carried the sloping roof, which was thatched with several layers of reeds and leaves. The walls were lined with reeds, then adorned with decorative, painted panels of stitched materials. The door at the front of the *whare* was a carved slab about 4 feet (1.2 meters) high. The builders lavished the ridge boards that covered the front edge of the roof with elaborate spiral carvings. A carved head or a complete ancestor figure stood at the apex of the front gable. The *whare* was devoid of furniture and served as a place where not only formal gatherings, but also speechmaking, singing, and dancing took place. The area in front of a meeting house often formed a *marae,* an open court for welcoming guests or conducting business.

Maori woodcarvers were fortunate to have abundant supplies of the *totara* tree at hand, a straight-grained, easily worked, and durable form of timber that was readily carved in the characteristic spirals and lacelike designs found on artifacts, houses, and canoes. Local greenstone supplied the Maori carvers with the tough-edged acres and axes needed for woodworking. At its most elegant, Maori art has an almost filigree quality in its delicacy, adorning the prow and stern pieces of great canoes, the handles of weapons, and the sides of *waka hula,* the oval caskets in which treasured heirlooms were stored. The Maori were also expert painters, basket makers, and mat weavers. Even tattooing was regarded as an artistic extension of wood carving and plaiting.

Maori artisans and farmers worked with the simplest tools, such as wooden digging sticks and clubs for breaking up the soil. The Maori lavished great care on the preparation of fishhooks, including trolling types that had a wooden shank and a shell inlay. But their greatest masterpieces were their seagoing canoes. The builders did not use outriggers, probably because there was an abundance of wide-bunked *kauri* trees to serve as hulls. Seagoing canoes were up to 46 feet long (14 meters), with planked gunwales lashed to the hull to give them more freeboard. Maori war canoes were 70 feet (21.3 meters) or more in length, composite vessels whose bow, stern, and central sections were joined with mortise-and-tenon joints. The upward sweeping extremities of the hull made for speed and graceful lines. The prow and stern boards, the stern post, and sometimes the gunwales and thwarts, were carved with intricate designs. Canoes of all sizes were vital to the Maori before European contact, for they were the only means of communication except for narrow, dangerous island paths. And they were essential in times of warfare.

The Maori acquired a ferocious reputation from early European visitors. But their warfare, like that of other non-Western societies such as the Aztecs, Khoikhoi, or Tahitians, was totally unlike European conceptions of military campaigning. The values of war, and of prestige gained through combat, permeated every aspect of Maori life. Most fighting was of short duration, conducted during the summer months between planting and harvest (Figure 15.8). One of the longest Maori battles in memory is said to have taken place in 1815, when two groups battled on a beach for the duration of two flood tides—some twelve to eighteen hours. Most battles consisted of sudden raids, ambushes by narrow forest paths, and a few minutes of ferocious hand-to-hand fighting with sharp-edged clubs or throwing sticks. Occasionally two exceptional warriors would engage in single combat. Maori warfare, like every other aspect of Maori life, was intricately linked to the acquisition of prestige and waged not so much to acquire land, but to avenge insults, gain prestige, and perhaps to obtain animal protein in the form of human flesh.

With such an emphasis on surprise attacks and unexpected raids, the Maori lived in constant fear of war. Guests at ceremonial feasts arrived armed to the teeth, and with good reason, for surprise massacres were not unknown on such occasions. The people of North Island lived in fortified villages protected by terraced earthworks. These *pas* were nestled on inaccessible promontories and cliffs, in strategically secure places where the risk of surprise attacks could be minimized. Cook observed many such settlements, like this one in Mercury Bay: "This village is built on a high Promentary—It is in some places quite inaccessible to man, and in others very difficult, except on that side which faced the narrow ridge of the hill on which it stands. Here it is defended by a double ditch, a bank, and 2 rows of Picketing; but not so near the Crown but what there was good room for men to walk and handle their Arms between the Picketing and the inner Ditch…Close within the inner Picketing was erected by strong Posts a stage 30 feet high and 40 feet in length and 6 feet broad. The use of this stage was to stand upon to throw Darts at the Assailants, and a number of Darts lay upon it for this purpose" (Beaglehole 1968, 198–9). The inhabitants were well prepared for a siege, as Cook saw from huge stockpiles of fern roots and dried fish.

The most elaborate of all Maori ceremonies took place before and after battle, for the gods played a major role in explaining any victory of defeat. The victors would eat the heart and eyes of the first enemy slain in battle. Sometimes when merely eating an enemy's flesh did not satisfy revenge, the bones would be kept and used for purposes that were considered insulting or degrading. They could be fashioned into ornaments and fishhooks, even into rings to tether the legs of a tame parrot. The eighteenth-century artist

15.8 "A New Zealand warrior in his proper dress and completely armed according to their manner," by Sydney Parkinson, 1773 (courtesy of the Alexander Turnbull Library, Wellington, New Zealand)

Sidney Parkinson once saw a human skull used as a canoe bailer. Sometimes the bones were broken up and burned in the fire to prevent relatives of the slain from collecting them for burial in a sacred place. The heads of detested enemies were sometimes preserved and taken home as trophies, often impaled on sticks or defensive palisades. The victors would remove the eyes, brain, and tongue, the latter through the basal foremen magnum. They would stitch the neck skin into a loop and smoke the head in an earthen oven. Such heads became treasured curios among early settlers. When the Maori found they could trade them for firearms and other European goods, headhunting became a minor industry. Some chiefs killed their slaves to satisfy the flourishing market in preserved heads.

Most Maori lived on North Island, organized in at least twenty tribes *(imi)*, which were in turn divided into subtribes (*hapu*) that claimed descent from common ancestors. The smallest social unit was the family *(whanau)*. The ownership of land was vested in *hapu* and *whanau,* this territory including both agricultural land and fishing grounds. While an individual might claim ownership of a tract of land, in practice it was vested in the communal hands of the kin unit to which he or she belonged, something that European settlers found hard to comprehend.

The leaders of Maori tribes were *ariki,* individuals who could claim direct descent from one of the legendary canoes of earlier times. A Maori *ariki* had far more powers and belonged to a much more exclusive social order than the *arioi* of Tahiti. He possessed the dual qualities of *mana,* personal magnetism and power resulting from his own achievements, and *tapu,* a form of personal sanctity inherited from his family ancestors. His people always treated him with respect and awe, as reveled by Sir Peter Buck's record of a chief's greeting: "*Haeri mai te mane, haere mai te tapu, haere mai te wthi*" ("Welcome to power, welcome to sanctity, welcome to dread") (Buck 1949, 347). An *ariki's tapu* was often concentrated in his head, so much so that his hair clippings were disposed of carefully so they could do no harm to others. In many respects the *ariki* was regarded as the *taumanu,* the resting place of the gods.

The free people of Maori society were the *rangatira,* almost a hereditary aristocracy. The *rangatira* were entitled to express their opinions in tribal gatherings. Commoners, *tutua,* often considered themselves to be *rangatira.* The distinction between these two rankings was sometimes blurred. The lowest class of Maori society was that of slaves, mainly prisoners of war. No matter how elevated the rank of a prisoner before capture, he lost all his *mana* when captured and was subject to the total whim of his captors. Some Maori were also *tobunga,* skilled people with a special expertise in canoe building, wood carving, or tattooing. Many were priests. The *tobunga aburewa* were the highest class of priests: scholars, philosophers, and guardians of tribal genealogies, as well as theologians. They received their training in special houses of instruction and were commonly credited with power over natural phenomena such as thunder and lightning. Lesser grades of the *tobunga* were responsible for the welfare of local gods and ceremonies of birth, death, marriage, and warfare. The Maori also had tribal genealogists and storytellers, who were the repositories of traditional history and local lore. Their chants were, and still are, a prized part of Maori life to which everyone was exposed from the earliest years of life.

Except for some minor, local variations, all Maori shared the same religious beliefs. Their major gods, known as *atua*, were invisible spirits created by the power of abstract thought, deities like Tane, the father of birds, trees, the progenitor of humans, and patron of canoe builders. Elaborate rituals surrounded Tu, the god of war, and Rongo, the patron of agriculture. Rongo supervised the growing, harvest, and storage of food, for this activity needed more assistance from the gods than any other part of Maori life. Tangaroa was in charge of the sea and the fish who swam in it. Whales, for example, were known as *te ika pipiha nui a Tangaroa* (the great spouting fish of Tangaroa). The Maori also paid attention to *atua kabu*, family gods and spirits, many of them guardians over sacred places.

Every aspect of Maori life was explainable through one or another of their gods, but the personal conduct of every Maori was guided by *tapu*, a form of prohibition. *Tapu* regulated contact between individuals, the consumption of foods, and protected sacred places. It radically affected the way the Maori behaved towards each other and towards the wider world, even Europeans. Chiefs were *tapu to* everyone. No one, for example, could cook food at a fire that a chief had blown upon. The consequence of violating *tapu* was misfortune, even death.

The Maori lived in a philosophical and spiritual world that no one could ever fully understand unless born into it. Their island environment was completely isolated from the outside world. Their challenges and opportunities for stimulation were unusually restricted, somewhat like those of the Tasmanians, who experienced an even longer period of isolation. Many of their thoughts and experiences were deeply involved in what can almost be described as a dream world, a subconscious environment that engendered a rationale for daily existence. This dream world placed severe restrictions on the activities of every Maori. Every social relationship, every proceeding was so imbued with religious implications that there was something sacred in almost every aspect of Maori existence.

Even a cursory examination of Maori oral traditions and values shows why they were so puzzled by European visitors, and why the early settlers failed so completely to understand their motives and society. Maori traditions were preoccupied with explaining the isolated world in which the people lived. It was a land of sea and sky, of sandy beaches and forest, a land that knew of no neighbors, a land whose acres were held in trust for future generations. But the *tobunga* would recite a prophecy that told of a day when strangers would inherit their land:

Kei tua i te awe mapara, he tangata ke.	(Behind this tattooed face, a stranger stands.
Mana e neho to ao nei—he ma.	He will inherit this world—he is white.)

CHAPTER 16

The Colonization of New Zealand

I think it is...conclusive that we have to attribute our peace with the natives more to the good sense which accentuates them than to the prudence and forbearance of Europeans.

New Zealand Government Report, 1842

THE MAORI ENJOYED SUCH A notorious reputation in the nineteenth century that many ships just sailed past New Zealand. Only the boldest whaling skippers dared confront the warlike inhabitants of this remote land. Those that did often recruited Maori seamen from their hosts. At times as many as thirty Maori were living at Parramatta near the convict settlement in Sydney. There they met a missionary named Samuel Marsden, an austere, humorless man of fearless demeanor who had established a model agricultural settlement for freed convicts. He became a strong advocate of their rights, took samples of fine Australian wool to England with him, and began the development of a flourishing wool trade with the mother country. Among his Maori visitors was a chief named Ruatara, who was impressed with Marsden's farming and his religious beliefs. He was among those who urged the chaplain to bring a mission to the Bay of Islands to counteract the evil ways of the whaling ships that visited New Zealand. Marsden himself had been shocked by the stories of Maori depredations with firearms obtained from visiting traders. Although he lacked education, Marsden was filled with fervor for spreading the gospel. He believed that the Maori should not only receive the word of God, but adopt the economic ways of the European as well.

With single-minded intensity, Marsden took his wool and his missionary zeal to England. He returned to Sydney with two lay missionaries in 1810.
But the fears raised by the *Boyd* massacre of the year before meant that no
captain would ferry the missionaries to their proposed base of operations.
Marsden waited more than three years. "No master of a vessel would venture for fear of his ship and crew falling a sacrifice to the natives," he wrote
in despair. Eventually he had to buy his own ship, the *Active,* and take her on
a trial visit to the Bay of Islands before the governor would allow him to found
his mission station.

"Behold, I bring you tidings of great joy"

SAMUEL MARSDEN LANDED AT OIHI in the Bay of Islands on Christmas Day
1814, accompanied, we are told, by "horses, sheep, cattle, poultry, and the
gospel." His party included a schoolteacher and two artisans, who were to
teach the Maori carpentry, as well as shoe and rope making. With a finely
developed sense of occasion, he preached the Gospel to the curious Maori
for the first time from the text, "Behold, I bring you glad tidings of great joy."
Marsden himself remained only two months, leaving a party of twenty-one
assorted Europeans behind him, all of them in one way or another associated with the Church Missionary Society. By 1819, the mission population
had risen to forty-five.

The resident missionaries faced extraordinary difficulties. They worked under very primitive conditions, were completely at the mercy of the local chiefs,
did not speak Maori, and lived in constant fear of their lives. So infrequent was
commercial shipping that only fourteen ships visited the Bay of Islands between
1816 and 1819. The missionaries did not make friends among the skippers
when they refused to accept convict stowaways from them. Their main concern was to lead the Maori to Christianity and to new economic ways by their
own peaceful example. There was no way the missionaries would encourage
disruption of their efforts by an influx of unruly and ill-disciplined settlers.

The first mission station was founded at Rangihoua on the northwest side
of the Bay of Islands (Figure 16.1). The missionaries would never have survived if it had not been for the protection of several Maori chiefs, among
them Ruatara. One of their most powerful allies was a northern chief named
Hongi Hika, a bloodthirsty warrior who visited England with one of the missionaries as part of an effort to translate the Gospel into Maori. Hongi was
introduced to George III and laden with valuable presents, including a suit
of armor, which he bartered in Sydney for powder and muskets. These guns
gave his people such military supremacy that they were able to subjugate
many tribes amidst scenes of horrible carnage. The missionaries became in-
voluntary witnesses to the enslavement and slaughter of hundreds of Maori.

16.1 *Mission station in the Bay of Islands. From Captain L. I. Dupenney's*
Voyage Autour du Monde *(Paris: Payot, 1826).*

There was little they could do. Marsden had laid out the policies they should follow. They were to civilize the Maori first, teaching them technical skills and the virtues of hard work. Only then could they learn the Gospel. Hardly surprisingly, there was little to show for twenty years of unremitting effort.

The work of these well-meaning and pious men went unrewarded for a long time. The missionaries came from a humanitarian background based on the belief that the English way of life and manners was the only Christian way. Quite naturally, the Maori were reluctant to become Europeans overnight or to adopt a religion they did not understand. Nor were Maori leaders in total sympathy with the idea of the Gospel of peace. "Fighting is the principal topic of their conversation," reported missionary Thomas Kendall in 1814. Cook himself had been bombarded with requests for assistance against hostile neighbors. The Maori were puzzled when he and the missionaries turned them down.

The Marsden mission coincided with the beginnings of a catastrophic change in Maori society brought about by the introduction of firearms. The people died in large numbers from European diseases. A combination of chronic warfare and epidemics reduced the Maori population by about 50 percent between 1800 and 1840. The chiefs were anxious to acquire iron tools and especially muskets. Unscrupulous whaling skippers and visiting ships would hand over occasional guns, which became prized symbols of prestige and power. The supply of firearms increased steadily, then with a rush after Hongi's visit to England. Hongi Hika used his treasured muskets to acquire enormous tracts of land from his neighbors. Instead of being a regular but well-controlled facet of Maori life, warfare became a means to an end, an over-whelming preoccupation that benefited no one and destroyed the very fabric of Maori society. And warfare as a way of life bred Maori chiefs who were totally devoid of compassion. They would torture or kill people without the slightest compunction. In the end, the constant and ever escalating bloodshed shook the faith of many less aggressive chiefs in the Maori way of life. They became disposed to listen to new teachers, who preached of peace and prosperity through agriculture rather than of war.

Until 1832, the missionaries were very much on the defensive. The missionary leaders in England had changed their policy about trying to civilize the Maori in 1822, when they appointed Henry Williams as an itinerant evangelist. "It is the great and ultimate purpose of this mission to bring the noble but benighted race of New Zealanders into the enjoyment of the light and freedom of the Gospel. To this grand end all the Society's measures are subordinate...Go forth...having no secular object in view," he wrote (Stock 1890, 213). In other words, souls were more important than agriculture.

Henry Williams's efforts soon met with limited success. Chief Waitangi was converted and baptized in 1824. By 1831, Williams had converted twenty adults and ten children in his coastal settlement (Figure 16.2). Seven years before, a Devonshire farmer named Davis had founded a model farm at Waimate that became a prototype for later agricultural efforts throughout New Zealand. This successful experiment made the missionaries' food supplies more secure. Davis's model farm also made a deep impression on the local people, who saw the benefits of European farming at first hand. It was one of the keys to the mission's eventual success. By 1832, much of the New Testament had been translated into Maori. A decade later, the missionaries claimed that they had printed over twenty thousand prayer books and five thousand copies of the New Testament. Copies of the Scriptures were to be found in villages throughout North Island. The sons and daughters of chiefs were brought into the missions to learn not only the Gospel, but also a whole world of new ideas, agricultural methods, and much more advanced technology.

But progress was slow. Initially, the chiefs restricted the missionaries to the coast. Then the interior was opened up in the 1830s. More and more Maori at least nominally accepted the new faith. The missionaries recorded 8,760 regular churchgoers in 1839, of whom 233 were regular communicants. Tribal wars virtually ceased by 1838. By the time the first large shiploads of settlers arrived in 1840, the missionaries' influence on the Maori was extraordinary. Bishop G. A. Selwyn, the first such cleric in New Zealand, was moved

16.2 *Missionaries, as they liked to think of themselves, interceding with the Maori. Unknown artist. (Courtesy of the Alexander Turnbull Museum, Wellington, New Zealand)*

to observe that "an essential change in all their moral habits" was going on in front of his eyes. Forty years after Marsden's first visit, the Church Missionary Society could boast of an organized church with twenty-one stations in four districts serving over twenty-five hundred souls.

The spread of Christianity among the Maori seems to have been fastest among the *rangatira* and the slaves. The chiefs, many of whom were also *tobunga*, were deeply involved in the worship of *Io*, a cult that was restricted to those of highest rank. This supreme being was considered to have close ties to the Christian God. The missionaries capitalized on the intellectual curiosity of the priests about these similarities, so much so that Maori leaders would often adopt Christianity on the basis of contact with their neighbors rather than a European missionary. One of the first results of conversion was that chiefs would free their slaves and allow them to return to their villages. The freed captives took the Word with them, sparking considerable interest in Christianity in areas far from the mission stations. Very often, the missionaries would arrive in a new area to discover that Christianity was already taking hold on the initiative of recently arrived slaves. Christianity came to the Maori at many levels: through the chiefs, through direct missionary effort, and through the lowest classes of society; and it brought many economically valuable innovations in its train. For a while, the Bible was sought as anxiously as muskets had been.

Soil and Sovereignty

THE GREAT ENEMY OF CHRISTIANITY in New Zealand after 1830 was not the Maori, but the few settlers who shared the land with the missionaries. In 1819, there were only seven non-missionary Europeans in the country. The number of visiting ships increased after 1820. Whalers landed regularly at the Maori settlement at Kororareka which became an exchange depot for the crews. By 1830, between ten and twenty Europeans were living at the village, with occasional influxes of whaling crews. The missionaries looked on this settlement with great disfavor, calling it a "plague spot of contamination." An Englishman named Edward Markham spent some time around the Bay of Islands in 1834 and wrote cynically that the Maori women would swarm to visiting ships and acquire more blankets in three weeks than the missionaries would give them in a year. "I believe the Sailors have done as much towards Civilising the Natives as the Missionaries have, or more, but in a more worldly view," he added with scorn (Simpson 1979, 24). Kororareka flourished mightily during the whaling seasons of the 1830s, when the world whaling trade expanded massively in response to a great demand for cheap oil and whalebone frameworks for ladies' corsets, and for such diverse products as umbrellas and fishing rods. "There are many spirit shops," wrote Charles Darwin, who called at the settlement on the *Beagle* in 1835. "The whole population is addicted to drunkenness and all kinds of vice." The missionaries maintained a rigid distance from Kororareka: "Here drunkenness, adultery, murder, etc., are committed...Satan maintains his dominions without molestation" (Wright 1959, 31).

The missionaries were opposed to large-scale European settlement on the grounds that it would defeat their evangelical efforts among the Maori. They pointed their warning fingers at Kororareka. In 1833, the powerful missionary lobby in London had persuaded the British Government to send out James Busby as British Resident to control whalers' excesses in the Bay of Islands area. His influence was minimal, and matters continued to deteriorate. Evangelical and humanitarian interests in England did not let the Colonial Office forget that more and more of Victoria's subjects were settling in New Zealand and that many of them were inflicting suffering on the local people. Reluctantly, the government decided to annex New Zealand as a crown colony. In January 1840, Captain William Hobson of the Royal Navy was sent out to sign an annexing treaty with the Maori. A governor was to be appointed to safeguard the interests of all New Zealand's population, whether European or Maori. The Treaty of Waitangi was the result.

The Treaty of Waitangi was not really a treaty at all. Rather, it was a statement of goodwill on both sides with no standing in international law. The Maori were to acknowledge the Queen of England as their ruler and be allowed to retain their lands. Should, however, land sales occur, the title could only be transferred to the Crown. The rights and protections of all British subjects were to be extended to the Maori.

The Maori were in no position to understand all the technicalities of the treaty. In any case, they regarded land as an inheritance from their ancestors, not as a commodity to be bought and sold like vegetables. Many chiefs refused to sign the pact. The missionaries, who were opposed to large-scale colonization but anxious to protect their flock, lobbied long and hard for the treaty among their converts. Hobson duly appointed himself governor at Auckland and assumed his job of protecting the interests of settler and Maori alike. Unfortunately, his efforts were weakened by powerful colonizing interests in London.

The first large-scale attempts at colonizing New Zealand had been made in 1826, when the New Zealand Company was floated to colonize parts of North Island. The venture failed when the Maori refused to protect the settlers. When the New Zealand Association was formed a decade later with the same objectives, both the Colonial Office and missionary interests opposed its charter, arguing that large-scale settlement would disrupt Maori life. The missionaries were, of course, anxious to protect their own interests. The organizers of the Association, however, were persistent. They formed the New Zealand Colonization Company in its stead and, in 1839, sent their first shipload of emigrants to North Island over the heads of the Colonial Office. Soon a flood of European immigrants was arriving in Maori country. By 1843, there were 11,489 Europeans living in New Zealand, nearly all of them in North Island.

At first relationships between the settlers and the Maori were excellent. The Maori proved to be willing workers who felled trees and often attached themselves to settler families. By 1848 the Maori were growing a great deal of produce for the new towns, even purchasing schooners and dominating the coastal trade of North Island (Figure 16.3). The progress of Maori agriculture was remarkable, especially in the north. Their chiefs were well aware of the fluctuations in the price of firewood, pork, flour, and other commodities they supplied to the settlers. However, as time went on and more immigrants arrived, the Maori found themselves competing with aggressive newcomers for land they had owned for generations.

The English and Scottish settlers who came to South Island found a treeless land with remote, high mountains, most of which was uninhabited country ideal for sheep farming. By 1861 the hills in the Otago region were supporting 600,000 sheep, the Canterbury area even more. The situation was different in North Island. The heavily forested land took much clearing and much of the best agricultural territory was controlled by warlike chiefs. The settlers found themselves in immediate conflict with the provisions of the

16.3 *Auckland market in the mid-nineteenth century (courtesy of the Hocken Library, New Zealand)*

Treaty of Waitangi, which had been devised ostensibly to protect the interests of the Maori. The treaty acknowledged the indisputable right of the Maori to the "soil and sovereignty" of New Zealand. The British government's primary reason for intervening in New Zealand and negotiating the treaty had been to protect the interests of the indigenous population. The Colonial Office argued that the only way settlers could purchase land was without endangering the "comfort, safety, and subsistence" of the Maori. Its agents also felt that, with the exception of cannibalism, the customs of the natives must be respected. Every possible assistance should be made for their "religious, intellectual, and social advancement." It was these humane objectives that were in Captain Hobson's mind when he assumed the governorship. Unfortunately, he died before he could implement coherent policies. Soon it was too late to prevent the Maori's loss of their land.

The damage had started before the New Zealand Colonization Company started operations. When rumors of impending large-scale settlement began circulating in Sydney, land speculators flocked to New Zealand and bought up as much land as they could for trifling sums. Edward Wakefield, the main instigator behind the Company, acquired millions of acres on either side of Cook Strait in 1839. Anxious to acquire land, he would summon a tribal meeting and display the goods he proposed to offer in exchange for the acreage.

After hearing long, eloquent speeches, the people would succumb to the tempting array of trade goods and sell their land for such miscellaneous merchandise as clothing, pocketknives, umbrellas, razors, looking glasses, and red nightcaps. All in all, Wakefield's land transactions cost him a mere £9,000. Thousands of new settlers arrived and the rush for Maori land mounted by leaps and bounds.

At first the chiefs did not contest the validity of land sales, except in a few isolated instances. The Maori worked hard, flocked to school, and accepted Christianity in unprecedented numbers, presumably because all three courses of action made sense to them. But they soon became disillusioned as a result of increased familiarity with Europeans, who pushed their way into the interior, cutting down trees, violating *tapu,* and grazing cattle on tribal lands. When the Maori started to retaliate in minor ways, they found they were not punished. This they conceived of as a sign of weakness. Soon the Maori became bolder in their dealings and more self-assertive.

Maori attitudes towards Christianity changed as well. Originally, many Maori had adopted the new religion in the belief that it would save them and teach them European ways. But Christianity failed to deliver. The missionaries lost much of their powerful *mana* in Maori eyes when they saw that the settlers treated the missionaries just like other people. The constant bickering between the different religious sects confused them. Eager converts were soon disheartened by the long lists of proscribed behavior that confronted them—restrictions on polygamy, premarital sexual intercourse, and nudity. Christianity had indeed given the Maori comparative freedom from tribal wars, slavery, and cannibalism, for the people had adopted it on the assumption that it would give them a new world order and tangible rewards akin to those of their own gods and the *mana* accompanying them. Once they realized that Christianity was no panacea for their new problems, they deserted the church in droves. They "broke the sabbath, danced again, and went to war." When their expectations were not met, the Maori simply returned to familiar values and customs whose essential validity had been proven again and again by centuries of experience. The Maori had expected too much of the Europeans, and the whites too much of the locals.

The land question came to a head after 1841, when Colonial Secretary Lord John Russell appointed William Spain as the Queen's Commissioner to adjudicate all land claims in New Zealand. Spain was extremely sympathetic to the Maori. His charge was to administer the law in such a way as to correct past injustices. The only way this policy could have been put into effect would have been to act at once. But Spain chose instead to carry out a minute inquiry into Maori land tenure. He paid special attention to Maori witnesses, so much so that hundreds of new claimants emerged to contest every unconsummated land deal. Dozens of land cases dragged on. Almost anything would have been preferable to the procrastination and deluge of claims that flooded into Spain's office. Once again, the Maori interpreted the government's acts as a sign of weakness. When the authorities let it be known that there was little they could do to protect settlers occupying disputed land, the Maori began to disrupt illegal settlements. They routed an armed posse of settlers at Wairau when they tried to seize Maori land. The casualties resulting from the affair caused a great furor and an official inquiry. The British government postmortem placed the blame fairly on the heads of the settlers, pointing out that the Maori had acted in self-defense.

Encouraged by this famous dispatch and the inaction on the part of the government, the Maori became even bolder. They menaced the infant settlements until Governor George Grey restored the Crown monopoly on the purchase of Maori land. He bought thousands of acres on the realization that the supply of land must slightly exceed the number of settlers that were to occupy it. But numbers were against the Maori. By 1850, 25,000 settlers were living in New Zealand, which was rapidly becoming a European country. A new constitution in 1852 gave the franchise to European property owners, but not to the Maori. Governor Grey attempted to minimize the effects of the new legislation by withholding authority over the Maori from the settlers, which was an effective measure only as long as he remained governor. The tragedy was that the Maori were proving to be progressive citizens of the new colony. By 1856, there was a higher proportion of literate Maori than whites in New Zealand. Unfortunately, by this time, the land hunger of an expanding European society was becoming acute, especially in the North Island, where the fabric of Maori tribal life was under constant threat of permanent disruption.

Despite the apparent progress of the Maori, confusion reigned. Their society was breaking down, with chief and commoner attending the same schools. Novel European ideas of land tenure and law added to the puzzlement. Maori leaders became increasingly concerned about the decline in their fortunes through land sales and contacts with Europeans. In 1856, a council of Maori chiefs bound themselves to sell no more land, not even to the government. Tensions between settlers and Maori came to a head at Waitara in 1860. The settlers of Taranaki had their eyes on a fertile tract of Maori land near the Waitara River. The local chief, Wiremu Kingi (William King), was anxious to retain this land as the only way of holding his tribe together. He refused to sell to the whites. When a minor chief tried to dispose of his land in the valley, Wiremu Kingi indignantly vetoed his plan. In an abrupt departure from Grey's policies, the government promptly announced that it would buy land from any Maori who could show title to it. The governor refused to support Kingi's veto. The chief withdrew angrily to fortify his land, and the Maori wars began.

"A child does not grow to be a man in a day"

MANY SETTLERS WERE READY FOR trouble, indeed had been expecting it for some time. They wanted a showdown with the Maori to show them just how advantageous it would be to give in to Europeans' needs. The same arguments were recited everywhere white farmers settled—in Kenya, South Africa, and South America. Here, as elsewhere, the settlers were confident in their strong line because they assumed—wrongly, as it happened—that the Maori were unable to unite in the face of a common enemy. The government was not prepared to climb down. After all, said the assistant native secretary, "It will never do for the Government to acknowledge an error to a Maori." The settlers flocked to join the militia, but efforts to subdue Kingi and his people by force were repulsed.

While the settlers were anxious to confront the Maori, the British authorities were still looking for a middle ground. In July 1860, they called an assembly of chiefs at which the Maori had a chance to air their concerns. The central point the chiefs made was that they wanted to retain their allegiance to the Queen and to become involved with European culture. But their people did not want to become subordinate members of a society that had contempt for their values. They were prepared to become involved with the development of a genuine biracial state, with institutions and laws that reflected not only settler interests, but those of the Maori as well. But the officials present could not look at the problem in anything else but an ethnocentric way. They were convinced that the Maori were still immature barbarians. "Children cannot have what belongs to persons of mature age," said the Chief Land Purchase Commissioner, "and a child does not grow to be a man in a day."

The government embarked on a military solution to the Maori without further ado, despite the urgings of some experienced judges and officials that the government recognize the legitimacy of Maori concerns. Many people in positions of responsibility were prepared to assume that the Maori would use the opportunities to create a genuinely biracial state in a thoroughly constructive way. The outcome, they argued, would be a form of racial integration that would bring Maori and settler culture together in a genuine partnership, and not just convert Maori culture into European culture. Such suggestions were anathema to settler interests, who stressed everything negative. "The colonist is exposed to daily provocations," one settler wrote. "His cattle for example, stray from his paddock; he follows them to a neighboring *pa*, and is compelled to redeem them by an exorbitant payment. In the course of the altercation a musket is, perhaps, pointed at him, or a tomahawk flourished over his head" (Simpson 1979, 92). Thus, the settlers argued, any compromise with the Maori would automatically lead to more trouble.

When it became clear that war was inevitable in Waikato country, the Maori were determined that it would be the settlers who started it. They preferred to settle their problems through the courts. The war began with a foolish incident. One evening the Maori were alarmed to see large fires burning on the hills around Auckland. They were puzzled and wondered if they were a sign of war. In fact these bonfires were to celebrate the wedding of the Prince of Wales. The Maori hastily called council meetings to discuss the strange fires, for no one had warned them of the impending celebration. Reports of their meetings reached settler ears. The authorities, thinking the Maori were planning an attack, responded by destroying a number of local villages close to the city, which were mainly occupied by older people. The inhabitants were evicted and left to wander homeless in the bush. Their possessions were expropriated, food supplies stolen by the troops. Not surprisingly, the Maori retaliated by killing two settlers. The government seized on the deaths as an excuse to commence formal hostilities. On 12 July 1863, British General Duncan Cameron invaded Waikato country at the head of 700 soldiers.

The Waikato wars went on for two long years. At best it was an unequal struggle. The Maori did not want to fight. Confronted by a total of 20,000 troops armed with up-to-date weapons and supported by artillery, armored steamers, and a naval brigade, the Maori withdrew from their fortified positions and only resisted when they had to. There were probably only as many as 400 Maori in the field at any one time. Cameron himself seems to have had serious doubts about the war, especially when the government insisted he continue to fight the Maori when both he and his opponents were arguing for a cessation of hostilities. The government's policy seems to have been to involve as many Maori groups as possible. Any Maori under arms was a rebel; therefore his lands were subject to confiscation. After two years of sporadic and often brutal skirmishing, as well as several horrifying atrocities by settler militia groups, the Waikato and their neighbors were considered punished enough. They had lost their land and possessions. Many of them were starving. The chiefs were allowed to sue for peace. Even the British soldiers who took part were sickened by the brutality of the settlers.

While the army was in the field, the settlers hastened to legalize their gains. They lobbied for passage of a series of Native Lands Acts that attempted to bring to an end two major obstacles to land acquisition from the Maori. The first was the Crown's right of purchase of land; the second, that favorite bogey of settlers, the communal ownership of land. The Native Lands Act of 1862 effectively removed the Crown's rights. The Suppression of Rebellion Act of 1863 authorized the governor not only to punish rebels, but also denied them the right of habeas corpus. In case anyone was in any doubt as to who these rebels were, the preamble to the act referred to "evil-disposed persons of the native race" (Simpson 1979, 148). An even more insidious measure was the New Zealand Settlement Act, which authorized the government to set up settlements in districts that were in the possession of a "considerable number" of rebels. The act was deliberately worded in such a way that the government could settle large numbers of ex-militiamen and newly arrived immigrants on plots they had been promised before the outbreak of war. The Colonial Office was appalled by these draconian measures, but did nothing to stop them beyond instructing the governor to ensure that the Maori were not abused.

Behind these new laws were a group of skilled and unscrupulous land developers, among them Thomas Russell and Frederick Whitaker, two of the founders of the Bank of New Zealand, and several land agents and ministers in the settler government. The British-appointed governor was confronted with the extraordinary position of working with a cabinet that consisted of five people actively engaged in land trading and settlement. This unscrupulous partnership now ignored the powerless governor and confiscated 1,202,172 acres of Waikato land alone and large tracts in Taranaki and the Bay of Plenty area as well. There is good reason to believe that the war was engineered deliberately by land development interests. It could have been dragged on even longer, for there were elements in the government who were quite willing to see the people of Waikato massacred, using, of all instruments, "loyal" Maori to do so—people who were anxious to pay off old scores.

Fortunately, the Russell-Whitaker government fell, and a more moderate successor arranged a peace settlement. Not that this government felt any more philanthropic than its predecessors. But its members worried about the expense of supporting the army, and were concerned about the political fallout from the war overseas. Many officers who had served with the British regiments in Waikato were writing openly to the papers to protest hostilities they felt were little more than a device to rob the Maori of their land. The leader of the new government was a settler named Frederick Weld, who believed that the New Zealanders should settle their own affairs and those of the Maori without the interference of London. He reached agreement with the Colonial Office that New Zealand would now pay for its own native policies, an arrangement that meant that all British troops were withdrawn by 1868, leaving locally recruited militia in their place.

With over three million acres of new land in its possession, successive land-speculator-dominated governments were able to do more or less what they pleased. The Native Lands Act of 1865 further strengthened their hand. This established a Native Land Court, where all disputes to land title were adjudicated. The new law was designed to ensure that communal title did not stand in the way of speedy purchase of Maori land. The Land Court was a pernicious institution, which operated on well-defined, settler-preferred lines. Hearings on ownership and title were forced in all sorts of ways. All a potential owner had to do was to suborn one of the many communal owners of a plot of land to accepting money that could be construed as payment for the property. Money for whiskey, threats, bribes, even compelled intoxication was used to sign over titles. When cases came before the court, any absent owner in a communal group lost his claim to ownership. The Maori could not afford the costly surveyors' fees involved in protecting their land. In any case, the surveyors were often in league with the land agents. And if a Maori group did defend their communal ownership, the land agents would tie up the case for months. Even if the Maori won, they were presented with exorbitant hotel and food bills for their long stay in town. All too often, they were forced to sell their acreage at a knock-down price to settle their debt. The hotel owners often worked in collusion with the land agents. Many Maori sold their land simply to avoid the lengthy and frustrating process of defending title.

Between 1865 and 1875, more than ten million acres of Maori land passed into settler ownership under conditions that seem unbelievable today. It became customary for the demoralized Maori to remark that the peace of the *paheka* was more to be feared than war. Meanwhile the settlers rationalized their brazen actions by arguing that the Maori were racially unfit to hold their lands, and believed that the Land Court was a beneficial institution.

Pal Mariri and *Ringatu*

THE MAORI EMERGED FROM THE decades of war and land grabbing with remarkable resilience. Many of them turned to intense spiritual movements, which was their way of grappling with the extraordinary disruptions of Maori society resulting from the disintegration of traditional culture.

In late 1862, a former Wesleyan catechist named Te Ua Hamene emerged as the spiritual leader of a new cult named *Pai mariri*, which means "good and peaceful." The cult provided an intellectual and spiritual alternative, a means of finding redress for grievances. "The Gospel is a *kopaki haoari* [a covering for a weapon]," cried one *tobunga*. There can be no doubt that the cult was originally peaceful in intent. Te Ua Hamene and his fellow priests were trying to develop a specifically Maori way to understand a world that seemed to have gone mad. The settlers thought *Pai mariri* was a violent and pagan sect, with "bloody, sensual, foul, and devilish rites." In fact the rituals were designed to suggest the Maori victory of the spirit, freedom from the contaminating ways of the foreigner. Many powerful chiefs joined *Pai mariri*, for they regarded it as a symbolic means of keeping *pakeha* at arms' length.

Pai mariri's doctrines did engender a form of fanaticism among its followers, but not the bloody and cannibalistic rites that settlers assumed were inevitably part of its ceremonies. Many myths surrounded the cult's brief existence, among them the legend that its members believed they were invulnerable to European bullets. The Maori had seen too much fighting to be so naive. But cult members did advance into battle shouting chants that ended with the words *Hapa, hapa, pai mariri hau,* secure in the knowledge that they were pure of spirit and uncontaminated by *pakeha.* Soon Maori warriors were known as *hau hau,* after the sharp explanation that ended the chant.

After the withdrawal of British troops in 1869, military operations against the Maori passed into the lands of local militia, who had no scruples about driving the people from their lands. Soon they were being paid five pounds for each Maori head they brought in. The continued skirmishes with the settlers led to the emergence of another resistance movement, founded by a charismatic Maori trader named Te Kooti. The settlers branded him as a troublemaker after he exposed schemes to enmesh local people in debt. So they deported him to the penal settlement on Chatham Island far off the east coast of South Island. While in prison, Te Kooti underwent a spiritual rebirth and acquired a fanatical following. He and his disciples overpowered their guards, seized a schooner, and forced the crew to sail them to the mainland. After years of bitter rebellion, he was allowed to live in peace in a remote part of North Island. There he attracted thousands of devotees with his religious cult, known as *Ringatu.* Te Kooti compared his followers to the Jews of the old Testament and their search for the Promised Land in the face of relentless enemies.

Like *Pai mariri, Ringatu* was an attempt to bring spiritual order into a chaotic world in which traditional values had no place. Adherents to *Ringatu* called themselves *tuwareware,* the forsaken. They used their beliefs as a means of survival in an alien world dominated by hostile Europeans. *Ringatu* was a place to stand, a place from which to defy the settlers. "In knowledge, the *pakeha* are but children, miserable beings and fools," cried one prophet. Like the Aztecs, the Tahitians, and the Northwest Coast Indians, the Maori turned inward on themselves, seeking spiritual strength from separatist cults. Many of them preferred to have no contact with Europeans whatsoever.

By the 1880s, many Maori living in areas affected by the wars were living in poverty. The selling of land continued, despite constant Maori resistance under such figures as Te Whiti, a chief of great *mana,* who advocated the refinement of *Pai mariri* doctrines into a finely tuned system of peaceful and passive resistance (Figure 16.4). The building of railroad lines frustrated attempts by the Maori to remain isolated, as settlers competed to acquire strategically placed lands close to the new tracks. Contrary to widely held assumptions, however, the Maori did not emerge from this traumatic period a dying people. Many tribes were demoralized; population densities had declined considerably. Many settlers, who now had little daily contact with Maori, assumed that they were finished. They thought of them as a listless, lazy, unreliable people. The old people, it was said, just smoked their pipes and asked "*E tuea te aha ?* [What is the use?]" Those Maori who were employed by *pakeha* were either under contract making roads or clearing forests,

*16.4   Te Whiti at the height of his powers in 1880. Portrait by Beatrice Dobie,
from* The Graphic, *1881.*

or earning wages as unskilled laborers. Thus, the settlers argued, the only solution was to educate the Maori to become Europeans or to use them as
unskilled employees.

Contemporary settler opinion comes across in pioneer New Zealand fiction of the time. The popular themes of early fiction followed predictable

tracks: a worthy, impoverished, but refined English family decides to emigrate to seek a new life. They learn all about New Zealand on the ship sailing out, a process that enables the author to turn the novel into a handbook for immigrants. The family buy land from friendly Maori, set up a school for them, and are in turn befriended and protected by the tribe when the wicked Wiremu Kingi rebels. Their new life is a triumph of hard work, moral rectitude, and Civilization among respectful and friendly natives. Another popular theme dwelt on the wars. The plot would mix up an officer hero, a Maori princess or attractive settler daughters, a sprinkling of *tobungas,* some bloodshed and military campaigns, and, of course, hostile savages. As one student of the New Zealand novel writes: "Mix well with muskets and inaccurate Maori, and serve up to a London publisher" (Stevens 1964, 74).

Popular novelists of international fame like G. A. Henty and Jules Verne also wrote about New Zealand and the Maori. Life was uncomplicated for Victorian novelists of the Henty type. For writers of this ilk, the differences between right and wrong, between virtue and vice, between civilized settler and uncivilized native were only too clear. Few Europeans, and certainly no novelists, had acquired a detailed knowledge of Maori life, nor did they bother to do so. So much was new and sensational about New Zealand that the aspiring novelist simply took advantage of cannibalism, geysers, tribal wars, and other popular topics to conjure up a grotesque stereotype of Maori life. Typical of the late nineteenth century was Alfred Grace's *Maoriland Tales,* published in 1901. A Maori girl is spurned by a white lover. She agrees to marry a Maori suitor if he will go to Auckland and bring her the head of her former lover's European wife. He does so, and she lived happily ever afterwards. At best, the Maori were depicted as naughty, lovable children who could be managed if you understood them. At worst, they were bloodthirsty cannibals.

The closing decades of the nineteenth century saw the Maori much concerned with a long-term question that still confronts them to the present day. What was to be their relationship to the dominant society, which seemed to feel the Maori were no longer a viable tribal society and as such willing to dispose of their land? By the end of World War I, it was clear to the Maori that they could no longer live apart from the Europeans. The more perceptive Maori realized their only hope was to acquire the education and qualifications that would allow them to assimilate into the mainstream of European politics and society. Today, sixty years later, the Maori live in a country that is more urbanized than France or Japan, a city dwellers' society in which they have a precarious and largely powerless role. In 1926, only eight out of every hundred Maori lived in the cities. Now the figure is over thirty per hundred. During the same period, the Maori have continued to lose their land. By 1965, the people owned just 3,680,585 acres of 66 million in New Zealand. Of these 3.6 million, no more than 695,000 acres can be used for a full range of agricultural purposes. One hundred seventy-five years of European contact and settlement have reduced Maori society to a parody of its former self. Fortunately, New Zealand is a welfare state, so a relatively secure "safety network" of social services provides some protection for even the most poverty-stricken members of society. In recent years, the Maori have challenged the Treaty of Waitangi in court and are pursuing major land claims aggressively. Of their own centuries-old lifeway, the Maori have been able to retain little, except their own image of a world radically different from that of the *pakeha.* This world is *tuanawaewae,* a place to repair to when the basis of all life—the land—is gone.

CHAPTER 17

The Legacy of Inequality

And I saw a new heaven and a new earth: for the first heaven and the first earth were passed away; and there was no more sea...And I heard a great voice out of heaven saying, Behold, the tabernacle of God is with men...And God shall wipe away all tears from their eyes; and there shall be no more death, neither sorrow, nor crying, neither shall there be any more pain: for the former things are passed away.

Revelation 21:1–4

HE KURA TANGATA, E KORE e rokohanga; he kura whemua ke rokohanga: "Take heed of this, that people perish or disappear; not so the land, which always remains." This Maori proverb epitomizes the attitude towards a people's individual identity in a world where the values of an industrial society are meaningless. Contrast this with a common attitude of Europeans in the nineteenth century, summarized in a work on New Zealand published in the 1820s: "We shall perhaps indeed arrive at the truest and most comprehensive estimate of the condition and character of the savage by considering him as a child in intellect and at the same time in physical powers and passions a man" (Simpson 1979, 83). The same attitude towards non-Westerners—"savages," if you will—prevailed wherever Westerners came into contact with other societies. Throughout the nineteenth century, the assumption was made that all non-Westerners were intellectually inferior to Europeans, that they did not have the white person's innate intelligence. These racial explanations for human differences did concede that more intelligent peoples would tend to behave more nearly like Westerners. However, cultural diversity was explained not in terms of nobility or peacefulness, nor in degrees of viciousness, but in terms of the civilized and the primitive, of progress and one's intellectual ability to become civilized (Figure 17.1).

The sorry chronicle of the Maori and their land was by no means unique to New Zealand. The same confrontation between totally incompatible cultural systems was played out in many parts of the world during the late nineteenth century and continues to this day in the Amazon rain forests and other remote areas. The Industrial Revolution launched a period of explosive growth, one that decimated tribal societies with very slow population growths but encouraged a massive expansion in world population under the impact of industrialization. By the 1990s, the world's population doubled every thirty-three years. Even more critical than the population explosion were radically increased rates of resource consumption, sparked by a global industrial civilization whose economies are based on the notion that constant expansion and ever accelerating consumption are desirable, indeed, should be the norm. The industrial civilization measures success by material wealth, by standard of living and rates of economic growth. These measures contrast dramatically with those of the relatively stable, non-Western societies the industrial West has supplanted and transformed. Within a few generations, the new industrial nations had stripped their own resources bare and were forced to look elsewhere. They were forced not only to look overseas for vital materials, but also to export millions of people to other parts of the world. By the 1990s, Americans alone were consuming fifteen times more energy than prehistoric farmers and seven times the world average in nonrenewable resources. The fundamental incompatibilities between industrial and nonindustrial societies are so profound that the enforced processes of what is often called "modernization" rarely seem to work effectively.

The contrasts between the Western and non-Western society are especially unsettling at a time when industrial civilization seems to be foundering in its own success. It is only now that anthropologists are beginning to comprehend some of the mechanisms, controls, and relationships that kept tribal societies in a state of dynamic equilibrium with their environments for thousands of years. And by now it is almost too late.

For five centuries, Europeans have debated their policies towards tribal societies, sometimes with passion, sometimes with insincerity, often with praiseworthy humanitarian concern. But rarely have they listened to the voices of the tribal societies themselves, and in most cases, the recommendation has been that indigenous peoples integrate themselves into the dominant society, blending the "best of both worlds" into a new, much more progressive future. No one was seriously concerned about peoples' real desires. Most policies towards indigenous peoples have been based on notions

*17.1 Missionary propaganda at its most romanticized and grotesque. A
Victorian tableau of a white missionary receiving gifts and respectful
attention from non-Western peoples from North America, Asia, Australia,
and New Zealand. This contrasts with the mayhem and war depicted in the
background. J. C. Wood, 1868.*

of progress and improvement. Progress has brought many things: penicillin, the tractor, the airplane, the refrigerator, radio, and television. It has also brought the gun, nuclear weapons, toxic chemicals, traffic deaths, and environmental pollution, to say nothing of powerful nationalisms and other political passions that pit human being against human being, society against society. Many of these innovations are even more destructive to non-Western societies than the land grabbing and forced conversions of a century and a half ago. Sometimes catastrophic change is forced on people under the guise of "economic development" or "modernization," and even today, as in the past, as a consequence of apparently trivial, short-term decisions by people acting in good faith.

Clash of Cultures has told the story of how Western civilization has established dominance by force or other means over various non-Western societies in the expectation that this dominance would remain permanent, even unchanging. In some cases, like the Khoikhoi and Tasmanians, this control has resulted in virtual or complete absorption or extinction for the weaker society. Others, like the Aztecs, the Tahitians, or the Maori, have undergone traumatic cultural change, loss of communally held land, and have been relegated to a subordinate role in the new social order. Still others, like the Kikuyu, managed to adjust to the realities of colonial rule and have survived with a highly modified traditional culture to achieve a dominant political role in a newly independent nation. One factor in the way people fared was the nature of the new social order. Sometimes, as in New Spain and New Zealand, the new government was rigid, even draconian in its governance. In others, like Brazil, it was content with a much more fluid stewardship. Often, these efforts at control, however flexible, were justified in the name of peace, health, happiness, and the perceived benefits of civilization. Almost invariably the primary concern was to protect the economic interests of the new government and its settlers, to control valuable natural resources for export to the world economy that flourished elsewhere.

The colonial administrators of the late nineteenth century were not concerned with the sovereignty of tribal nations, sovereignty that had been recognized as valid by such authorities as Bartolomé de las Casas and others centuries before. Their concern was to extend imperial control. For example, at the height of colonial expansion in 1888, the Institute of International Law at a meeting in Lausanne, Switzerland, condemned wars of extermination and other atrocities, but argued at the same time that sovereignty could be achieved simply by extending government control over a new region. The devices used to obtain such control were either military force, or dubious pacts like the Treaty of Waitangi, in which the Maori ceded their land and mineral rights, and the right to make laws, wage war, and administer justice to a remote queen and her government. Treaties like this were all too often elaborate shams. Lavish gifts were proffered, messages of peace read. But the threat of force was always in the background.

Next came large-scale, well-organized programs of base camps, tax collecting schemes, and levies of forced labor that established governance over previously independent societies. At this point, the tribal society was no longer in control of its own affairs. The colonial power was firmly in charge, either through elaborate schemes of direct rule that tied French colonies to the homeland, or through protective legislation that provided a form of welfare governance for indigenous peoples who were minorities and were of little use for labor and other development purposes. The most widespread system was that of indirect rule, established by the British in Africa, where the government recognized tribal entities and ruled through chiefs and tribal councils. This system was an effective way of maintaining order, collecting taxes, and acquiring adequate supplies of local labor. In due time, this system gave way to a new, independent government controlled by an educated elite who simply took over the old system and replaced many appointed chiefs with elected officials and a local bureaucracy. The situation was well summed up by the eminent anthropologist Bronislaw Malinowski: "The government of any race consists rather in implanting in them ideas of right, of law and order, and making them obey such ideas" (1929, 23).

Most tribal societies were almost powerless to resist Western civilization on equal terms. They lacked the political organization and the allies within the dominant society to make significant political gains. It is only belatedly, and in recent years, that regional, national, and international organizations have emerged to support the causes of tribal societies. Such organizations have taken many forms, but their primary focus has been in keeping traditional cultural values alive and in organizing widely scattered, sometimes antagonistic, and often demoralized peoples into larger political units to confront external threats. Some are political pressure groups, others operate on a larger scale and bring blatant cases of exploitation and illegal land grabbing into the national and international spotlight. There are, for example, at least five major regional organizations in Colombia, South America, formed to fight for control of Indian lands. Indigenous peoples have become active on the international scene as well, especially since the early 1970s. The year 1975 saw the founding of the World Council of Indigenous Peoples, at an assembly on Nootka tribal lands on Vancouver Island. Fifty-two delegates from nineteen countries formed an international organization of indigenous peoples that has achieved official status as a Non-government Organization of the United Nations. This affiliation enables it to present the case of indigenous peoples on the widest possible international canvas. The work of this body has borne fruit in many directions, not least in a powerful declaration by the 1978 UN Conference to Combat Racism and Racial Discrimination (Article 21):

> *The Conference endorses the right of indigenous peoples to maintain their traditional structure of economy and culture, including their own language, and also recognizes the special relationship of indigenous peoples to their land and stresses that their land, land rights and natural resources should not be taken away from them.*

Today, a bewildering array of organizations claims to support the interests of indigenous peoples. Many of these are little more than special interest groups with political or spiritual axes to grind. Undoubtedly the most successful are those who provide financial and technical support and strengthen tribal societies' capacity for self-defense and support. The Aborigines Protection Society of the 1830s was the first of these organizations. Some of the most successful modern-day organizations attempt to help traditional societies with basically nonpolitical approaches, supporting development and adjustment, as well as self-determination. Unfortunately, such small-scale efforts are a tiny drop in an ocean of misunderstanding and neglect, in which many, diverse special interests are fishing and seeking short- and long-term advantage— to the detriment of the very societies they sometimes purport to assist.

Until very recently, industrial states have always assumed that tribal societies will ultimately be integrated and assimilated fully into the larger polity, whatever the cost in human terms. Victorian writers like Herman Merivale even described them as "feeble survivals of an obsolete world" (1861, 510). Today, the debate rages over "what can be done about" the few surviving tribal societies still relatively untouched by Western civilization. Should they be isolated in human zoos or be preserved as tourist curiosities, as "smiling, friendly natives busily entertaining tourists with their quaint, primitive and exotic ways" (*Cultural Survival Quarterly*, 1983, 3:3)? Or do tribal societies have the right to remain permanently outside any modern state structure and to reject any attempts to "modernize them?" The answers are complicated, perhaps even beyond our power to address.

Certain deeply held sentiments common to much of humankind have tended to exacerbate the clash of cultures. Social stratification, the determination that one group in a society is considered superior to another, has been deeply ingrained in human society since at least the beginnings of farming some ten thousand years ago. The Sumerians, the ancient Egyptians, the Chinese, the Maya, and later the Aztecs and Inca all grappled with the problem of the inequality of human beings. They did so by using unexplained divine forces as the justification for enormous numbers of people to toil unquestioningly for the good of the state—and the few nobles who ran it. This form of social structure, one in which a few ruled and many labored, was taken for granted in many non-Western societies. It prevailed in nonliterate societies, where the knowledge of earlier generations was communicated verbally through brittle and transient human memories. Here tradition and community were all-important, the common good placed above that of the individual. Similar beliefs were an important legacy of Greek and Roman civilization in the West, but were soon modified by a set of contrary ideas that taught that all people were equal before God.

These Christian doctrines maintained that every individual, however insignificant, had at least some equality in terms of law and opportunity. As time went on, the individual became more important. The nuclear family of husband, wife, and children began to replace the kin group and the extended family as the rationale for technical advance, exploration, and learning. Then came the printing press, the ability to store knowledge for everyone to share, an opening of a vast reservoir of human experience and learning for anyone who could absorb it. The result was the Renaissance, which fostered free inquiry and personal initiative. This initiative was shackled by the centralized governments of the new nation states that were emerging from the feudal kingdoms of medieval times. However, personal initiative was encouraged by a Church that itself was highly controlled and stratified. But it taught, even if it did not always believe, that the individual was all important, and that theoretically, at any rate, everyone had equal opportunity.

These notions of social inequality and equality at the same time were contradictory doctrines. The one provided the assumptions that organized European civilization. The other was an article of faith, read daily from Christian pulpits everywhere, acted on sometimes, but always in the public consciousness. It was this basic contradiction, together with technological superiority, that provided the internal strength that enabled the Western nations to overrun the rest of the world. Their political unity and their technological advantage were the tools used to dominate others. The combination of individualism, political unity, and social discipline enabled them to achieve total domination. Yet the same contradiction made it inevitable that their colonies would rebel.

No single factor caused the resulting complex and ever-changing relationships between Europeans and the multitude of societies with which they came in contact. An enormous diversity of situations arose as a result of contact and affected each side's perspective of the other's—the conscious and unconscious beliefs of the dominant culture, its assumptions about its own institutions, the sophistication and complexity of the host society, and the motives of the visitors. Even the numbers of men relative to women among the visitors and each society's attitudes to sex affected the relationship that developed in the decades that followed. Only one factor seems to have played an even vaguely dominant role: that of the human will and its ability to make conscious decisions—whether profoundly important or apparently trivial.

The power of human will wreaked awesome change among the people described in these pages. The Khoikhoi lost much of their cattle as a result of dozens of feckless, spur-of-the-moment decisions that decimated their breeding stock for future generations. Their individual deeds in themselves were on a small scale and far from momentous. In contrast, the Spanish Crown decided early on to unify New Spain on the basis of a common faith—Catholicism. Time and time again, the Crown supported the Indians against the settlers, the people against the nobles, even if the support at the time was ineffective and thousands of miles away from Mexico. In the long term, conscious policy decisions in faraway Spain prevailed and set political and economic trends that profoundly affected the relationship between Hispanics and Indians for centuries. Only rarely can decisions of this magnitude with such momentous long-term consequences be overturned, and then only by the most prodigious effort of all parties concerned. Almost invariably, the decisions made subsequent to European contact set the course for generations, dividing the new society rigidly along lines that separated the conquerors from the conquered, the colonists from the colonized.

It was only in the nineteenth and twentieth centuries that the descendants of the host societies acquired the very Christian individualism propagated by their masters, and began to rebel. Their newly acquired independence caused such unrest that the relationship between master and servant, ruler and ruled, has been completely reversed since World War II, a tremendous event that is still hard for Westerners to assimilate and explain. This process has been assisted by the deeply ingrained feelings of Christian charity that give and have always given Western society tendencies towards humility and feelings of guilt, even apology. It was this same disposition that caused many people in earlier centuries to talk of Noble Savages, and to undertake the ambitious humanitarian projects that are one of the more heartening features of our relationships with other societies.

Ever since Sumerian times, the bluff of kings and rulers has worked. Thousands of people have accepted the unquestioning notion that social inequality is an inherent part of their world. Social stability—not necessarily political order—has persisted for centuries, even millennia. People have gone about the business of planting and harvest, of trading, paying taxes, getting married and having children, despite a weighty backdrop of momentous political change. The social order had been taken for granted until the "infection of European individualism," as Philip Mason calls it, took hold. This happened when Europeans taught the ruled the basic truths about the admixture of conformity and individualism that makes Western society work. It was—and is—inevitable that the ruled would seek independence, and that there would be violence and social disorder before their colonial rulers saw that they were in earnest and independence was negotiated. The lesson was not lost on nationalists from many nations, nor on American Indian leaders and Afro-Americans: whites do not listen until violence begins.

This revolt is, of course, part of a much wider uprising, of poor against rich, of youth against age, even female against male. Every facet of this vast revolt is part of the new reality, that people everywhere have rejected the accepted notion that inequality is part of the established order. Inequality was for long the cement that held entire societies, civilizations, and even empires together. "No alternative to inequality has yet been found that is consistent with freedom," writes Mason (1970, 326), so much so that African-Americans were once excluded from North American society, the society of the equal and the free. Why? Because they were not perceived of as human. The revolt against racial dominance is especially bitter, not only because of the insulting views of nineteenth-century writers, of whom New Zealand novelists were only a few; but also because of the Caribbean experience—the brutality of slavery and colonialism—that convinced blacks that the ambition to being white was worth striving for.

The ways in which people have classified one another have changed constantly through the centuries. The Dutch originally thought of themselves as quite separate from the Khoikhoi, not only on grounds of color, but on religious, linguistic, and a host of obvious cultural criteria as well. Within a century, the Khoikhoi were gone from the Cape. They had moved elsewhere, been killed, or assimilated into the fringes of European society. By this time the people of color worshipped the same God and enjoyed a watered-down version of European culture. So the Dutch shifted their mental ground and considered the Cape Coloreds a people apart solely on the basis of their color. Such simplistic views may persist for centuries, as they did in South Africa until the 1990s, reinforced by government regulations and laws that became more and more grotesque. In less extreme cases, the passage of time sees the boundaries of color, culture, language, and religion no longer coinciding. This is due in part because of gradual cultural change, and also because increased European migration and vastly improved communications have shrunk physical distances and reduced cultural distances between different, once widely separated cultures. In societies like Mexico where this intersection of different groups is recognized, it can become a social strength. In others, like South Africa, the boundaries became more and more artificial, and social tensions became acute and unbearable, forcing ultimate change. The question for the next century is not whether the sorts of social inequalities described in these pages are justified, nor even whether they work to the betterment of humankind: it is, what social cement is going to evolve to take its place?

History shows us there is no easy road to harmonious relations between people of different cultures or ethnic background. The categorical contrast between the civilized and the primitive originated in classical times and persisted into this century. Today we know it is a false and empty one. Countless anthropological studies have shown that people from other societies are as capable as we are of showing high regard for human life, and on occasion just as impelled to show great altruism and unselfishness toward others. By the same token, societies such as the Aztecs or Tahitians were just as capable of exploiting one another unmercifully. Every culture, whether that of the Tasmanians, the Yahgan, or the Maori exhibited the same range of behavior as we do. Their traditional cultures should not be idealized any more than ours. Nor is it a valid notion to assume, as many early missionaries did, that other societies will willingly surrender their cultures to our own, or reject their values completely.

In today's world, many non-Western societies stand in the middle of a ferocious material and ideological crossfire of industrialists, arms companies, fundamentalist missionaries, political ideologues, and even, unfortunately, a few anthropologists. Their beliefs and philosophies are under constant assault. Yet many of them, like the Hopi Indians of the American Southwest, some of the Maya Indians of the Yucatán, or a few bands of Australians, still cling on to their ancient philosophies of living harmoniously with the natural environment. The nineteenth-century missionary working in New Zealand, southern Africa, and Tahiti soon found it was impossible to eradicate an entire culture. Unfortunately, the same lesson must be relearned again and again to this day.

The inability of humankind to comprehend others heightens the mounting tensions in our industrial and nuclear world. The same inability has haunted us ever since Bartolemeu Dias encountered the Khoikhoi at Mossel Bay and Christopher Columbus landed on San Salvador. The apparent failure of generations of intelligent and perceptive people to solve this problem may tempt one to wonder if there is hope for the future. The answer must be a resounding yes, for the most lasting legacy of the clash of cultures had been the rejection of inequality as a means of suppressing individual ambitions. The diverse industrial society will have to achieve harmony by allowing people to express their diversity in a civilization where no one group has overriding priority and where the humblest and most poverty-stricken of people can win esteem in many ways. Humanity has the capacity to achieve such a society, but is prevented from doing so by its own fear, greed, and jealousy, qualities that will always be with us. The task will become harder and more traumatic as natural resources become scarcer, petty nationalisms boil over, and political passions rise. Some idealists say that technology is the wave of the future, that computers and other mechanical artifices will enable humankind to shape radically new societies. Others predict that we will destroy ourselves in a nuclear or environmental holocaust. More likely our hopes and aspirations for the future lie not in microcomputers or awesome weapons, but in humankind's most remarkable and distinctive asset—successive generations of people who care passionately about eradicating injustice and creating a better world for everyone. Such people are usually a tiny but fortunately vocal minority, individuals who feel so strongly about justice that they are prepared to suffer hardship—even death—for their beliefs. It is they who overthrow empires, move societies, and shake the foundations of complacent conformity. The world is fortunate that such people have been among us since long before the Age of Discovery.

We humans are still on a quest for a kind of earthly paradise. We started off with dim myths of the Garden of Eden, then searched for paradise on earth. Then paradise turned into a utopia of Noble Savages, a dreamlike land where people lived simply with nature and each other. The nineteenth century changed this vision into disillusioned reality and banished the Noble Savage to oblivion. Today, we live in a world of far greater complexity, where computers, the Web, steamships, airplanes, and world wars have made everyone far more accessible. Societies once far removed from another have mingled and migrated until the stereotypes and perceptions of even half a century ago are rapidly becoming meaningless. But now we are searching for a new world, a new utopia where the injustices and inequalities of centuries will be eliminated and hunger unknown. The search is overladen with catchwords such as "human rights," "computer age," and "green revolution." But it is a search, nevertheless, and conceivably a less idealistic and impractical one. This time, perhaps, there are enough people on earth who reject the age-old evils of inequality and racism, who are prepared to transfer their thoughts into concerted action. Perhaps a new faith will be born that will carry us closer to what is probably an ever-elusive ideal.

"And I saw a new heaven and a new earth: for the first heaven and the first earth were passed away; and there was no more sea." Two thousand years ago, the twenty-first chapter of the Book of Revelation offered hope for the future. Doubtless future generations and new faiths will help humankind define its idealism in a world where the traditional institutions and symbols seem increasingly bankrupt and irrelevant. Since civilization began, people have puzzled about the world without and clothed it in myths and stereotypes that reflected their own fears and deeply held beliefs. The world of reality has always functioned apart from these puzzlements. But today, for the first time, the outside world is readily accessible to most of us and the curtain of myth is harder to draw. Perhaps myth and reality will finally begin to coincide. *Clash of Cultures* tells a tragic tale; yet from its lessons comes a message of hope that one day, perhaps, humankind will be able to create at least some just societies on earth.

Guide to Sources

THE LITERATURE ON THE GENERAL subject of cultural contact between Western civilization and other human societies is gargantuan and beyond the scope of one scholar to master. The reader wishing to delve more deeply into the subject is best advised to start with the general accounts mentioned below and then to consult a specialist in a particular culture area before plunging into the scattered and often polemical academic literature.

The sources consulted in the writing of this book comprised more than 800 references in several languages ranging from entire monographs to scattered manuscripts in the British Museum Reading Room. The list that follows covers mainly secondary summaries, travelers' accounts, and general studies that are widely available in good university, college, and public libraries. Most contain useful bibliographies that act as signposts for more detailed reading. For clarity, and on the assumption that most readers will be English-speaking, I have concentrated on books rather than articles in English.

1. Prologue

THE LITERATURE ON THE AGE of Discovery and clash of cultures is growing rapidly. The following list can but guide the reader to a few general works that should be combined with more specialized references cited in later chapters. Henri Baudin's *Paradise on Earth* (New Haven: Yale University Press, 1969) is a fundamental essay for anyone interested in the clash of cultures. It describes changing European perceptions of paradise and utopia through the centuries, and has been a major inspiration for this book. Eric R. Wolf, *Europe and the People Without History* (Berkeley: University of California Press, 1982) is another definitive work of seminal use in the writing of this book. It covers the impact of European capitalism and industrial development on what Wolf calls "people without history." The theoretical chapters in Wolf will be of great use to readers interested in scholarly perspectives on the clash of cultures. For a review of world systems approaches, see Stephen K. Sanderson (ed.), *Civilizations and World Systems* (Walnut Creek, CA: Altamira Press, 1995). The whole problem of acculturation theory in anthropology is covered by two classic works: Robert Redfield, *The Primitive World and Its Transformations* (Ithaca: Cornell University Press, 1953) and Melville J. Herskovitz, *Acculturation* (New York: J. J. Augustin, 1938). Edward Spicer's *Cycles of Conquest* (Tucson: University of Arizona Press, 1961) deals with the American Southwest, but has many lessons for other areas as well. The Kikuyu are described by Greet Kershaw in John Middleton and Greet Kershaw, *The Kikuyu and Kamba of Kenya* (London: International African Institute, 1965). Leonard Thompson's *Survival in Two Worlds: Moshoeshoe of Lesotho 1786–1870* (Oxford: Clarendon Press, 1975) is a study of one of the most remarkable figures of nineteenth-century African history. By far the most comprehensive account of Atlantic voyaging is Samuel Eliot Morison's great work, *The European Discovery of America*, 2 vols. (New York: Oxford University Press, 1971 and 1974). For the Pacific see J. C. Beaglehole, *The Exploration of the Pacific*, 3rd ed. (Palo Alto: Stanford University Press, 1966). Inga Clendinnen's *Aztecs* (Cambridge: Cambridge University Press, 1991) offers an elegant analysis of the challenge of historical and non-traditional sources. Eric Williams's *Capitalism and Slavery*, rev ed. (Chapel Hill: University of North Carolina Press, 1994) is a classic.

2. The Khoikhoi of the Cape of Good Hope

THE CONTROVERSIES SURROUNDING EARLY anthropological observations are well described by Margaret T. Hodgen, *Early Anthropology in the Sixteenth and Seventeenth Centuries* (Philadelphia: University of Pennsylvania Press, 1964). The basic source on the Khoikhoi is historian Richard Elphick's *Kraal and Castle* (New Haven: Yale University Press, 1977). Elphick's book is a comprehensive account of the history and anthropology of the Khoikhoi written elegantly for a specialist audience, but readable all the same. See also Elphick's *Khoikhoi and the Founding of White South Africa* (Johannesburg: Raven Press, 1985). Read this in conjunction with the brilliant chapters on hunters and herders by Monica Wilson in *The Oxford History of South Africa*, vol. 1, edited by Leonard Thompson and Wilson herself (Oxford: Clarendon Press, 1969). Two invaluable, indeed vivid, compilations of early writings on the Khoikhoi are: R. Raven-Hart (ed.), *Before Van Riebeeck: Callers at South Africa from 1488 to 1652* (Cape Town: C. Struik, 1967) and the same author's *Cape Good Hope, 1652–1702*, 2 vols. (Cape Town: A. A. Balkema, 1971). Writings on the archaeology of the Khoikhoi are scattered, and are best found in articles in recent numbers of the *South African Archaeological Bulletin*. Andrew Smith, *Pastoralism in Africa* (Johannesburg: University of the Witwatersrand Press,

1992) gives an admirable archaeological synthesis. See also: Alan Barnard, *Hunters and Herders of Southern Africa* (Cambridge: Cambridge University Press, 1992). No one should miss Carmel Schrire's *Digging Through Darkness* (Charlottesville: University of Virginia Press, 1995), an account of an excavation of an outlying Dutch trading post, which throws light on Khoikhoi/Dutch relations. J. S. Marais's *The Cape Coloured People, 1652–1937* (Johannesburg: Witwatersrand University Press, 1962) is an authoritative study of race relations at the Cape in more recent centuries.

3. The Aztecs

A NUMBER OF BOOKS SUMMARIZE the rise and fall of the Aztec civilization, among them Frances Berdan, *The Aztecs of Central Mexico* (New York: Holt, Rinehart and Winston, 1982), Richard F. Townsend, *The Aztecs* (London and New York: Thames and Hudson, 1992), and Michael Smith, *The Aztecs* (Oxford: Oxford University Press). Inga Clendinnen's *Aztecs* (Cambridge: Cambridge University Press, 1991) offers a perceptive analysis of the civilization and the Conquest. The tragic events of the Conquest are best experienced through the eyewitness accounts of Bernal Diaz, *History of the Conquest of New Spain* edited by J. H. Cohen (Baltimore: Pelican Books, 1963), or through Bayard Morris's edited *Five Letters of Cortés to the Emperor* (New York: W. W. Norton, 1928). The Aztec side of the story has been brilliantly translated by Arthur O. Anderson and Charles E. Dibble, *The Florentine Codex,* vol. 12 (Salt Lake City: University of Utah Press, 1971), or in the same authors' *The War of Conquest* (Salt Lake City: University of Utah Press, 1975), a distillation of and commentary on the last volume of Sahagun's great work. Another fascinating sixteenth-century account is Diego Duran's *The Aztecs: The History of the Indies of New Spain,* translated by Doris Heyden and Fernando Horcasitas (Norman: University of Oklahoma Press, 1994). William Arens's *The Man-Eating Myth* (New York: Oxford University Press, 1979) discusses cannibalism. For archaeology, try Smith and Townsend, already cited, and Muriel Porter Weaver, *The Aztecs, Maya, and Their Predecessors,* 3rd ed. (New York: Academic Press, 1991). Finally, no serious reader should miss W. H. Prescott's *The History of the Conquest of Mexico* (New York: Harpers, 1843). For all its romantic excesses and ethnocentric viewpoints, the book is a classic.

4. The Consequences of the Spanish Conquest

HUGH HONOUR'S *THE NEW GOLDEN Land: European Images of America* (New York: Pantheon, 1975) deals with changing visual perceptions of the American Indian. See also Benjamin Keen, *The Aztec Image in Western Thought* (New Brunswick: Rutgers University Press, 1971). Charles Gibson's *The Aztecs under Spanish Rule* (Palo Alto: Stanford University Press, 1964) is the definitive work on the fate of the Indians, but should be amplified by Lewis Hanke's works, notably his *The Spanish Struggle for Justice in the Conquest of America* (New York: American Historical Society, 1949), *Bartolemé de las Casas: An Interpretation of his Life and Writings* (The Hague, Netherlands: Martinus Nyhoff,1951), and *All Mankind is One* (De Kalb: Northern Illinois University Press, 1974). Some other useful works are: Robert Ricard, *The Spiritual Conquest of Mexico* (Berkeley: University of California Press, 1966), which covers missionary endeavors, and George Foster's *Culture and Conquest: America's Spanish Conquest* (Chicago: Quadrangle Books, 1960), which is a much-quoted anthropological source. Colin M. Maclachlan and Jaime Rodriguez, *The Forging of the Cosmic Race* (Berkeley: University of California Press, 1980) is a fascinating and readable account of the emergence of the *mestizo* in Mexico.

5. The Land of the Rising Sun

STEVEN WARSHAW'S, *JAPAN EMERGES: A Concise History of Japan from Its Origin to the Present* (Berkeley: Diablo Press, 1989) is a useful summary that formed a basis for this chapter. See also: George Sansome's monumental *A History of Japan*, 3 vols. (Palo Alto: Stanford University Press, 1958–63), which discusses the forces that formed Japanese society. Gina Barnes's *China, Korea, and Japan* (London: Thames and Hudson, 1994) ably describes the archaeology of Japan. Eric Wolf's *Europe and the People Without History* (Berkeley: University of California Press, 1982) and John Keay's *The Honorable Company: A History of the British East India Company* (New York: HarperCollins, 1991) cover the general European mercantile background. Jeffrey Massim's *Warrior Government in Early Medieval Japan* (New Haven: Yale University Press, 1974) is very helpful, as is Charles R. Boxer's *The Christian Century in Japan, 1549–1650* (Berkeley: University of California Press, 1956). Michael Cooper's *They Came to Japan* (Berkeley: University of California Press, 1956) is an admirable summary of eyewitness accounts of early Japan, 1543–1640. Roger Pineau (ed.), *The Japan Expedition 1852–1854: The Personal Journals of Commodore Matthew C. Perry*. (Washington DC: Smithsonian Institution Press, 1968) gives the best account of Perry's mission. W.G. Beasley's *The Meiji Revolution* (Palo Alto: Stanford University Press, 1972) is authoritative.

6. The Great Dying

ANN RAMENOVKY'S *VECTORS OF DEATH* (Albuquerque: University of New Mexico Press, 1989) summarizes earlier literature and depopulation estimates, then bolsters them with archaeological data. Linda A. Newson's *Life and Death in Early Colonial Ecuador* (Norman: University of Oklahoma Press, 1995) is an important study of depopulation based on tribute records, covering three ecological zones of the Andean region.

7. Noble Savages: The Tahitians

HOXIE NEALE FAIRCHILD WROTE WHAT is widely regarded as the definitive study of the Noble Savage nearly three quarters of a century ago: *The Noble Savage: A Study in Romantic Naturalism* (New York: Columbia University Press, 1928). This, and Baudin's *Paradise on Earth,* were major sources for this chapter. Bernadette Bucher's *La Sauvage aux seins pendants* (Paris: Hermann, 1977) analyzes European images of savages, while Bernard Smith's *European Vision and the South Pacific, 1768–1850* (Oxford: Clarendon Press, 1960) looks at European responses to later art. J. C. Beaglehole was the doyen of Pacific historians. His *The Exploration of the Pacific,* 3rd ed. (Palo Alto: Stanford University Press, 1966) is a classic, and no one can write about Captain Cook without his *The Life of Captain James Cook* (Palo Alto: Stanford University Press, 1974) at his or her side. Cook's journals appeared in three volumes under Beaglehole's editorship between 1955 and 1969, *The Journals of Captain Cook on his Voyages of Discovery* (Cambridge: Halkluyt Society), and have been used extensively here. Beaglehole also edited *The Endeavour Journal of Joseph Banks 1768–1771* (Sydney: Angus and Robertson, 1962). Patrick O'Brian's recent biography of Joseph Banks, *Joseph Banks: A Life* (Boston, MA: David Godine, 1993) is also recommended reading. The Tahitians themselves are brilliantly described by Douglas Oliver in his monumental *Ancient Tahitian Society* (Honolulu: University of Hawaii Press, 1974). Pacific voyaging is covered in Ben Finney, *Voyage of Rediscovery* (Berkeley: University of California Press, 1994).

8. The Van Diemeners and 9. "The Noble Savage Is a Dog!"

THE TASMANIANS HAVE ATTRACTED MANY writers in recent years, but the most comprehensive, if dull, account is probably that of H. Ling Roth, *The Aborigines of Tasmania* (London: Kegan Paul, 1890). D. M. Davies's *The Last of the Tasmanians* (London: Frederick Muller, 1973) and Robert Travis's *The Tasmanians* (Melbourne: Cassell, 1968) are widely read popular accounts. Lyndall Ryan's *The Aboriginal Tasmanians.* (Vancouver: University of British Columbia Press, 1943) combines a careful description of aboriginal life with a discussion of Augustus Robinson. N. J. B. Plumley's *Friendly Mission: The Tasmanian Journals and Papers of George Augustus Robinson, 1829–1834* (Hobart, Tasmania: Tasmanian Historical Association, 1966) is probably the most useful source on Tasmanian life before European contact. Robinson's journals are a mine of fascinating information, while Christine Cornell's *The Journal of Post Captain Nicholas Baudin* (Adelaide: Libraries Board of South Australia, 1974) gives insights into the early days of European contact. N. J. B. Plumley's *An Annotated Bibliography of the Tasmanian Aborigines* (London: Royal Anthropological Institute, 1969) lists all early references. N. G. Buthin's, *Forming a Colonial Economy* (Cambridge: Cambridge University Press, 1994) is a useful source on the transformation of Tasmania into a farming region. Alex Graeme-Evans' *Tasmanian Rogues and Absconders* (Launceston, Tasmania: Regal Publications, 1994) is a two-volume study of convicts and the treatment of aborigines. Sharon Morgan's *Land Settlement in Early Tasmania* (Cambridge: Cambridge University Press, 1992) describes the growth and expansion of colonial Tasmania, also the treatment of aborigines with special reference to the work of Augustus Robinson. Finally, no general reader should miss Robert Hughes's *The Fatal Shore* (New York: Random House, 1986), a popular account of early Australian history, including Tasmania. On the archaeological side, readers may benefit from looking at Richard Cosgrove, Jim Allen, and Brian Marshall, "Pleistocene Occupation of Tasmania." *Antiquity* 64 (242):59–78 (1990).

10. The Word of God

A GENERAL WORK BASED ON a BBC television series is useful as a starting point: Julian Pettifer and Richard Bradley, *Missionaries* (London: BBC Publications, 1990). Richard Elphick's "Africans and the Christian Campaign in Southern Africa," in Howard Lamar and Leonard Thompson (eds.), *The Frontier in History,* (New Haven: Yale University Press, 1981), 270–307, provided the major historical inspiration for the arguments in this chapter. Colin Newbury's *Tahiti Nui: Change and Survival in French Polynesia 1767–1945* (Honolulu: University of Hawaii Press, 1980) describes missionary activities in the south Pacific, providing a clear path through a veritable flood of self-serving evangelical literature. So does the same author's *The History of the Tahitian Mission, 1799–1830* (London: Cambridge University Press, 1982). William Ellis's *Polynesian Researches* (London: Fisher, Son and Jackson, 1829) provides an eyewitness perspective, as does James Wilson's *A Missionary Voyage to the Southern Pacific Ocean...* (London: T. Chapman, 1799). Robert I. Levy's *Tahitians: Mind and Experience in the Society Islands* (Chicago: University of Chicago Press, 1975) is a superb study of recent cultural change in Tahiti. For Herman Melville's writings, see Charles Roberts Anderson, *Melville in the South Seas* (New York: Columbia University Press, 1939). Other useful sources: Oliver, Douglas. *The Pacific Islands,* 3rd ed. (Honolulu: University of Hawaii Press, 1989), and the same author's comprehensive *Native Cultures of the Pacific Islands.* (Honolulu: University of Hawaii Press,

1989). See also Victoria S. Lockwood, Thomas G. Harding, and Ben J. Wallace (eds.), *Contemporary Pacific Societies: Studies in Development and Change.* (Englewood Cliffs, NJ: Prentice Hall, 1993). On Pacific whaling see John R. Spears, *The Story of the New England Whalers* (New York: Macmillan, 1908), and Elmo Paul Hohman, *The American Whaleman* (New York: Longmans Green, 1928).

11. The Fuegians and 12. Missionaries at the end of the Earth

PHILIP L. CURTIN'S *THE IMAGE of Africa: British Ideas and Actions 1780–1850* (Madison: University of Wisconsin Press, 1964) and Winthrop D. Jordan's *White Over Black* (Chapel Hill: University of North Carolina, 1968) are definitive studies of slavery and racial attitudes that were drawn upon for this chapter, and, for that matter, throughout this book. E. Lucas Bridges's *The Uttermost Part of the Earth* (New York: E. P. Dutton, 1949) tells the vivid story of early missionary endeavors, as well as providing unique, first-hand insights into Yahgan life. Eric Shipton's *Tierra del Fuego: The Fatal Lodestone* (London: Charles Knight, 1973) will interest casual readers. The classic anthropological study is long outdated: Samuel Lothrop's *The Indians of Tierra del Fuego* (New York: Museum of the American Indian, 1928). However, Lothrop's study is still useful, simply because it was written while some traditional cultures could still be observed. Try also John M. Cooper's chapter, "The Yahgan," in Julian Steward (ed.), *Handbook of South American Indians, Vol. I* (Washington, DC: Bureau of American Ethnology, 1946), 81–106. Robert FitzRoy's *Narrative of the Surveying Voyage of his Majesty's Ships Adventure and Beagle between the Years 1826 and* 1836 (London: Henry Colburn, 1839) describes the kidnapping of the Fuegians and should be combined with the bizarre but little-known story of Allen Gardiner in John W. Marsh and W. H. Stirling, *The Story of Commander Allen Gardiner, R.N.* (London: James Nisbet, 1887). George Stocking's *Race, Culture, and Evolution* (New York: Free Press, 1968) describes the early years of the Aborigines Protection Society and other developments in early anthropology.

13. Furs and Firearms: The Hurons of Eastern Canada

THE DEFINITIVE WORK ON THE Huron is Bruce G. Trigger's *The Children of Aataensic: A History of the Huron People to 1660* (Montreal: McGill-Queen's University Press, 1976). I have drawn heavily on this work for this chapter. Trigger's *The Huron: Farmers of the North* (New York: Holt, Rinehart and Winston, 1969) is a historical ethnography that fills in many details of traditional life. Elizabeth Tooker's *An Ethnography of the Huron Indians, 1615–1649* (Washington, DC: Bureau of American Ethnology, Bulletin no. 190,

1964) is fundamental. W. Vernon Kinietz's *The Indians of the Western Great Lakes 1615–1760* (Ann Arbor: University of Michigan Press, 1940) covers the wider historical picture. There is a rich literature on the Jesuits in eastern Canada. Try Cornelius J. Jaenen's *Friend and Foe: Aspects of French-Amerindian Cultural Contact in the Sixteenth and Seventeenth Centuries* (Toronto: McClelland and Stewart, 1976) and James Moore's *Indian and Jesuit: A Seventeenth-Century Encounter* (Chicago: Loyola University Press, 1982). For the prehistoric background, see Brian M. Fagan, *Ancient North America*, 2nd ed. (London: Thames and Hudson, 1995).

14. Northwest Coast Indians

Cook's journals and Beaglehole's *Life* are key sources here, as is Robin Fisher's *Contact and Conflict: Indian-European Relations in British Columbia, 1774–1890* (Vancouver: University of British Columbia Press, 1977). Herman Merivale's *Lectures on Colonization and Colonies* (London: Longman, Green, Longman, and Roberts, 1861) lays out British attitudes towards colonization very well. Franz Boas, *Kwakiutl Ethnography*, edited by Helen Codere (Chicago: University of Chicago Press, 1966), and Ronald P. Rohner (ed.), *The Ethnography of Franz Boas: Letters and Diaries of Franz Boas Written on the Northwest Coast from 1886 to 1931* (Chicago: University of Chicago Press, 1969) are basic sources. Helen Codere's *Fighting with Property: A Study of Kwakiutl Potlatching and Warfare 1792–1930* (Seattle: University of Washington Press, 1966) describes the potlatch, the ceremonial feast of the Northwest Coast. So does D. I. Cole and I. Chaiken's *An Iron Hand Upon the People: The Law Against the Potlatch on the Pacific Northwest Coast* (Seattle: University of Washington Press, 1990). See also Aldona Jonaitis, *Chiefly Feasts: The Enduring Kwakiutl Potlatch* (Seattle: University of Washington Press, 1991). Leland Donald's *Aboriginal Slavery on the Northwest Coast of North America* (Berkeley: University of California Press, 1997) argues that slaves and slavery were central to Northwest hunter-fisher societies. Phillip Drucker's *Cultures of the North Pacific Coast* (San Francisco: Chandler, 1965) and *The Northern and Central Nootkan Tribes* (Washington, DC: Bureau of American Ethnology, 1951) are good summaries of traditional culture. See also May Beck's *Heroes and Heroines: Tlingit-Haida Legend.* (Anchorage: Alaska Northwest Books, 1989), which recounts original Haida-Tlingit myths with reference to their similarity to Western and Greek equivalents. On the topic of William Duncan see John Arctander's *The Apostle of Alaska: The Story of William Duncan of Metlaktla* (New York: Revell, 1909).

15. The Maori and 16. The Colonization of New Zealand

Cook's Journals and Beaglehole's *Life* again provide a foundation for all reading on early New Zealand. Maori traditional culture is described by Sir Peter Buck in *The Coming of the Maori* (Wellington, New Zealand: Whitcombe and Tombs, 1949), an account that is somewhat outdated and unreliable, as is Eldon Best's *The Maori*, 2 vols. (Wellington, New Zealand: Whitcombe, 1924). See also Andrew P. Vayda, *Maori Warfare* (Wellington, New Zealand: Polynesian Society, 1960). Raymond Firth's *Primitive Economics of the New Zealand Maori* (London: Routledge, 1929) is authoritative. Keith Sinclair, A *History of New Zealand*, rev. ed. (London: Allen Lane, 1980) is one of the best summaries of the subject, while Harrison M. Wright's *New Zealand, 1769– 1840: Early Years of European Contact* (Cambridge: Harvard University Press, 1959) is very useful. David P. Millar's "Whales, Flax Traders, and Maoris of the Cook Strait Area: A Historical Study in Cultural Confrontation," *Dominion Museum Records in Ethnology* 2, no. 6 (1971), is an admirable analysis of interaction between Maoris and outsiders. Tony Simpson's *Te Riri Paheka: The White Man's Anger* (Martinborough, New Zealand: Alistair Taylor, 1979) is a vivid popular account of colonization, war, and land grabbing. Harold Miller's *Race Conflict in New Zealand, 1814–1865* (Auckland, New Zealand: Blackwood and Janet Paul, 1966) is a more specialized study. Anyone interested in resistance and revitalization movements should read Anthony Wallace, "Revitalization Movements," *American Anthropologist,* 58(1956): 264–281. All these sources contain excellent bibliographies. The nineteenth-century New Zealand novel is discussed by Joan Stevens, *The New Zealand Novel 1860–1960* (Wellington, New Zealand: A. H. and A. W. Reed, 1964). Archaeology: Janet Davidson, "New Zealand Prehistory." *Advances in World Archaeology* 4 (1985):239–292. Also: Peter Bellwood, *The Polynesians* (London: Thames and Hudson, 1987) and Atholl Anderson, *Prodigious Birds: Moas and Moa-Hunting in Prehistoric New Zealand* (Cambridge: Cambridge University Press, 1992), and the same author's "The Chronology of Colonization in New Zealand." *Antiquity* 65 (1991):767–795.

17. The Legacy of Inequality

Philip Mason's Patterns of Dominance (London: Institute of Race Relations, 1970) provided the major inspiration for this chapter. John H. Bodley's *Victims of Progress*, 3rd ed. (Mountain View, CA: Mayfield, 1992) is a useful source on modern attitudes, reactions, and policies.

References

MANY OF THE REFERENCES IN the text come from primary sources, others from secondary ones that are more accessible to the general reader. I have tended to use secondary sources here wherever possible, simply because they are more readily available in public and university libraries. Details of primary sources will be found in these works, and also in the "Guide to Sources."

Beaglehole, J. C.

1955–67 *The Journals of Captain Cook on his Voyages of Discovery.* 3 vols. Cambridge: Cambridge University Press.

1962 *The Endeavour Journal of Joseph Banks, 1768–1771.* Sydney: Angus and Robertson.

1966 *The Discovery of the Pacific.* Palo Alto: Stanford University Press.

1974 *The Life of Captain James Cook.* Palo Alto: Stanford University Press.

Bougainville, Louis A. de

1772 *A Voyage Round the World.* Translated by John Reinhold Foster. London: Nourse and Davis.

Boxer, C.R.

1951 *The Christian Century in Japan.* Berkeley: University of California Press.

Chimalpahín Cuauhtlehuanitzen, Domingo Francisco

1965 *Relaciones originales de Chalco Amquemecan escritas par Don Francisco de San Antón Muñón Chimalpahín Cuauhtlehuanitzen.* Edited by S. Rendón. Mexico City: Fondo de Cultura Económica.

Clendinnen, Inga

    1991   *Aztecs.* Cambridge: Cambridge University Press.

Curtin, Philip L.

    1964   *The Image of Africa.* Madison: University of Wisconsin Press.

Darwin, Charles

    1839   *The Voyage of the* Beagle. London: John Murray.
    1871   *The Descent of Man.* London: John Murray.

Davies, D. M.

    1973   *The Last of the Tasmanians.* London: Frederick Muller.

d'Urville, Jules Sebastien Cesar

    1834–5   *Voyage pittoresque autour du monde.* 2 vols. Paris: L.Tenre.

Diaz, Bernal

    1963   *The Conquest of New Spain.* Translated by J. M. Cohen. Baltimore: Pelican Books.

Dixon, George

    1789   *A Voyage Round the World: but more Particularly to the North-West Coast of America.* London: G. Goulding.

Duran, Diego

    1994   *The Aztecs: The History of the Indies of New Spain.* Translated by Doris Hayden and Fernando Horcasitas. Norman: University of Oklahoma Press.

Earle, Augustus

    1832   *Narrative of a Month's Residence in New Zealand In 1827.* London: John Murray.

Ellis, W.

    1829   *Polynesian Researches.* 2 vols. London: Fisher and Jackson.

Elphick, Richard

    1977   *Kraal and Castle.* New Haven: Yale University Press.

Fagan, Brian M.

    1977   *Elusive Treasure.* New York: Charles Scribners' Sons.

Fairchild, Hoxie Neale

1928   *The Noble Savage: A Study in Romantic Naturalism.* New York: Columbia University Press.

Fisher, Robin

1977   *Contact and Conflict: Indian-European Relations in British Columbia, 1774–1890.* Vancouver: University of British Columbia Press.

FitzRoy, Robert

1839   *Narrative of the Surveying Voyages of His Majesty's Ships Adventure and Beagle between the years 1826 and 1836.* 3 vols. London: Henry Colburn.

Forster, George

1777   *A Voyage Round the World in His Brittanic Majesty's Sloop, Resolution, Commanded by Captain James Cook, during the years 1772, 3, 3 and 5.* 2 vols. London: White, Robson, Elmsly, and Robinson.

Gomara, Francisco Lopez de

1964   *Cortés.* Translated by Lesley Byrd Simpson. Berkeley: University of California Press.

Hakluyt, Richard

1903–5   *The Principall Navigations, Voiages and Discoveries of the English Nation...* (originally written in 1589). Glasgow: J. Maclehose and Sons.

Hanke, Lewis

1949   *The Spanish Struggle for Justice in the Conquest of America.* New York: American Historical Society.

Hawkesworth, John

1773   *An Account of the Voyages Undertaken by the Order of His Present Majesty for Making Discoveries in the Southern Hemisphere...* London: Strahan and Cadell.

Hodgen, Margaret T.

1964   *Early Anthropology in the Sixteenth and Seventeenth Centuries.* Philadelphia: University of Pennsylvania Press.

Jaenen, Cornelius J.

1977 "Missionary Approaches to Native Peoples." In *Approaches to Native History in Canada,* ed. D. A. Muise, 5–15. Ottawa: National Museum of Man.

Lansdowne, Henry W.

1927 *The Petty Papers: Some Unpublished Writings of Sir William Petty.* 2 vols. Boston: Houghton Mifflin.

Lattimore, Richard A.

1959 *The Works and Days.* Ann Arbor: University of Michigan Press.

Leon-Portilla, Miguel

1963 *Aztec Thought and Culture.* Translated by Jack Emory Davis. Norman: University of Oklahoma Press.

Levy, Robert I.

1973 *Tahitians: Mind and Experience in the Society Islands.* Chicago: University of Chicago Press.

Lubbock, Sir John

1865 *Prehistoric Times.* London: Williams and Norgate.

Malinowski, Bronislaw

1929 "Practical Anthropology." *Africa* 2, 1:22–38.

Mason, Philip

1970 *Patterns of Dominance.* London: Institute of Race Relations.

McGhee, Robert

1984 "Contact between Native North Americans and the Medieval Norse: A Review of the Evidence." *American Antiquity* 49:4–26.

Melville, Herman

1847 *Omoo.* Evanston: Northwestern University Press. (Quotes and pagination are from the Newberry Library edition, 1968.)

Moerenhout, Jacques-Antoine

1837 *Voyages aux iles du Grand Ocean...* 2 vols. Translated by Douglas Oliver. Paris: A. Bertrand.

Montaigne, Michel de

1948   *Of the Canibales.* Translated by Donald Frame. Palo Alto: Stanford University Press.

Moorehead, Alan

1966   *The Fatal Impact.* New York: Harper and Row.

Morison, Samuel Eliot

1971   *The Discovery of America. Vol. 1: The Northern Voyages.* New York: Oxford University Press.

Newberry, Colin

1980   *Tahiti Nui.* Honolulu: University of Hawaii Press.

Ogilby, John

1670   *Africa.* London: T. Bowles.

Oliver, Douglas

1974   *Ancient Tahitian Society.* 3 vols. Honolulu: University of Hawaii Press.

Pitt-Rivers, George H. Lane-Fox

1927   *The Clash of Culture and the Contact of Races.* London: Routledge.

Prescott, William

1843   *History of the Conquest of Mexico.* New York: Harpers.

Raven-Hart, R.

1967   *Before Van Riebeeck.* Cape Town: C. Struik.

Sahagun, Bernardino de

1950–82 *The Florentine Codex: General history of the Things of New Spain.* 12 vols. Translated Arthur O. Anderson and Charles E. Dibble. Salt Lake City: University of Utah Press.

Schrire, Carmel

1995   *Digging Through Darkness.* Charlottesville: University of Virginia Press.

Shipton, Eric

1973   *Tierra del Fuego: The Fatal Lodestone.* London: Charles Knight.

Simpson, Tony

1979   *Ti Riri Pakeha: The White Man's Anger.* Martinborough: Alistair Taylor.

Stevens, Joan

1964   *The New Zealand Novel 1860–1960.* Wellington, New Zealand: A. H. and A. W. Reed.

Tedlock, Dennis

1995   *Popol Vuh.* New York: Simon and Schuster.

Thompson, Leonard

1975   *Survival in Two Worlds: Moshoeshoe of Lesotho 1786–1870.* Oxford: Clarendon Press.

Tippett, Alan R.

1971   *People Movements in Southern Polynesia.* Chicago: Moody Press.

Topsell, Edward

1607   *The Historie of Fowre-Footed Beastes ...* London: J. Williams.

Trigger, Bruce G.

1976   *The Children of Aataentsic: A History of the Huron People to 1660.* 2 vols. Montreal: McGill-Queens University Press.

Valliant, George

1972   *Aztecs of Mexico: Origin, Rise, and Fall of the Aztec Nation.* Rev. ed. Baltimore: Pelican Books.

Wolf, Eric

1982   *Europe and the People Without History.* Berkeley: University of California Press.

Wright, Harrison M.

1959   *New Zealand, 1769–1840: Early Years of Western Contact.* Cambridge: Harvard University Press.

Index

About the Author

BRIAN FAGAN IS PROFESSOR OF anthropology at the University of California, Santa Barbara, and a well-known writer and lecturer on archaeology. He has written several widely used textbooks, and a number of popular books. He edited *The Oxford Companion to Archaeology* (Oxford University Press, 1996), and wrote *Snapshots of the Past* (AltaMira Press, 1995).